Jammu and Kashmir

The Blunders and Way Out

Jammu and Kashmir

The Blunders and Way Out

Bhim Singh

HAR-ANAND
PUBLICATIONS PVT LTD

First published: 2011

Published by Ashok Gosain and Ashish Gosain for:
HAR-ANAND PUBLICATIONS PVT LTD
E-49/3, Okhla Industrial Area, Phase-II, New Delhi-110020
Tel: 41603490 Fax: 011-41708607
E-mail: info@haranandpublications.com
Website: www.haranandpublications.com

Printed in India at Vinayak Offset.

Preface

Jammu Kashmir Hai Ladakh and Gilgit was the real name given to the presently known State of Jammu and Kashmir. Kashmir Valley has been an emotional, historical and spiritual constituent of the Great Bharata since pre-Christ era. The fourth Buddhist Conference was organized by King Kanishka some 100 years before Christian era in Kashmir. King Kanishka had established his kingdom from Patliputra to Kandhar during his emperorship. Kashmir was in his kingdom. The ancient monument of Mahabharta era built by the Pandvas during their exile is the living document in the history that Kashmir formed integral constituent of Hastinapur (Delhi). The popular route to Kashmir from Delhi had been via Lahore-Rawalpindi and Muzaffrabad, (a district of Kashmir province) which was occupied by Pakistan military in October 1947 and has been placed as capital of the POK styled as 'Azad Kashmir' by Pakistan. Kashmir has suffered worst type of conversion of Kashmiri Brahmins commonly called as 'Kashmiri Pundits'. Those who had studied history of conversion into Christianity in Latin America shall understand the woeful history of Kashmir. Ancestors of Pt. Moti Lal Nehru, the father of Pt. Jawahar Lal Nehru were among the suffering migrants from Kashmir Valley during the rule of Mughal Emperor, Aurangzeb in the 16th century. Recent migration of Kashmiri Pundits from the Valley had a horrifying backdrop of history of Kashmir. Sheikh Mohd. Abdullah, the tallest Kashmiri Muslim leader proudly and loudly used to claim that his ancestors were Kashmiri Brahmin. There is a small section of Kashmiri Muslims in the Valley who are related to other families from Iran or

Central Asia. This was one of reasons that composite culture called Kashmiriyat remained integral part of the society. Foreign imported militancy and terrorism has not changed the composite culture of the State.

Kashmir has a tragic history for being ruled by different clans and dynasties for centuries. To understand the basic characteristic and in-depth cultural heritage of the people of Kashmir one has to share the experience of the chain of authors of Raj Trangini, one of the greatest written documents authored by a galaxy of the Kashmiri intellectuals dating back to more than 3000 years. The composite culture of Kashmir today described as Kashmiriyat is a perfect reflection of brotherhood which the English speaking intellectuals describe as 'secularism'. It was this composite culture and the historical background that the Kashmiris rejected creation of State of Pakistan and two Nations theory propounded by the British Colonizers in the thirties to weaken the Indian sub-continent.

In 1846 the Great Dogra intellectual, diplomat and a conqueror founded the present State of Jammu and Kashmir with the Union of four regions. He had consolidated Jammu Ladakh and Kashmir joined in 1846 and conquered Gilgit-Baltistan by 1856 before his death.

Ladakh was a Buddhist culture and the people drew their cultural and spiritual inspiration from Tibet, ruled by the famous Lamas. Ladakh, Kargil and Baltistan were integrated with Jammu Dogra State by 1840 after the world-famed Dogra General Zorawar Singh conquered this Himalayan belt under the supervision of Maharaja Gulab Singh. Kargil and Baltistan (Askardu in POK) were Muslim majority areas and wedded to Shia culture of Iran. The Gilgit region comprising Chitral, Hunza, Astore, Dardistan etc. became part of Jammu and Kashmir State by 1857 under the command of another Dogra General Hoshiara Singh and General Baaz Singh. This culture was totally different from that of Dogras, Kashmirirs or Ladakhis. This shall be perfect statement that the formation of Jammu and Kashmir was totally an unnatural union with no similarity of culture, language, geography or even ethnicity. It cannot be described as the Wonder in the World history. Beyond imagination, how the Dogra rulers who hailed from Jammu region called Dogras managed to govern J&K, a heterogeneous conglomeration of territories. J&K was an Unnatural Union, geographically, demographically or economically.

The Sikhs lost battle to the East India Company in 1844. The East financial crises by 1842 the State of Jammu and Ladakh were founded by the Dogra Maharaja Gulab Singh. About 20 small States rather principality in Jammu region from Poonch to Ramnagar and Kishtwar were integrated into Jammu State patronized by the Kingdom of Punjab. In fact, it was Maharaja Ranjit Singh of the Punjab who decorated Gulab Singh as the Maharaja of Jammu in 1820 in a brief ceremony held at the banks of River Chenab in Akhnoor, 29 kms. to the west of Jammu City. India Company imposed war indemnity on the Sikh ruler. The Sikh rulers were in worst and could not afford to pay war compensation which was fixed as Rupees one crore (gold coins). Gulab Singh came out in support of the youthful Maharaja Dalip Singh and offered to pay the compensation. The Punjab government agreed to release Kashmir province (Valley) from its territory and handover its administration to Maharaja Gulab Singh. The people of Kashmir Valley had been agitating against the authoritarian and oppressive rule of the Punjab Governor and they found a great relief in Maharaja Gulab Singh who took over as Kashmir Governor. The Dogra ruler had to pay Rs.75 lacs (gold coins) to the East India Company to buy freedom for the depressed people of Kashmir from Punjab Governor rule. The first message that Maharaja Gulab Singh delivered to the Kashmiris was that he opened the gates of all mosques in the Valley, removed the debris of earth etc. The Treaty of Amritsar enabled Maharaja Gulab Singh to establish the State of J&K in 1846. By 1850 state of J&K, Hai Ladakh and Gilgit was established as it existed in 1947 when the last ruler of J&K, Maharaja Hari Singh acceded to the Union of India when attacked from Pakistan side. The Maharaja's declaration was supported by all sections of the people of J&K. The Dogra ruler had acceded entire State comprising 84,000 sq. miles of area to the Union of India. The greatest tragedy in the history of J&K has been that Indian leadership failed to liberate the areas which were occupied by the so-called raiders with the help and support of Pakistan in 1947.

More than one-third of the area of Jammu and Kashmir has remained illegally occupied by Pakistan, part of it is called 'Azad Kashmir' and the major chunk Pakistan has annexed as its province called Gilgit-Baltistan under the so-called 'Reform Package' of November 2009. This was violation of UNCIP Resolution of August 13, 1948. This area is about 28,000 sq. miles. This area, Pakistan has segregated from the so-called 'Azad Kashmir'. Gilgit-Baltistan is literally under the strategic defence space for China's expansionist designs since 1963 when China managed to grab about 5,000 sq. miles of our territory in Karakoram from Pakistan to build its National Highway connecting Beijing with Peshawar. This agreement between Pakistan and China to lease out this area of J&K to China in the Gilgit region was in total violation of the UNCIP Resolution of August 13, 1948. The Govt. of India remained a silent spectator. The political leadership in India demonstrated their ignorance about J&K. This is important to know that Indian leadership has committed blunders after blunder right since 1947.

A series of blunders which have been committed vis-à-vis J&K ever since the State acceded into the Union of India. There is need to find a way out.

BHIM SINGH

INTRODUCTION

BLUNDERS

The blunders committed vis-à-vis Jammu and Kashmir by the national and the local leaders have remained unaccounted by the historians and the political pundits for different reasons though. Horrifying blunders include, Treaty of Amritsar, 1846 signed between Maharaja Gulab Singh and the East India Company, which made the great Dogras a perpetual slave of Kashmiri rulers, Ordinance on the State Subject by Maharaja Hari Singh in 1927, Congress wedding with National Conference in the forties only to denounce Dogras and support 'Quit Kashmir' movement in 1946. Persuading Maharaja Hari Singh to reach Jammu to sign Instrument of Accession which he signed on October 26, 1947, Lord Mountbatten's blunder in fixing a condition though a letter to the Maharaja which was illegal after the acceptance of the Instrument of Accession on October 27, 1947, Nehru's arrogance and unsolicited declaration to hold plebiscite in J&K at Lal Chowk in 1947 only to denigrate the Maharaja, unilateral declaration by Prime Minister to observe ceasefire on January 1, 1948, restraining the Indian Army led by General Cariappa from liberating occupied areas from Pakistan, allowing deliberate Gilgit fall in the hands of Pakistan by November 16, 1947, followed by tragic fall of Mirpur in Jammu region on November 25, 1947. Introduction of Article 370 in the Constitution of India may be conveniently added in the list of blunders.

The Blunders include, National Conference usurped (acquired) landed property of the citizens in J&K without compensation in 1951, dismissal and arrest of Prime Minister, Sheikh Abdullah on August 9, 1953, promulgation of Constitution for J&K with a preamble sans secularism and fundamental rights. Dismissal and arrest of Prime Minister, Bakshi Ghulam Mohd. in 1964 only defeat no confidence motion moved by him in the Assembly was never highlighted as a blunder committed by Delhi favourite Govt. of G.M. Sadiq. Sending Sheikh Abdullah on a special deputation to Pakistan in 1963, cost Nehru his life, return of Haji Peer to Pakistan, a strategic defence security point in J&K, surrendering Chhamb sector in Akhnoor area to Pakistan in 1971, signing Simla Agreement in 1972 by releasing 98,000 Pak-soldiers without seeking final settlement of J&K, the so-called Indira-Sheikh Accord in 1975 transferring power to Sheikh Abdullah thus dismantling the nationalist gains of two decades, killing of four students inside GGM Science College, Jammu in 1966 and injuring hundreds and later killing four students in Kishtwar during Congress rule the State in 1975 are all unaccounted blunders committed by the National and state leadership. In the long list of blunders dismissal of Farooq Abdullah in 1984 and then dismissing G.M. Shah's government after 20 months, taking over Mata Vaishno Devi Shrine from the Hindu owners which amounted to a religious invasion are included. Rigging of Assembly elections in 1987 and Udhampur by-election in 1988 were the latest blunder that brought a U-turn change in the mind of the Kashmiri leaders. The latest blunder committed by the Central leadership was imposition of a young, inexperienced and inefficient young man as the Chief Minister of J&K.

Why the children of those who fought against Pakistan raiders and infiltrators in 1947, 1965, 1971 and at all the times are fighting against India today? Let the echelons of power ruling Delhi dig out an answer to this question. The conflict shall be settled. If 'Shaitan' dies, no one shall visit the Church. The leaders have been responsible for the present State of Affairs which suits their political interest.

Khalil Jibran's 'Prophet' has depicted the truth beautifully how a priest saved 'shaitan' when shaitan reminded the church going priest that the day he (shaitan) died no one shall visit his Church and the priest would die of starvation. The ghost of Pakistan is source of earning bread for the unemployed politicians. This is the first attempt to reveal the hidden truth to the new generations about the 'situation' in J&K. They are the best judges of tomorrow.

CONTENTS

BLUNDERS 1

Treaty of Amritsar, 1846
Unnatural Union

This treaty was signed at Amritsar on the 16th day of March, 1846, corresponding with the 17th day of Rabi-ul-Awwal, 1252 Hijri. The signatories were Sir Henry Hardinge, G.C.B. Governor-General, on behalf of the British government, and Maharaja Gulab Singh of Jammu-Ladakh (in-person) which was ratified by the seal of Henry Hardinge, G.C.B. Governor-General. Thus Kashmir a Punjab province entered into an unnatural Union with Jammu-Ladakh. Maharaja Gulab Singh had to pay Rupees one crore as war indemnity to the British Empire on behalf of the Punjab Ruler in exchange of the province of 'Kashmir'. The Dogra Maharaja could manage only Rs.75 lacs with the result 'Chamba' region remained outside the domain of the Agreement. The Dogras paid that huge sum to buy freedom for the suffering 'Kashmiris'. He, however, managed to retain Bhaderwah region in Jammu State, which was in the regime of Raja of Chamba.

Kashmir province was transferred from the territorial control of the Punjab to the State of Jammu-Ladakh. Hence a new State came into being, State of Jammu and Kashmir as is known today. Money was contributed by the Dogras of Jammu and other friends of Maharaja Gulab Singh from Punjab and other areas. The major revenues had come from General Zorawar Singh's contribution that he donated the Maharaja in 1940 after conquering Ladakh region. Maharaja Gulab Singh failed to raise Rupees one crore. He could only pay Rs.75 lacs (gold coins) with the result Dogra districts of Kangra and Chamba presently in the present State of Himachal Pradesh, could not be made part of the State. A U-turn in J&K history of tragedy continued. A strong Dogra ethnic hold remained outside the State of J&K.

This was the first blunder committed by the founder of J&K State which during the past three and half centuries reduced the Dogras of Jammu, the Ladakhis and the Gilgitis into political serfs. The great Dogras known for their velour, chivalry and sacrifices were lost their identity and entity. The people of Jammu and Ladakh lost peace and they are still passing through the darkness of the 16th century in 21st century because there is no peace in the Kashmir Valley. The Dogras paid Rs. 75 lacs in gold coins to liberate their Kashmiri brethren from suppressing and oppressing of the Punjabi Governor. Maharaja was advised to give up his claim on Kupwara and Uri sectors and take Kangra as the Punjab administrator was interested to retain its connection. The British were keen to have space in Kashmir belt. The Maharaja did not intend to disintegrate Kashmir, instead, had to accept the painful decision to leave Chamba and Kangra the backbone the Dogra culture and history for the sake of Kashmir.

Rupees 25 lacs changed the tide of the direction and events forever in the history. Maharaja Gulab Singh's human touch with Kashmir, his passion to revive human dignity needs special attention. At what cost he raised desired revenue is also a matter of unimaginable vision, commitment and passion to liberate the Kashmiris from the clutches of the authoritarian Governor. It was only after 100 years that National Conference stood to oppose the Treaty.

Instead of expressing gratitude the NC tried to exploit and oppose it. They kept mum once they got into power. Abrogation of the Treaty of Amritsar shall provide freedom to the people of Jammu and Ladakh from the Kashmiri rulers so that they could live as honourable citizens of India with full democracy and fundamental rights.

The Treaty, the Masterpiece

Article 1: The British government transfers and makes over, forever, independent possession, to Maharaja Gulab Singh, and the heirs male of his body, all the hilly or mountainous country, with its dependencies, situated to the eastward of the river Indus, and westward of the river Ravi, including Chamba and excluding Lahore, being part of the territory ceded to the British government by the Lahore state, according to the provisions of Article 4 of the Treaty of Lahore dated March 9, 1846.

Article 2: The eastern boundary of the tract transferred by the foregoing article to Maharaja Gulab Singh shall be laid down by commissioners appointed by the British government and Maharaja Gulab Singh respectively, for that purpose, and shall be defined in a separate engagement, after survey.

Article 3: In consideration of the transfer made to him and his heirs by the provisions of the foregoing articles, Maharaja Gulab Singh will pay to the British government the sum of seventy-lacs (seven and half millions) of rupees (Nanakshahi), fifty lacs to be paid on ratification of this Treaty, and twenty-five lacs on or before the 1st of October of the current year, AD 1846.

Article 4: The limits of the territories of Maharaja Gulab Singh shall not be, at any time, changed without concurrence of the British government.

Article 5: Maharaja Gulab Singh will refer to the arbitration of the British government any disputes or questions that may arise between himself and the government of Lahore, or any other neighbouring state, and will abide by the decision of the British government.

Article 6: Maharaja Gulab Singh engages for himself and heirs, to join with the whole of his military force, the British troops when employed within the hills, or in the territories adjoining his possessions.

Article 7: Maharaja Gulab Singh shall never to take, or retain in his service any British subject, nor the subject of any European or American State, without the consent of the British government.

Article 8: Maharaja Gulab Singh engages to respect, in regard to the territory transferred to him, the provisions of Articles 5, 6, 7 of the separate engagement between the British government and the Lahore Durbar dated 11th March, 1846.

Article 9: The British government will give its aid to Maharaja Gulab Singh in protecting his territories from external enemies.

Article 10: Maharaja Gulab Singh acknowledges the supremacy of the British government, and will, in token of such supremacy, present annually to the British government one horse, twelve perfect shawl goats of approved breed (six male and six female), and three pairs of Kashmir shawls.

This treaty consisting of ten articles have been this day settled by Frederick Currie, Esq. and Brevet-Major Henry Montgomery Lawrence acting under the directions of the right.

Maharaja Gulab Singh, a chieftain of Akhnoor who was coroneted by Maharaja Ranjit Singh of Punjab in 1920 on the banks of the romantic river of the Chenab, managed about 22 principalities of Jammu region from Kotli to Kishtwar to Ramnagar. Ramnagar was at that time around 1825 a principalities of the forefathers of this author known as Chanotras. They were brutally massacred by the new invaders under Gulab Singh. The Fort of Ramnagar stands as witness to this 'grave massacre'. Thus founded Jammu State! General Zorawar Singh (author's ancestral line) by 1840 annexed Baltistan, Kargil and Ladakh. By 1942 State of Jammu and Ladakh was established by Dogra Maharaja Gulab Singh. Humanitarian approach of Maharaja Gulab Singh to seek liberation of the 'oppressed' people of Kashmir Valley by paying Rs.75 lacs. from the Dogra Treasury in 1846 as war indemnity to the East India Company and not go well with the annals of history. Had Kashmir Valley not integrated with Jammu-Ladakh State, the Valley would have remained with Punjab and finally gone with Amritsar. The Kashmiriyat was saved by the Dogra Maharaja at the cost of Jammu Pradesh. The Maharaja left Kangra and Chamba, the Dogra dominated regions to choose Kupwara and Baramulla instead. Let historians wake up to these parts of the hidden history.

Legal Revolutionary Era (1857-1885)

Jammu and Kashmir remained under Dogra kings from 1846 to 1952. The first ruler of J&K, Maharaja Gulab Singh died in 1857. Maharaja

Ranbir Singh succeeded and ruled till his death in 1885. His period witnessed a unique era of transformation of legal jurisprudence in J&K. Maharaja Ranbir Singh introduced Criminal Penal Code which continued to be named after him, Ranbir Penal Code (Indian Penal Code). The civil and criminal justice delivery system was updated at par with the functioning of judicial and administrative institutions in the United Kingdom. It is interesting to note that a Sessions Judge was vested with powers to issue any writ or order. Even today a writ can be issued by a District Sessions Judge. Historical temples were also raised. The state capitals were changed. Srinagar became the summer capital whereas Civil Secretariat worked in Jammu during winter. It was an era of consolidation and reconciliation and progress.

100 Years of Dogra Rule

The Dogra rule which lasted for one hundred and six years from November 1846 to August 1952, was one of the most peaceful and progressive periods in the long history of J&K though the Monarch was abolished in 1952 by a resolution of the nominated Constituent Assembly. The credit for opening much of this far flung mountainous territory of snow covered peaks, deep ravines, extensive valleys and arid Himalayan plateaus to modern civilization and social and political influence, goes to its Dogra rulers. The Kashmir valley which is the most celebrated and coveted part of the State is particularly indebted to them.

The first agenda of Gulab Singh after establishing the State of Jammu and Kashmir in 1846 was to consolidate it and provide an effective and efficient administration and develop communication. He cleared all Mosques and Shrines of all debris and encroachments.

Jammu Province covered the entire territory from the Ravi to the Jhelum lying south of the Pir Panchal range. It included the whole of Jammu region together with Mirpur area of the Dogri-Pahari speaking sector.

A number of efficient and capable administrators like Mehta Basti Ram gave modern administration to Ladakh for the first time. They built the fort and bazar of Leh, laid plantations for a perennial supply of fuel, built and repaired bridle roads linking Leh with Srinagar, Lahaul, Yarkand and Gartok, surveyed the traditional Ladakh-Tibet frontier and made a land settlement for the first time. Baltistan with its main town of Askardu was put under the charge of another administrator. Later, both Ladakh and Baltistan were joined together and put under the charge of one administrator who had his headquarters at Leh in summer and Askardu (Baltistan) in winter. Askardu (Baltistan) has been under illegal occupation of Pakistan since 1947.

As a compromise settlement with the Raja of Chamba, who claimed Bhaderwah as a part of his kingdom was allowed to transfer his allegiance to the British instead of the Dogra King in return for renunciation of any claim on Bhaderwah. This settlement was reached in the Treaty of Amritsar. Maharaja Gulab Singh failed to pay full war indemnity of rupees one crore imposed on the Sikh Govt. It was unique diplomacy of highly talented Maharaja that he managed to bring Bhaderwah with his empire.

It is interesting to mention that the people of Kashmir persuaded Dogra Maharaja Gulab Singh to take care of the Kashmiris and improve their situation who had been feeling suppressed under the Punjab Governor in 1846. The Dogra Maharaja crowned his son Ranbir Singh as the Maharaja of J&K in his life time and took over as Governor of Kashmir couple of years before his death in 1857.

Maharaja Ranbir Singh, Founder of Rule of Law (1858-1885)

The most outstanding achievement of Ranbir Singh, who is considered to be the greatest of the Dogra rulers, was the Hero of re-conquest of Gilgit and annexation of the Frontier States of Hunza and Nagar. He organized a big expedition to which almost every Dogra family contributed a soldier in 1860 under the command of Colonel Devi Singh. Chitral also accepted his sovereignty in 1876. Chitral, Pakistan has illegally declared as its District.

After having thus re-established the prestige of the Dogra army, he turned his attention to internal reforms. The Ranbir 'Dand-Vidhi', the code of laws, both civil and criminal, which he got prepared, established his reputation as a law-giver. He reorganized his army on the British model which is the order of judicial system today in J&K.

His spirit of independence and the originality and initiative he displayed in the organization of his civil and military administration were not to the liking of the British. They, therefore, made another attempt to force a British Resident on Jammu and Kashmir in 1873. Maharaja Ranbir Singh too refused to yield in the matter on the plea that there was no provision in the Treaty of 1846 giving authority to the British Government to appoint a Resident.

British Intrigues Gentleman Rule (1885-1925)

Maharaja Pratap Singh was coroneted as third Dogra King in 1885 who expired in 1925. A history of political turbulences with difficult times vis-à-vis the British Rule in Delhi. Maharaja Pratap Singh demonstrated tremendous amount of patience to ensure that the state continues to survive. He died issueless.

It was Hari Singh, son of Maharaja Pratap Singh's younger brother Amar Singh who succeeded him after a lot of inner turmoil and domestic conflicts in 1925. He was highly qualified and experienced in the practical politics of J&K. His contributions for the upliftment of all the regions are worth taking into account.

Having got a Resident appointed which eventually brought down Jammu and Kashmir to the level of other Indian States like Hyderabad and Gwalior, the British now made a determined bid to have a more direct control over the State The Maharaja was charged with conspiring with Russia against the British and was forced to hand over all his powers to a five members State Council which ran the administration under the guidance of the British Resident for many years. In the meantime, the British interest in the Pamirs and the frontier states of Chitral, Hunza was aroused by the continued advance of Czarist Russia in Central Asia. As a result, the British decided to have a more effective control over the Mehtar of Chitral. The military campaign launched for the purpose between 1889 and 1895 was conducted by the State Forces but under the command of British officers. After the successful termination of the campaign, Chitral passed under direct control of the British in practice. But in theory it continued to be a feudatory of Maharaja of Jammu and Kashmir.

This campaign brought the strategic importance of Gilgit region to the notice of the British. The publication of White's book, 'Where Three Empires Meet', which gave a graphic account of this campaign and the valor of Dogra troops, put Gilgit on the map of the world. The result was a concerted effort on the part of the British Government to bring the whole of Gilgit area under its direct control. For the moment a British political agent was stationed at Gilgit to watch British interests though administrative control remained in the hands of the State Government.

Maharaja Pratap Singh got back full powers in 1905 after an attempt to completely oust him had been foiled by the timely revelation of the machinations of the Political Department of the British Government of India in the 'Amrit Bazar Patrika' of Calcutta and raising of the issue in the British House of Commons by some opposition members. He ruled for twenty years more till his death in 1925.*

The modernization of Jammu and Kashmir State began during the reign of Pratap Singh. Kashmir was linked to Rawalpindi, Abbotabad and Sialkot by motorable roads, first rate Arts and Science Colleges

*100 years of Dogra Rule in J&K by Balraj Mandhok.

were opened in Jammu and Srinagar, foreign administration was streamlined with the help of British experts, a hydro-electric plant, among the first few of its kind in India, was set up at Mehura near Baramulla and new holiday resorts like Gulmarg and Pahalgam were developed in the Valley.

Maharaja Hari Singh Era of Democracy!

Hari Singh succeeded to the thorny throne of J&K in 1925. His very first declaration at the time of his coronation that, "My religion is Justice," surprised (many religious bigots). His proclamation was great, unique and a sweeping message of secular ethos to which he stood till his last. His urge to develop and modernize his State and introduced democratic era which had witnessed in England. This urge was partly the result of a new awareness in his mind about the importance of his State and a distrust of the British whose bullying attitude had created a strong suspicion in his mind.

His misunderstanding with the British Resident began from the very day of his coronation and continued to grow in the following years due to his spirit of self-dependence. British Empire was shocked by his declaration at the first Round Table Conference in London in 1930, "While Indian Princes valued British connection, they had full sympathy for the aspirations of their motherland (India) for an equal and honourable place in the comity of nations." This outspoken support to the 'seditious' demand for independence by a representative of Princely India, which had been given a disproportionately high representation at the Round Table Conference to counterbalance the popular representatives from British India, came as a bomb shell to the British diehards in England and the Political Department in India. When the viceroy reminded that he was a Maharaja and should mind his limits, Great Dogra King shot back, "I am an Indian first and then a Maharaja." This opened the flood volcanoes against the Maharaja which he faced boldly and courageously till his death in 1961 in exile in Bombay. The strategic importance of Jammu and Kashmir State and the British plan to have a more direct control over Gilgit made this spirit of independence and defiance in Hari Singh all the more galling to them, so they decided to break him. To that end they had recourse to the convenient method of building up popular 'Muslim' pressure on communal line.

These political developments did not deter Hari Singh from pursuing his plans for the modernization of Kashmir Valley and democratization of the political system. Apart from the meager resources of the State, he spent huge sums from his accumulated family treasures as well as his own privy purse to beautify the Valley and equip it with modern amenities for Indian and foreign tourists. It would be no exaggeration to say that the modern establishment which have made Kashmir valley such a rage with foreign tourists are mainly his contribution to this 'Paradise' on earth. Had he bestowed even a fraction of the interest and money he lavished on Kashmir Valley on his own homeland of Jammu which also abounds in places of great natural beauty and is the richest part of the State from the point of view of human, forest and mineral resources?

Maharaja introduced Praja Sabha (Parliament) through electoral process in 1939. Constituted a Cabinet of the elected representatives Mirza Afzal Beg and second in command in Kashmir leadership, was a Revenue Minister in the Maharaja's Cabinet.

Maharaja enacted a law 'State Subject' restricting citizenship right only to the permanent residents which alone could save the State and its composite culture. The Maharaja opened all public places and temples for the depressed classes (Harijans) in the thirties in spite of the strong resentment of high caste society. He banned child married and smoking by minors etc. He enacted law against prostitution. Banned killing of female-infants! He himself took up a 'plough' to till the land thus introducing a revolutionary concept that 'tilling of land' was an honour to the tiller. Maharaja was designated a Major General for his contribution in Second World War.

BLUNDERS 2

Introduction of 'State Subject'

It was a revolutionary era with several changes he made in the customary, criminal and civil legal systems in the state. His most revolutionary notification with far-reaching effect was a law dealing with the basic, civil and political rights of a person born in J&K called as '**hereditary state subject**'. Maharaja Hari Singh experienced that many wealthy and influential rich men and high flying British and Indian bureaucrats were planning to purchase immoveable property in J&K. The Maharaja told his advisors that he would not allow J&K to be converted a rich men colony like South Africa. In spite of a strong reservation from his Durbar mostly from Kashmir officials, the Maharaja came out with a unique notification to shut the doors of the busy bodies and rich intruders from entering J&K to settle. His law which has given J&K a distinction in the property right was described as a blunder by many critics of the Maharaja. It was this 'blunder' that barred the outsiders from purchasing the immoveable properties in J&K from the local residents. There is a strong opinion in India that had the Maharaja not introduced such a law, the demography in J&K would have naturally undergone a sea change in population. Those who raised 'Quit Kashmir' slogan in Kashmir against the Dogras forgot these were Dogra kings who have protected their eternal right to property and land.

Royal Proclamation, 1927
Saviour of Kashmiris!

No. I-L/84. The following definition of the term 'State Subject' has been sanctioned by his Highness the Maharaja Bahadur (Vice Private

Secretary's Letter No. 2354, dated the 31st January, 1927 to the Revenue Member of Council) and is hereby promulgated for general information.

The term State Subject means and includes—

Class I. All persons born and residing within the State before the commencement of the reign of His Highness the late Maharaja Gulab Singh Sahib Bahadur, and also persons who settled the rein before the commencement of samvat year 1942, and have since been permanently residing therein.

Class II. All persons other than those belonging to Class-I who settled within the State before the close of samvat year 1968, and have since permanently resided and acquired immovable property therein.

Class III. All persons, other than those belonging to Classes-I and II permanently residing within the State, who have acquired under a rayatnama any immovable property therein or WIZO may hereafter acquire such property under an ijazatnama and may execute a rayatnama after ten years continuous residence therein.

Class IV. Companies which have been registered as such within the State and which, being companies in which the Government are financially interested or as to the economic benefit to the State or to the financial stability of which the Government are satisfied, have by a special order of His Highness been declared to be State subjects.

Note I. In matters of grants of the State scholarships State lands for agricultural and house building purposes and recruitment to State service, State subjects of Class-I should receive preference over other classes and those of Class-II, over Class-III, subject, however, to the order dated 31st January, 1927 of his Highness the Maharaja Bahadur regarding employment of hereditary State Subjects in Government service.

Note II. The descendants of the persons who have secured the status of any class of the State Subjects will be entitled to become the State Subject of the same class. For example, if A is declared a State Subject of Class-II his sons and grand sons. Will ipso facto acquire the status of the same Class-II and not of Class-I.

Note III. The wife or a widow of a State Subject of any class shall acquire the status of her husband as State Subject of the same Class as her husband, so long as she resides in the State and does not leave the State for permanent residence outside the State.

Note IV. For the purpose of the interpretation of the term 'State Subject' either with reference to any law for the time being in force or otherwise, the definition given in this Notification amended up to date shall be read as if such amended definition existed in this Notification as originally issued. The notification was modified in 1932 as under;

State Subject

(Issued by order of His Highness the Maharaja Bahadur dated Srinagar, the 27th June 1932, (14th Har, 1989, published In Government Gazette dated 24th Har, 1989).

No.13L/1989: Whereas it is necessary to determine the status of Jammu and Kashmir State Subjects in foreign territories and to inform the Government of Foreign States as to the position of their nationals in this state, it is hereby commanded and notified for public information, as follows:

1. That all emigrants from the Jammu and Kashmir State to foreign territories shall be considered State Subjects and also the descendants of these emigrants born aboard for two generations. Provided that, these nationals of the Jammu and Kashmir State shall not be entitled to claim the internal rights granted to subjects of this State by the laws, unless they fulfill the conditions laid down by those laws and rules for the specific purposes mentioned therein.
2. The foreign nationals residing in the State of Jammu and Kashmir shall not acquire the nationality of the Jammu and Kashmir State until after the age of 18 on purchasing immovable property under permission of an ijazatnama and on obtaining a rayatnama after ten years continuous residence in the Jammu and Kashmir State as laid down in Notification No.-l-L. of 1984, dated 20th April, 1927.

3. Certificates of nationality of the Jammu and Kashmir State may, on application, be granted by the Minister-in Charge of the Political Department in accordance with the provision of Section-I of this Notification.

The Maharaja revolutionary induction to raise the social and political life of a common subject.

This gave a life line to the State Subjects and lasting security for generations.

Today the residents of J&K are protected by this notification of the Maharaja and not by virtue of Article 370 of the Indian Constitution. How great was the Dogra Maharaja as secularist of the highest order. 87% was the Muslim population in his State. He had no compulsion nor there was any pressure or a demand to this effect. The Dogra Maharaja could have brought back of Hindus from Jammu or even Punjab if he so wished and settled them in Kashmir or elsewhere. Instead, the Dogra king stood to his commitment, "**My religion is Justice**" and reserved this '**piece of heavens**' for the sons and daughters of the soil.

Could they who started 'Quit Kashmir' campaign against Hari Singh justify their movement?

This law forms part of the present legal system which differentiates J&K status from other Indian States.

BLUNDERS 3

Congress Support to 'Quit Kashmir'

National Conference led by Sheikh Mohd. Abdullah started '**Quit Kashmir**' movement against the Dogras least realizing that the Dogras were the founder of the State of J&K. Sheikh Mohd. Abdullah patronized by Pt. Jawahar Lal Nehru was under his political influence and that was the reason that he started '**Quit Kashmir**' movement against the Dogras. Indian National Congress had launched '**Quit India**' against the British rule. British were foreigners. The Dogras were citizens of J&K. Nehru's ancestral relationship with Dogras may not be cordial. It was Nehru's influence on the school master Sheikh that made him to think as would be Sultan of Kashmir. The Sheikh used Muslim cards against the Maharaja. Nehru had many scores to settle with the Dogra Rajput Maharaja. NC's '**Quit Kashmir**' created communal divide for the first time. Ram Chander Kak was appointed Prime Minister by the Maharaja keeping his understanding and visionary approach in mind, came under fire from the Nehru's Congress when he dealt the agitation with strong hand. Sheikh Abdullah was put in jail for exciting violence by Ram Chander Kak. This movement was the beginning of sowing discords of contempt and hatred between the Dogras and the Kashmiris. This movement ultimately took a communal turn and created animosity between the Dogras and the Kashmiris. Sheikh Abdullah and his political partners were arrested in May, 1946 and later convicted also for causing a threat to the security of the state and its secular character.

It was another blunder of Nehru to support Sheikh's communal and anti-Dogra '**Quit Kashmir**' movement in 1946. Mr. Nehru, the Prime Minister elect of India breaching all the norms and ethics decided to go to Kashmir in support of the NC, 'Quit Kashmir' movement. Nehru acted against the advice of Governor-General Lord Mountbatten and moved by road from Delhi to Rawalpindi. He tried to enter J&K via Kohala Bridge, bordering J&K with British India, thus undermining the State Authority.

There were two trespasses of J&K by the VVIPs. Nehru trespassed in 1946. He was arrested under the orders of J&K Prime Minister, Ram Chander Kak and released the same day by the Maharaja and flown back to Delhi.

There was another alleged 'trespass' into J&K by Dr. Shyama Prasad Mukherjee in 1953 via Lakhanpur after the State's Accession with India. He was arrested by Sheikh Abdullah and taken to Srinagar jail where he was declared dead in prison.

Blunders 4

Arrest of Nehru at Kohala, 1946

Nehru was chosen to be the first Indian Prime Minister. He was getting panicky to learn that the 'Quit Kashmir' movement against the Dogra Maharaja was failing. He decided via Rawalpindi to drive to Srinagar in support of Sheikh Abdullah. At Kohala Bridge which connected J&K with British India, the Prime Minister in waiting Pt. Jawahar Lal Nehru was stopped and arrested by the local SHO in July, 1946 on the direction of the Prime Minister of J&K, Pt. Ram Chander Kak. Nehru was released on the hot intervention of Lady Mountbatten. On her personal request to Maharaja Hari Singh. Nehru was released and flown back to Delhi. His hatred towards Maharaja Hari Singh and Mr. Kak did not end. He declared while boarding helicopter at Kohala that, **"I will teach him a lesson. How he dared arrest the would be Prime Minister of India."** The two never met again in their life time. Nehru became Prime Minister and tried to wreck vengeance to the extent he could do till the Maharaja lived. The Saga of history of Jammu and Kashmir from 1946 till this day is the Saga of the blunders that created unbearable wounds in the heart of every citizen of Jammu and Kashmir. The history shall record what price Pt. Ram Chander Kak had to pay for enforcing law and order in 1946. It proved a disaster for his life, his human dignity and respect. It needs a separate chapter how Ram Chander Kak was humiliated, his property confiscated and was forced to quit his home state. Blunder after blunders by the men in power! However, the Maharaja released Sheikh Mohd. Abdullah after he addressed a letter of apology from jail. Quit Kashmir movement could not gather any support except from Mr. Nehru and the Congress. Muslim Conference led by Chaudhary Abbas of Jammu confronted Abdullah and National Conference. This, however, blunders sowed the thorny seeds of hatred and conflict between Kashmir and Jammu.

BLUNDERS 5

Humiliation and Dismissal of Kak

Ram Chander Kak was chosen as Prime Minister of Jammu and Kashmir in 1946 by Maharaja Hari Singh during the key transitional period of 1946-47 when the British were preparing to Quit India. He was also a pioneering archaeologist who excavated the leading sites of antiquities in Kashmir and wrote definitive text on them. The Praja Sabha (elected Parliament) approved this appointment. He was made minister of military affairs in 1941 and became Prime Minister in Hari Singh's government.

This was a difficult time for the Govt. when 'Quit Kashmir' movement was getting Nehru's blind support for Abdullah. Abdullah was jockeying for power and he used Nehru to strengthen his case. Nehru's vengeance against Kak and the Maharaja never subsided for the reason that Nehru's entry to J&K was stopped at Kohala on the orders of Mr. Kak in July, 1946.

Kak thought it most prudent to buy time and improve Kashmir's bargaining position. He recommended that Kashmir remain independent of both India and Pakistan for a transitional period of at least one year, and then take a decision on accession. Mountbatten—after asking for and receiving a note from Nehru—visited the Maharaja on June 19, 1947 and urged him to take a decision on accession. Mountbatten favoured Accession of J&K with Pakistan before 15th August, 1947.

Sheikh was already on warpath with Ali Mohd. Jinnah, the latter had rubbished the Sheikh publicly in Srinagar. Jinnah's speech in Jammu in 1946 deserves attention.

"As regards the Mussalmans, as I said, we are vitally concerned with their welfare, but I regret that although Sheikh Abdullah and his party and the Muslim Conference discussed matters with me in Delhi and in Lahore before my arrival here, and were good enough to accord me a great reception, and were anxious that I should hear both sides and bring about a settlement, when I, after careful consideration, suggested that the Mussalmans should organize themselves under one flag and on one platform, not only my advice was not acceptable to Sheikh Abdullah but, as is his habit, which has become a second nature with him, he indulged in all sorts of language of a most offensive and vituperative character in attacking me. My advice to the Mussalmans is that the differences can only be resolved by argument, discussion, exchange of views, and reason, and not by goondaism and one thing that I must draw the attention of Kashmir Government about is that goondaism must be put down at any cost, and there should be constitutional liberty of speech and freedom of thought, which is the elementary right of every citizen under any civilized form of Government."

This condemnation of the Sheikh by Mr. Jinnah on the eve of India's partition sowed the seeds of hatred and scorn between Mr. Jinnah and Abdullah. Abdullah got several assurances from Nehru that the former shall be the Sultan of Kashmir after 'Hari Singh' exit. Nehru-Sheikh agenda reached the climax, to oust Hari Singh by any means and all means. Several senior leaders visited Srinagar to persuade the Maharaja to out 'Kak' and then hand over power to the Sheikh.

Shockingly, Mahatma Gandhi and Kriplani also met the Maharaja with the same agenda.

BLUNDERS 6

Gandhi's Blunder, 1947

On August 1, 1947 Mahatma Gandhi visited the Maharaja and suggested removal of Kak as Prime Minister. Mahatma Gandhi was assured by Abdullah that if Kak was ousted, a plebiscite will return a vote in favour of India. Pt. Ram Chander Kak was dismissed as Prime Minister on August 11, 1947. The British Indian government returned Gilgit that was leased out to Britain in 1934, for a period of 60 years. Brig. Ghansara Singh was deputed to Gilgit as Governor in 1947.

When Sheikh Abdullah became Prime Minister of Kashmir, he imprisoned Kak and then externed him. After this, Kak retired from public life and left Kashmir for good. A history that has never been written till day. The blunder may be attributed to the intellectuals and the historians.

Gandhi ji was persuaded by Nehru to meet Maharaja Hari Singh on two accounts. Gandhi ji advised the Maharaja to dismiss Pt. Ram Chander Kak and hand over power to the Sheikh. Nehru knew that the Maharaja would not care for Nehru's advice. Nehru visited Srinagar to meet Abdullah in jail. But Kak refused to oblige Nehru. Nehru persuaded Gandhi ji to fulfill his mission in Kashmir. Maharaja had met Gandhi ji during 'Round Table Conference' in London in 1930 where the Maharaja roared saying, "I am an Indian first then a Maharaja." Maharaja honoured Gandhi ji. Sheikh Abdullah was released, Kak was removed. Later Sheikh Abdullah was made Administrator of J&K on October 30, 1947 under Prime Minister, Mehr Chand Mahajan.

This did not satisfy Nehru. Nehru insisted that Mahajan should be replaced by Abdullah. Sardar Patel who had good influence over the

Maharaja prevailed up him to satisfy Nehru. Mahajan was too replaced on March 5, 1948. Mahajan left humiliated. This was Nehru's command as Prime Minister of India that no one cared to defy. The Sheikh was brought in to humble and disgrace Maharaja and establish his (Sheikh) authority to accomplish the 'Quit Kashmir' agenda. The Maharaja was forced to go on exile. Even the Maharani was not spared. She had to leave J&K too. The Maharaja died in Bombay in 1961 and the Maharani spent rest for life in Kangra's Taragarh Palace. She died in 1967.

BLUNDERS 7

No to Military Assistance

36 days after State's Independence Pakistan after having signed 'no-war pact' with the Maharaja's government invaded the State. On August 15, 1947, J&K assumed a status of an independent and sovereign state. The Maharaja offered friendship to both India and Pakistan, her immediate neighbourers—Pakistan responded but India chose to keep silent. Pak-sponsored raiders ransacked Muzaffrabad district, tramped Uri and entered Baramulla by October 27, 1947. Dr. V.P. Menon reached Jammu to seek Maharaja's signature on the Instrument of Accession to fulfill Nehru's condition to accede first and then ask for Army. The Indian Army reached Srinagar on the morning of October 27, 1947.

Nehru vetoed every move of the Maharaja to secure militancy assistance from the Dominion. Even Sardar Patel whom it was said that he was sympathetic towards the Dogra Maharaja failed to twist Nehru. Mahatma Gandhi who was considered a **'most just'** leader failed to demonstrate his impartiality. Maharaja chose both Accession and as well safety of his people. His correspondence, mainly his letters addressed to Lord Mountbatten show his passion and love for his people and the country.

The Qabaili invasion aided by Pak-army was, in fact, a naked Pak-aggression, which started on October 22, 1947 taking over Muzaffrabad and crossed to Uri on October 23, 1947. Maharaja's army had only 12 Battalions with 12000 soldiers and some officers. Brig. Rajinder Singh was the Commanding Army Chief in 1947 who was deployed with about 125 Dogra soldiers on October 24, 1947 from

Srinagar to stop the enemies at Baramulla at all costs, 'to the last man and last bullet.'

J&K armies comprise, J&K Rifles with about 12000 strength who fought the invaders along more than 700 kms. border with Pakistan. Almost entire force perished while the great Dogra (both Muslims and non-Muslim soldiers) armies fought in defence of their motherland resisting the invading Pak-army who came to fight in the cloak of the 'raiders'. Brig. Rajinder Singh, Chief of the Staff of the J&K Army wrote the history as the saviour of Kashmir in his own blood. He along with over 100 Dogra soldiers stopped the enemy at Buniyar between Uri and Baramulla town till the dawn of October 27, 1947. While Maharaja was signing the Instrument of Accession in Jammu, Dogra soldiers under the command of Brig. Rajinder Singh were fighting against the invaders to keep them away from entering Baramulla. When Indian Army came to salute Brigadier and his men, they touch that everyone was martyred but the enemy had run away. Brig. Rajinder Singh died, "Last man to the last bullet." Last instance of heroism and patriotism that Chief of Army Staff laid down his life for his motherland in world history. A great Saga of Dogra history of sacrifice!

Maharaja to Mountbatten
October 26, 1947

"My dear Lord Mountbatten,

GRAVE EMERGENCE

I have to inform Your Excellency that a grave emergency has arisen in my State and request the immediate assistance of your Government. As Your Excellency is aware, the State of Jammu and Kashmir has not acceded to either the Dominion of India or Pakistan. Geographically my State is contiguous with both of them. Besides, my State has a common boundary with the Union of Soviet Socialist Republics and with China. In their external relations the Dominion of India and Pakistan cannot ignore this fact. I wanted to take time to decide to which Dominion I should accede or whether it is not in the best interests of both the Dominions and of my State to stand independent, of course with friendly and cordial relations with both. I accordingly approached the Dominions of India and Pakistan to enter into Standstill Agreement with my State. The Pakistan Government accepted this arrangement. The Dominion of India desired further discussion with representatives of my Government. I could not arrange this in view of the developments indicated below. In fact the Pakistan Government under the standstill agreement is operating the post and telegraph system inside the State. Though we have got a standstill agreement with the Pakistan Government, the Government permitted a steady and increasing strangulation of supplies like food, salt and petrol to my State.

Armed Invasion

Afridis, soldiers in plain clothes, and desperadoes with modern weapons have been allowed to infiltrate into the State, at first in the Poonch area, then from Sialkot and finally in a mass in the area adjoining-Hazara district on the Ramkote side. The result has been that the limited number of troops at the disposal of the State had to be dispersed and thus had to face the enemy at several points simultaneously, so that it has become difficult to stop the wanton destruction of life ad property and the looting of the Mahura power house, which supplies electric current to the whole of Srinagar and which has been burnt. The number of women who have been kidnapped and raped makes my heart bleed. The wild forces thus let loose on the State are marching on with the aim of capturing Srinagar, the summer capital of my government, as a first step to overrunning the whole State. The mass infiltration of tribesman drawn from distant areas of the North-West Frontier Province, coming regularly in motor trucks, using the Manwehra-Mazaffrabad road and fully armed with up-to-date weapons, cannot possibly be done without the knowledge of the Provincial Government of the North-West Frontier Province and the Government of Pakistan. In spite of repeated appeals made by my Government no attempt has been made to check these raiders or to stop them from coming into my State. In fact, both radio and the Press of Pakistan have reported these occurrences. The Pakistan Radio even put out the story that a provisional government has been set up in Kashmir. The people of my State, both Muslims and non-Muslims, generally have taken no part at all.

Offer of Accession

With the conditions obtaining at present in my State and the great emergency of the situation as it exists, I have no option but to ask for help from the Indian Dominion. Naturally they cannot send the help asked for by me without my State acceding to the Dominion of India. I have accordingly decided to do so, and I attach the instrument of accession for acceptance by your Government. The other alternative is to leave my state and people to freebooters. On this basis no civilized government can exist or be maintained.

This alternative I will never allow to happen so long as I am the ruler of the State and I have life to defend my country. I may also inform your Excellency's Government that it is my intention at once to set up an interim government and to ask Sheikh Abdullah to carry the responsibilities in this emergency with my Prime Minister.

If my State is to be saved, immediate assistance must be available at Srinagar. Mr. V. P. Menon is fully aware of the gravity of the situation and will explain it to you, if further explanation is needed.

In haste and with kindest regards,

Yours sincerely,

Sd/-

Hari Singh

October 26, 1947

Nehru to Mahajan

New Delhi
October 26, 1947

My dear Mr. Mahajan,

I gave you a hurried note today just before you left. I have not even got a copy of it. I have therefore drafted a slightly fuller note and I am enclosing it. There is no essential difference between this and the previous note.

I think, it is important for Sheikh Mohammad Abdullah to go to Srinagar immediately as the situation there requires urgent handling and his presence will be helpful. I am suggesting to him therefore to go straight to Srinagar tomorrow morning. He will come to Jammu whenever the Maharaja so desires.

We have decided to send more troops to Srinagar tomorrow as at first intended. Probably, we shall be able to send 400 by air tomorrow I am quite sure that our troops will render a good account of themselves. Apart from other officers we are wending one of our senior and experienced officers, namely Brigadier Hiralal Atal to accompany the troops. He knows Kashmir and his presence ought to be of great help.

Yours sincerely,
Sd/-
Jawahar Lal Nehru

Ruler signed Instrument of Accession October 26, 1947

The Defence Committee met under the chair of Lord Mountbatten on October 25, 1947 only to reject Maharaja's request. Let him sign 'Accession' first and then we shall consider his request for military help.

Mr. V. P. Menon, Secretary in States Ministry was sent to Srinagar to explain to Maharaja the position on October 25, 1947. He met

Maharaja. Menon found conditions grave in Srinagar. Advised Maharaja to leave for Jammu so that the Hari Singh could sign the Accession in a safe place.

Mr. Menon did not take it safe to fly with the documents to Srinagar on October 26, 1947. It was on his advice that the Maharaja with the Maharani and Yuvraj left Srinagar by car and reached Jammu in the morning of 26.10.1947. Menon succeeded in making Hari Singh a little soft towards Sheikh Abdullah. V.P Menon returned to Jammu on October 26, 1947 and called on the Maharaja at Amar Singh Palace. The Maharaja signed the Instrument of Accession.

Nehru's Advisory to Mehr Chand Mahajan October 26, 1947

The Defence Committee of the Cabinet of the Government of India considered the situation in Kashmir and the request made by the Government of Jammu and Kashmir State for help against the raiders who had entered their territory and caused great loss. The suggestion that the Kashmir State should accede to the Indian Union was also considered. The Committee came to the following conclusions, which were subsequently confirmed by the Cabinet:

(1) In view of the request made by the Kashmir Government for help against raiders who have entered their territory, the Government of India have decided to give such help. In furtherance of this decision they are sending troops by air tomorrow morning to Srinagar. They intend reinforcing these troops by air as well as by the land route via Jammu, as the defence of Kashmir has become their responsibility now and they intend to discharge it to the best of their ability;

(2) His Highness, the Maharaja, in accordance with his wishes and the wishes of a large number of his people, will agree to Jammu and Kashmir State acceding to the Indian Union. The Government of India will accept this accession provisionally

subject to their declared policy that such matters should be finalized in accordance with the will of the people. Any reference to the people can only take place when law and order have been fully established;

(3) H. H. the Maharaja will invite Sheikh Mohammad Abdullah to form an Interim Government after the Mysore pattern.

BLUNDERS 8

Mountbatten to Maharaja

My dear Maharaja Sahib,

Your Highness' letter dated October 26, 1947 has been delivered to me by Mr. V.P. Menon. In the circumstances mentioned by Your Highness, my Government has decided to accept the Accession of Kashmir State to the Dominion of India. **In consistence with their policy that in the case of any State where the issue of accession has been the subject of dispute, the question of accession should be decided in accordance with the wishes of the people of the State, it is my Government's wish that, as soon as law and order have been restored in Kashmir and its soil cleared of the invader, the question of the State's Accession should be settled by a reference to the people.**

Meanwhile, in response to Your Highness's appeal for military aid, action has been taken today to send troops of the Indian Army to Kashmir, to help your own forces to defend your territory and to protect the lives, property, and honour of your people. My Government and I note with satisfaction that Your Highness has decided to invite Sheikh Abdullah to form an interim Government to work with your Prime Minister.

Sd/-

Mountbatten of Burma

October 27, 1947

Mountbatten formally signed the acceptance on 27th October and returned a copy of Instrument under cover of a letter to Maharaja. And the First Contingent of Indian troops landed at Srinagar Airport in the morning of October 27, 1947.

Arrival of Indian Army

On the other hand, the Indian Army arrived in Srinagar on October 27, 1947. Lt. General P.C. Sen who as Brigadier functioned as Commander of 161 Infantry Brigade in Srinagar during 1947-48, wrote in his book, 'Slander was the Thread', "These volunteers moved across the mountains and forests with speed and gave accurate information the army about enemy's strength, location and movements." While the army pushed back the invaders, there are several instances where people put up a gallant resistance and stopped the advance of the invaders. The most glaring examples of people's resistance were the martyrdom of Mohammad Maqbool Sherwani and Master Abdul Aziz.

The sacrifice of Master Abdul Aziz too was exemplary. The invaders who raped the nuns and wanted other non-Muslim women to hand over to them, Master Abdul Aziz, a tailor by profession, held the holy Quran in his hand and said that they can touch the women only over his dead body and the holy Quran. The brutal killers did not spare him.

Abdullah appointed administrator October 30, 1947

Maharaja was under a constant pressure from Delhi to empower Abdullah as Prime Minister. Mehr Chand Mahajan was the Prime Minister and the Maharaja did not want to disturb the status quo. Sheikh was resting in Delhi. He had left Kashmir before the Pak-aggression fearing for his life because Jinnah did not like him. During the Pak-aggression he was Nehru's guest in Delhi. After the Maharaja agreed to empower him, the Sheikh left for Srinagar. Lord Mountbatten's personal persuasion made the Maharaja agreed to provide some job to Sheikh. On October 30, 1947, the Maharaja reluctantly issued the declaration.

"We are hereby pleased to command that pending the formation of the Interim government as agreed upon and in view of the emergency that has arisen. I charge Sheikh Mohammad Abdullah to function as the Head of the Administration with power to deal with the emergency.

Sheikh Mohammad Abdullah be sworn in by the Chief Justice or any other Judge of the High Court at Srinagar."

With J&K becoming legal and constitutional part of Union of India, the troops were rushed to the state to push back the invaders and vacate aggression from the territory of the state. The first batch of Indian Army troops arrived at Srinagar airport immediately after the Accession was signed. On October 30, 1947 an Emergency Government was formed in the State with Sheikh Mohammad Abdullah as its head. The Army fought sustained battle against invaders. The Dogra Infantry resisted at the entry points. The arrival of Indian Army pushed the enemy away from the Valley.

Sd/-

Hari Singh, Maharaja

On Record

Sheikh Abdullah was invited by Maharaja to work as administrator in the Interim Government and work under Prime Minister, Shri Mehr Chand Mahajan.

Most of the area of Jammu Province of J&K fell to Pakistan after October 27, 1947. In Kashmir except Muzaffrabad, all the occupied areas had been cleared of the Pakistani raiders by November 10, 1947. It was on 01.01.1948 that India approached UN Security Council with a complaint against Pakistan. India had every opportunity and capability to liberate all occupied areas of J&K. Why it did not? Needs careful study?

Maharaja announced formation of popular government on 05.03.1948 in State. Relations between Maharaja and Sheikh remained uneasy as the Sheikh wanted Maharaja to quit. Maharaja's

Prime Minister Mehr Chand Mahajan was nearly made defunct. He was replaced by Sheikh Abdullah as Prime Minister.

It was 1st May, 1949 that Sardar Patel suggested Hari Singh for a temporary exit from the State. It was suggested that Yuvraj Karan Singh shall act as Regent in his absence. Maharaja had no option but to accept the same. He communicated his consent from Imperial Hotel New Delhi where he was lodging. Some security and economy related conditions before Patel on 06.05.1949.

BLUNDERS 9

Fall of Gilgit November 16, 1947

Brig. Ghansara Singh, the last Governor of Gilgit wrote in his prison's diary of Astore (Gilgit) established blunder of the Govt. of India headed by Pt. Jawahar Lal Nehru allowing fall of most strategic area just for Abdullah's sake. The minutes of the diary of the Gilgit Governor he wrote in Gilgit prison are the most important documents to prove unforgivable blunder of Nehru. This wrote Brig. Ghansara Singh in his cell.

1. "Prior to my appointment as Governor of Gilgit, I was working as Brigadier General Staff of Jammu and Kashmir State Forces. I was appointed Governor of Gilgit by Maharaja Bahadur, Hari Singh at a time when the partition of the country was in the offing, and the circumstances then prevailing in that part of the state, were too challenging. Shortly after my appointment as Governor, I came to know that the then Prime Minister of the State, were too challenging. Shortly after my appointment as Governor, I came to know that the then Prime Minister of the State, Shri Ram Chander Kak was not interested in my appointment but wanted one of his own favourite to be sent there. He had to however bow before the wishes of the Maharaja. The basic aim of sending me there was to relieve the British Political Agent and head the agency as its first Governor from the State. It would be relevant to mention here that Gilgit at that time was ruled by the British as the then Jammu and Kashmir government had given it over to them on lease for a period of 60 years. Now on the termination of British rule in India, Gilgit was automatically to come back to the State and the Government's take over was quite imminent.

2. "It was essential for me that before departure for Gilgit, I should have a wide range of discussions with the Prime Minister and fully understand the existing situation and threat, vis-à-vis, the policy to be followed in dealing with different type of situations. On 20th day of July 1947, I went to the Prime Minister. I told him, that I had once before been to that part of the State, and knew most of the problems confronting the people inhabiting this region. I strongly objected to the retention of British Officers in Gilgit Scouts as this would unnecessarily create problems and hamper in the independent disposal of cases. The Prime Minister refuted the idea. It was decided that Major General H.L. Scott, who was Chief of the Jammu and Kashmir State forces, would go with me to see my requirements on the spot and report to the government. On 21st July, 1947 I was to proceed to Gilgit but could not get a plane. On 24th July, 1947 again I was to proceed to Gilgit but could not get a plane. On 24th July, 1947 at 2.00 p.m., I got a message from Chaudri Niaz Ahmed, the then Foreign Secretary that the Prime Minister wanted to leave for Gilgit that evening and to reach there in two days time. I was surprised to receive this message. It was quite impossible by all stretches of imagination to cover a distance of more than 200 miles in two days on Ponies. I immediately contacted the Prime Minister who quoted the incident of Raja Ram Singh the uncle of Maharaja Hari Singh, who had earlier covered the same distance in two days time. I repeatedly pleaded, that it was not possible for me to reach Gilgit within two days, as my resources and facilities were not in consonance with that of Raja Ram Singh, but the Prime Minister would not agree to it. I met Major General H. L. Scott, and told him all about the discussion that I had with the Prime Minister. He was surprised to see such an attitude of the Prime Minister. The next day there was a meeting at Palace, in which the Prime Minister and General Scott took part, General Scott raised the point of my going by road and the impossibility of reaching Gilgit by 1st August, 1947 the date of taking over. General Scott on return told me that His Highness told the Prime Minister to arrange for a plane. Thus, due to the intervention of General Scott and solicitude of Maharaja Bahadur, I got mental relief.

3. Before my departure, I learnt from the State Political Department that all officers of the British government had opted to serve Pakistan. The State Civil Officials, who had to replace them, had hardly been detailed. Therefore, I know I was being sent alone to take over the whole of the Gilgit administration single-handed.

4. I had been to Gilgit once before, and as such before going to Gilgit I met and told the Chief Minister that I was being sent there all alone. No Civil Officer was detailed to go with me to take over the charge of different departments. I was directed to meet Pt. Anant Ram the then Revenue Minister who told me that he had detailed one Shri Sehdev Singh, who would be relieved from Leh, to move to Gilgit as Tehsildar, when in peace time there used to be a Wazir Wazarat also. The Medical Department alone detailed one Assistant Surgeon L. Hans Raj, who accompanied me. Thus, I had to go only with one Doctor, when there were four British officers to help the Political Officer. The State had not prepared any budget and I had to wait for it. I was not allowed to carry on with the budget. That was being carried on by the Political Agent in Gilgit. No responsible officer put me in picture of the situation prevailing in the Agency. Though one Pt. Sham Lal, the then Political Secretary informed me about the whole situation. He told me that Scouts and the whole Civil Establishment had already opted for and had even drawn T.A. etc. for their move. I was not given any judicial powers, which were most urgently needed in the Frontier. Al the controlled articles were consumed by the British Officers before their move and thus naturally the British Officers had planned a scheme to discredit the State Administration and to bring about Pakistan.

5. From the above facts it will be quite clear to readers that I was pushed away by the responsible officers of the State without equipping me with the necessities of administration. On my own initiative, I had sent one telegram to Raja Noor Ali Khan, the then Revenue Assistant at Astore and one Telegram to Captain Durga Singh, Company Commander, 5th Kashmir Light Infantry at Ratoo to meet me at Gilgit on or about the 1st of August, 1947.

6. I reached Gilgit on 30th July, 1947 to take over as Governor of Gilgit and its Agency.

7. At that time Lt. Colonel Bacon, a British officer was the Political Agent. He was assisted by three or four British Officers in the Administration.

8. The general impression was that the British officers did not like the change over, but the Gilgit public, however, was highly pleased with the transfer of power and they welcomed the change, but were surprised to find that I had come all alone. The same evening Major Brown, the Commandant, and JCOs of Gilgit Scouts came to pay respects to Major General Scott and to me. During the course of our conversations Sub-Major Babur Khan of Scotts and all the JCOs clearly stated that they wanted to serve Pakistan. They will serve the State if their demands were adequately met. Major General Scott noted down all their demands, which were about a dozen in number and promised that he will obtain sanction and communicate the same to the Governor and they need not worry and must serve the State. After dispersal, I told Major General Scott, that 3 or 4 demands were most unreasonable and these will not be acceded by the Government but he promised for obtaining special sanction.

9. Similarly the next day the whole civil establishment in Gilgit came to meet me and stated that they all had opted to serve Pakistan. They would serve the State in case they were given higher rates of their pay. I had no authority from my Government to settle this issue or give any such assurance. I promised to recommend their case for sympathetic consideration to the Government, but they stopped work in all the offices.

10. No other establishment was with me, except a few officers. There was one Raja Noor Ali Khan, a Revenue Assistant, and one Dr. Hans Raj Gupta with me. I had to lock up the Agency Office and put a military guard over it in the absence of office establishment. Revenue Assistant took over the treasury and Dr. Hans Raj Gupta took over the charge of the Hospital without usual paraphernalia of the office. Lt. Colonel Bacon hesitated to handover, in absence of hands, but I told

Bacon that I would be responsible for Agency offices and will personally compensate for any shortages.

11. Thus the whole charge of the Gilgit and Gilgit Agency was taken over. The office work was at standstill for want of establishment. After a few days some of the non-local clerks showed inclination for service and gradually it was ascertained that he scouts, as well as the civil employees had taken this attitude of non-cooperation at the instigation of some of the British officers. To augment my difficulties they had completely spent or distributed all the controlled articles. There was not a yard of cloth and not an ounce of sugar left for the whole area. Thus my point of view, which I had earlier expressed to the Prime Minister, regarding retention of British officers at Gilgit was realized. General Scott also saw the whole situation. I gave him the following most urgent points for immediate decision of the government—

(a) Demands put forth by Gilgit Scouts.

(b) Demands put forth by the civil establishment regarding grades and pay.

(c) Sanction to permit me to operate the then Budget or alternatively to send me State Budget if sanctioned by the Government.

(d) Acquisition and control of one wireless set installed in Gilgit by the British Government but now controlled paid and maintained by Pakistan authorities from Peshawar. Necessity of acquisition was pointed out to General Scott on the spot, as this was the only means of maintaining communications with Srinagar.

(e) Dire need of more doctors.

(f) Urgency of the appointment of an officer for Chilas outpost, lying vacant, etc.

12. General Scott was given all these points by me. He promised to personally see that all these points were decided immediately on return to Srinagar.

13. On 3rd or 4th August, 1947 revolution started at Yasin. The Political Agent Lt. Colonel Bacon had imprisoned some of the leading men of Yasin, who had revolted against the Raja.

14. They were granted interviews and were patiently heard. Whole Gilgit and Gilgit Agency was watching this agitation with great panic, as it was a test case for me. The Methar of Chitral was supporting the cause of the locals against the Raja. The Methar was interested in the installation of one of his relative (khuswaqats) as a Raja in place of the present one who came from Nagir. After a few days agitation grew stronger. The Methar started sending telegrams to His Highness the Maharaja Bahadur to intervene. I knew this was a legacy left by the British for me. I appreciated that the change of Raja at pressure of the Methar of Chitral would tell heavily on new administration so I decided to support the old Raja and not to yield to the threats of the Methar. Raja of Punial helped me in quelling this agitation most peacefully without resorting to any force.

15. At this time I was sitting like a dummy at Gilgit, I had no powers to operate the Budget, no powers of a District Magistrate, no powers to operate criminal offences in the Agency. I had no controlled articles such as cloth, sugar or kerosene oil for the public. Nothing was decided about any of the point given to General H. L. Scott for decision. Telegrams were sent incessantly to the Foreign Secretary and the Prime Minister but no replies were sent to my queries, about important point sent through General Scott. Further, I noted that there was no officer at Chilas post, so I sent Captain Sayeed, now with the Scouts, to Chilas on tour. On his return he reported that one Captain Hamilton (Late Scout Officer) on his return to Peshawar had openly said at Chilas, that the people need not worry, as they will bring Pakistan there within sixth months' time.

16. During this period companies of 6th Kashmir Infantry started from Srinagar to relieve one Company of 5th J&K Infantry at Bunji. The leading Company was commanded by one captain Hussain Khan. They shouted slogans of Pakistan from Bandipur. I got applications from the locals of Gurez and Astore that the Military party often shouted Pakistan slogans, as they approached villages and they should be adopted. I sent these applications to Major General Scott and to Brigadier Rajinder Singh emphasizing the need for not sending this Battalion.

17. I got message from Major General Scott that the Statement given in the applications were corroborated by a responsible police officer of Kashmir Police Force. This officer had personally heard these slogans at Warwam near Koorgbal and that a proper enquiry may be held and persons involved may be arrested and sent to Srinagar under escort.

18. Raja Noor Ali Khan, my Revenue Assistant, in the meantime went to Astore on tour and reported that the military detachment had actually shouted Pakistan slogans in Astore area too. Lt. Colonel Abdul Majid Khan in the meantime reached Bunji. I called him at once to Gilgit. I told him the whole story and gave him all the secret messages sent by Major General Scott directing him for immediate action and report. On return to Bunji after two days he informed me on phone that, on enquiry it was found that there was no truth in the allegations of the shouting of Pakistani slogans and that only religious slogans were shouted by the Company. He sent enquiry papers and the same were forwarded to the Chief of the Staff.

Gilgit Scouts

19. The services of two of the British officers were retained by the State. Consequently the Gilgit scouts were commanded by Major W.A. Brown-assisted by Captain Matheson, Captain Mohammad Sayeed and Lt. Haider of the Kashmir Army. One Babur Khan, uncle of the Mir of Nagir was Subedar Major of the Scouts. The Headquarters of the Scouts was at Gilgit.

6th Kashmir Infantry

20. 6th Kashmir Infantry, less than about two companies, compoused of Sikhs and Muslims in almost fifty-fifty ratio was commanded by Lt. Colonel Abdul Majid Khan and was stationed at Bunji a place about 34 miles short of Gilgit. Captain Ishan Ali, Captain Hussain Khan, Captain Mohmmad Khan, Captain Baldev Singh, Lt. Raghunath Singh and Lt. Sukh Dev were the State Officers in the Battalion.

21. At this time the civil administration was running most smoothly. His Highness's birthday was approaching and Durbar was to be held. The preparations were afoot to celebrate it in a big way. Lt. Colonel Abdul Majid Khan and both Mohammedan and Sikh Dogra officers were called from Bunji to Gilgit to participate in the celebrations. Mirs, Rajas, Civil and Military officers all collected.

22. Later, I knew that, during their stay at this very particular time Mohammedan officers of J&K State Forces contracted scout officers and decided to establish Pakistan in Gilgit.

23. After about one and a half month, I received a letter from General Scott saying that he was hooted by certain officers when he went to the Prime Minister to talk about Gilgit affairs. He stated that none was keen to settle Gilgit matters and as such I should not expect any decision or help from these quarters. On receipt of this information, I was definite that I was doomed.

24. By this time I was in full picture of the Gilgit situation. I knew the attitude of the Scouts. I knew the behaviour of 6th Kashmir Infantry. I knew the grouses of the civil local employees. I knew the attitude of certain Mirs. I wrote a D.O. letter each to Pt. Ram Chander Kak, General Janak Singh who took over as Prime Minister and Mr. Batra, the then Deputy Prime Minister. In these three D.O. letters, I vividly depicted the entire picture of the situation in Gilgit. I stated that in case the state accedes to Indian Union, the Gilgit province will go to Pakistan but no action was taken. I never got replies to my Dos from any of these quarters and my difficulties remained just the same.

25. A few days later, I heard at Gilgit that General H.L. Scott was relinquishing his duties of the Chief of the Staff and as a matter of right and routine I was entitled to the post of the Chief of the Staff. I pointed out to General Janak Singh, the then Prime Minister, about my right. I got an evasive reply. I heard that Kangra intrigue was going on underneath against me. After a few days I got information from my friends that General Janak Singh with the help of his Kangra party had succeeded in getting his son Kashmir Singh from the Indian Army as Military Adviser in place of General H.L. Scott. It would not be out of

place to state that since the disbandment of 7th Infantry (Composed of half-Sikhs and half-Kangra Dogras) Kangra gentry in J&K State service with the exception of a few reasonable persons were working against me, in spite of my clear confession that I had not the least hand in the disbandment of that unit. My personal feeling is that they got the right opportunity to get me deprived of my well-earned claim for the post of the Chief of the Staff of Jammu and Kashmir State Forces. After serving the state most faithfully and loyally for more than 27 years no worse treatment could be meted out to any one in the Service.

26. About ten days before the revolution I went to Bunji and my main object was to find out as to what strength was available with me in the event of any emergency. Lt. Colonel Abdul Majid Khan told me that there was only one Mohammedan Coy of Capt. Hussain Khan, which was fit for operations wherever needed. The Sikh Coy consisted of raw recruits who would be fit after 3 to 5 months time, when they fire their musketry course. So I had to depend on one Mohammedan Coy alone.

27. It was here at Bunji that one Telegraph Officer a Kashmiri Pandit secretly informed me that there was a rumour in Kashmir that one major Sher Ali of 4th J&K Infantry had joined hands with Pakistan troops, and they had taken Muzaffrabad and were at Baramulla.

28. With full knowledge of the events and told lack of cooperation on the part of the J&K Authorities in Srinagar, I prepared myself to lay down my life along with my colleagues for the sake of the state, which our forefathers had once extended to that part of the country.

29. I had a very good occasion to slip away from Bunji but as my other colleagues and on Muslim public could not be evacuated, so I decided to go back to Gilgit and to die on the spot, along with them. On arrival at Gilgit, I learnt that the State had acceded to Indian Union and Pakistan troops had reached Pattan near Srinagar.

30. Further rumours about the Gilgit's invasion by Swat and Chitral started. I contacted the Mirs and Governors except Raja of Punial as there was no telephone communication. All promised and assured me of their loyalty and support. The Raja of Punial was called

by me. He reached Gilgit the same evening, when I was arrested. He was not allowed by the commandant of the Scouts to see me.

31. There were conflicting news about the fall of Srinagar. There was a sensation among the Scouts. Major Brown, Lt. Gulam Haider and Subedar Major Babur Khan of the Scouts were holding secret meetings and were in touch with Bunji Mohammedan officers. Hindu and Sikh shopkeepers came to me and requested to call state army detachment, from Bunji.

32. I had a great problem I had to weigh the two, i.e., the Gilgit Scouts and the 6th J&K Infantry. I knew the attitude of the Mohammedans of 6th J&K Infantry will be more destructive, than that of the Gilgit Scouts. The Mohammedans of the 6th Infantry knew what had happening at Poonch, near their homes (a regular war). After critical examination of these pros and cons, I decided that I should depend on Gilgit Scouts, as they had not seen disastrous actions of East and West Punjab. The second consideration was that it will bring no credit if we died at the hands of our own Mohammedans. It would be rather a credit to us if we were killed by Gilgit people whom we have once conquered. With these impressions, I did not want Mohammedans of the 6th Infantry to be in Gilgit before time. I informed my subordinates about the gravity of the situation. They decided to shoot their women folk in case of emergency, before they fall in the hands of the Scouts.

33. On 3rd October, 1647 in the afternoon I contacted on phone Lt. Colonel Abdul Majid Khan at Bunji and ordered him to reach Gilgit immediately with as much force as he could muster.

34. On the night between 31st October, 1947 at 1 November, 1947 at 2.00 a.m. about 100 Gilgit Scouts led by Major Brown, Lt. Haider Khan and Sub. Maj Babur Khan surrounded my house.

35. Hearing foot noise on my wooden planked verandah I got up and saw about 8 men on the side. I never thought of scouts but suspected them as Pakistanis. I got revolver and slipped to the other room. My orderly was there. I told him to take a rifle. My driver with his gun also reached there. I had a revolver, my orderly had a rifle and

my driver was with a D.B. Gun. I went to my office room and outside I saw a lot of soldiers surrounding the Bungalow.

36. When I came back to my orderly's room I saw six men pushing my bathroom door and trying to break it open. I thought they will enter the house. One round was fired in the air to frighten them away. They started firing in reply. We occupied three rooms, one by each. Both sides exchanged fire. After about one hour MMG bursts started on my bungalow Skylight smashed and bullets were striking right and left.

37. It was Lt. Haider of Scouts, son of Colonel Sher Ali, pensioner of J&K State who started machine gunning. It was stopped after a short while. Afterwards rifle fire from both sides continued till 4.00 a.m.

38. In the morning Pandit Mani Ram, Naib Tehsildar, and a Police Inspector were sent to me. The scouts were still surrounding my Bungalow. Both these officers came to me and said that the scouts' officers say that I should surrender within 15 minutes and in case of surrender all non-Muslims and civil officials will be safely sent to Bunji, as they want to establish Pakistan in Gilgit Agency only. In case these terms were not accepted, all non-Muslims would be shot dead. On, this ultimatum I called Raja Noor Ali Khan and Mr. Sehdev Singh, Tehsildar. They came to me and requested for acceptance of the terms and return to Bunji, Battalion Headquarters. To these terms, I agreed. As I had ordered Lt. Colonel Abdul Majid Khan on 30 October to reach Gilgit immediately so I was expecting him at any time. Had he reached Gilgit as ordered the picture might have been different, but to our misfortune, Captain Hussain Khan of 6th J&K Infantry instead reached Gilgit same morning, at about 9.00 a.m. leaving his coy behind at Pari, half way between Gilgit and Bunji. They lay ambush for us in case we try to escape from Gilgit. Captain Ishen Ali of 6th Infantry also reached Gilgit.

39. Thus Major Brown, Captain Ihsan Ali, Capt. Hussain Capt. Sayeed, Lt. Haider, Sub. Major Babur Khan and Wazir Walayat Ali (Revenue Assistant, Kashmir State, on leave at Gilgit) formed a provisional Government, headed by one local, Sub Rais Khan.

40. After hearing the news of my arrest, people from the surrounding villages collected. They protested against this action.

It is said that some slabs of detonators were collected from the PWD stores and were shown to the villagers. They were told that these were the hand grenades, which had been distributed by the Governor to all the non-Muslims of the Bazar for destruction of Muslim Houses. Thus these ignorant people were duped for the time being but after a few days they again came to know the real position. They cursed this action but were helpless in face of the revolution.

41. Mohammedan Officers of the State intervened and disagreed to the first decision and compelled Scout Officers to ask for the surrender of Bunji Garrison of non-Muslims. Instead they started arrangements to attack Bunji. Captain Matheson, the 22nd British Officer at Chilas Post, was instructed from Gilgit by this Provisional Government to occupy Astore and to cut off line of withdrawal of Bunji Garrison. Major Brown and Capt. Hussain arranged attack on the Sikh detachment from Gilgit side. 6th Infantry had one outpost of non-Muslims at Janglot. Mohammedans of 6th Infantry and Gilgit Scouts raided this post at night and shot all, except one person who crossed river Indus on a log of wood. It was there that one Sub. Jamit Singh of 5th Infantry, younger brother of Col. Joginder Singh, was killed along with his men.

42. The Sikh Company at Bunji hearing about the happening of Gilgit and the massacre of their outpost at Janglot fled to find their way back to Astore. This line of withdrawal was already cut off by Captain Matheson with the help of Scouts from Chilas. Therefore, this company could not find any way. They stuck up to the Hills for a fortnight but had nothing to eat, so after starvation, fell back to Bunji and were captured.

43. Neither any of the Mirs, nor any of the Rajas were at Gilgit at this time, it was purely a military government, and an army revolution. Public had no say in it.

44. In this Government, two influences began to work. Gilgit Scout Officers were in favour of Pakistan alone and they did not want

to slaughter any non-Muslims. On the other hand Mohammedan Officers of the State Forces were totally against keeping any non-Muslim alive. They wanted either to shoot them or to convert them. Lt. Haider Khan volunteered to shoot me. Thrice, timings were fixed to shoot all non-Muslims, but somehow or the other this was avoided by local people. Life was most insecure. A great panic prevailed. All civil officials with their families were threatened. Bazar people were harassed and in general pandemonium reigned.

45. Major Brown ruled Gilgit and Capt. Hussain became General at Bunji. He went to Astore, took over the treasury and started shooting all selected Hindu and Sikh rank and file on minor pretexts.

46. Capt. Mohd. Khan married a Kashmiri Pandit's girl. At Astore and Bunji he forced conversion. The maxim of the day was either all non-Muslims should be slaughtered or forcibly converted to Mohammedanism.

47. From Gilgit, Major Brown sent wireless messages to Peshawar authorities, intimating them that Pakistan Government had been established at Gilgit and they must recognize it.

48. On 3rd November, 1947 flag-hoisting ceremony was performed at Gilgit in Scouts lines by Major Brown, where all Civil Officers of the State, except myself were called and directed to salute the Pakistan Flag.

49. It was on 3rd November, 1947 that Lt. Colonel Abdul Majid Khan and Sub. Major Babur Khan came to me. Sub. Major brought one typed telegram, in which they had written charge of Gilgit as handed over to Gilgit Government, etc.

50. I refused to sign the telegram saying that I had not handed over, but it was forcibly taken over. On my refusal, I was plainly told that in case of my refusal, all non-Muslims would be shot dead. I offered myself to be shot, as I told Sub. Major that I was the culprit who had not requested authorities to join Pakistan and that the civilians had no hand it. He said that there is no question of one man; it is a question of all non-Muslims. If I want all to be slaughtered, I may not sign and

those were the instructions of the provisional government. Thus I was forced to sign the telegram.

51. After a fortnight, one Sardar Mohammed Alam came by air from Peshawar and took over as Political Agent in Gilgit. Air Service started with vigour. Civil and Military Officers of the regular Pakistan Army poured in. One Colonel Mohammed Aslam Khan, son of Brigadier Rehmat Ullah Khan, pensioner of J&K State Forces arrived with two other regular officers. In short Pakistan Civil and Military Officers took over the administration. There was never any Azad Government in Gilgit. The Military Officers contacted Peshawar and Pakistan took over Gilgit and started administration properly. Gradually things came to be normal. During this period Major Brown and Capt. Hussain Khan fell out with each other, each wanted to take greater credit for the revolution.

52. But as soon as Pakistan Officers reached they transferred both Major Brown and Capt. Matheson to Peshawar and took over Command of both the Scouts, as well as the Mohammedan troops of the State, under the command of Captain Hussain Khan.

53. The Pakistan Air Force, started work with great keenness. Monoplanes were used for conveying officials; Dakotas were used for dropping arms, ammunition, clothing and ration from Peshawar. Fresh recruitment started in Gilgit, about two thousand recruits were enlisted.

54. Rifles, 3 "mortars and guns were dropped both at Gilgit and Bunji. This I knew through some soldiers from Gilgit Scouts who would disclose the information to my men. I could see are droppings in Gilgit from my own quarters and this was very freely done."

Governor Ghansara Singh's detention in Gilgit

55. "On 1st November, 1947 at 8.45 a.m. I was imprisoned by Sub. Major Babur Khan, of the Scouts and was removed from my Bungalow to one of the Indian Officers Quarters in Gilgit Scouts Lines. I was surrounded by more than one hundred scouts all armed and in

uniform. Major Brown and Lieutenant Haider were there said to be in Radio Station. These Scouts were the same lot who had laid siege of Bungalow since last midnight, led by Maj. Brown. A few days later all the unit employees of Scouts lines were also moved down to Scouts lines.

56. "In the beginning for several days we were getting information through orderlies that we would be sent back to Srinagar, and that the transport was being collected. Sometimes there were rumours that the Kashmir Government had been informed to take over their prisoners at Burzil. In fact the Gilgit scouts officers did not want to keep us in Gilgit, but the Mohammedan officers of the 6th Jammu and Kashmir Infantry did not like to send us back, because of the fact that we would disclose their actions against the Government. As such they prevailed over Gilgit Scouts. For several days nights were most unforgettable. At odd hours alarms were sounded practically every night for a month. Sometimes machine gun firing and at others rifle firing was going on for hours together. Captain Hussain Khan by new started loot and forced, conversion at Astore. Messages from Mohammedans of 6th J&K Infantry personnel were pouring in Gilgit to either shoot all Kaffirs or to convert them.

57. "Once night Scouts and a few townsmen started looting non-Muslim houses and shops. All shopkeepers along with their families ran away to the riverbed and polo ground. Some naked and some half clothed, spent the whole winter night outside under the sky. Early in the morning Khan Mohammad Alam Khan, the Pakistan Political Agent in Gilgit came to the Bazar to see this happening. Males and females all in tears related their woeful tales and losses sustained. Scouts took away a lot of booty to their homes. This raid was made mostly by Scouts with a few other townsmen.

58. "A few days later Bazar Hindus and Sikhs were all converted. Beards of the old Sikhs were shaved in front of the quarter guard of the Scouts. There was great harassment. Most of the Kashmiri Pandits out of terror, adopted Islam. For a few days such converts were well fed and

entertained. They were all the preachings. Now they could move freely in the bazar and working in their shops.

59. "There were three or four Sikhs living with out civil officers, who were not converted. Sardar Arjan Singh Contractor being one of them. Outside contacts and movements started from all directions. Sometimes officers from Peshawar were coming sometimes Mirs and Rajas were coming. Parties from Bunji were visiting Gilgit or detachments from Chitral were coming to reinforce Gilgit garrison. One Pathan Assistant Political Agent from Peshawar was always leading processions to receive such persons or parties. No Muslim leader of Gilgit was participating, except under threat or coercion.

60. "I was kept in one room continuously for three months. There was one W.C. and no bathroom in it. My servants, one Sardar Makhan Singh, his son Roshan Singh and one Sansar Singh were put with me in the same room. I was not allowed to get out of my room. I did not see the sun. There was one skylight in my room where from I could see whether it was day or night. I could not take bath for three months, as there was no arrangement. During daytime, I was all-alone as my orderlies were allowed to sit outside in the sun I was given no book or any paper. My orderly had one Ramayan, which I would read all the day. In the morning I would take my meals at 11.00 a.m. and in the evening at 5.00 p.m. as after dark my orderlies were not permitted to go outside to bring my food. Most strict watch was kept one my orderlies. They were not allowed to talk or contact anybody.

61. "At 7.00 p.m. the Guard Commander would lock up the room and none could go out even to answer the call of nature. Days and nights were very cool. There was no arrangement to keep the room warm. As money was a great problem, so I had to buy five seers of fuel to warm ourselves both in the morning and evening. No officer or any man could come to find my difficulties during this period. I had to purchase all edibles from my own pocket to feed all my servants. I spent all I had. There was a balance of my 15 days pay in the office. I asked for it, and got Rs.100 for such expenditure.

62. "I had secretly kept a razor blade with me. For want of exercise and good food I grew weak and lean. Many a times when all alone I thought of committing suicide. I several times felt my throat to find out which will be the right place to try. At times I felt if I fail to finish my self it may bring a bad name for me. I will be considered as a coward not to have borne the hardship I was put to.

71. "During winter months it was nearly impossible to sleep from 7.00 p.m. to 8.00 a.m. Many a times we were awakened by fake alarm practices of the Scouts. We had to concoct stories but our stock soon exhausted. Sometimes at 11.00 p.m., sometimes at 12, sometimes at 1 or 2 at night I used to get up. My friend Makhan Singh would at most times wake me up by his words, *Wah Guru, Wah Guru*. We were all fed up with him, as he was the only one who would care much for home and death. We would bring tales that all will be slaughtered this evening at 8.00 a.m. We liked that because we thought that this would bring us easy death. Sometimes my Kashmiri washer man would also bring such a news but the occasion never materialized. After a month or so one Lieutenant Col. Aslam Khan came to see me. He mentioned a lot of stories about revolution in Jammu and Kashmir State and also told me that, all the Mohammedan officers in the Jammu and Kashmir State Army have been slaughtered. As such no question of repatriation would arise. State prisoners will be treated as Pakistani prisoners by the Kashmir State and the Pakistani authorities will treat me as an army prisoner and that the army will in future issue rations to me and to my servants.

63. "For three months it was nothing but a great tragedy to spend time. Life was a mere burden. No news from home, nor news from abroad, no books or papers to read and no getting out of the room. After 3 months, Mirs and Rajas were called by the Political Agent. None was allowed to see me one day Mir of Hunza's younger brother quietly visited me in the evening as Hunza Scout Guard was on duty that day. He saw me locked up in one room and promised that he would relate this to the Mirs and Rajas. After a fortnight I do not know how it came out that I was shifted to another quarter, where I could sit in the

sun. Major Anwar Khan, the Brigade Major in Gilgit came to remove me to other place and accompanied me to that quarter. I saw the sun rise and sun set after a weary three months.

64. "After a few days Lieutenant Colonel Mohammed Aslam Khan came to see me again and brought a present of a few tins of cigarettes and a few cakes of bath soap. It was a luxury for me after six months' time. He ordered to issue soap from the stores for washing clothes. As a man I cannot forget his presents and the soap I got after months and months. Major Anwar Khan, his younger brother came to me, when I called him. His look for told me that he felt my captivity. During this time one brother of Mohammad Aslam Khan in the Air force, came to pick up Lieutenant Colonel Aslam Khan for Peshawar. He was new to the place. He flew low and his plane crashed and he along with one comrade died on the spot.

65. "Col. Aslam Khan was replaced by one Col. Jilani (a Pathan from Peshawar) Col. Jilani came to see me and asked about food being provided to me. I told him that I get dal and bread. He asked if I was getting any vegetables. I replied in the native, as I was not getting them for the last six months. He then started narrating his own story and told me that he himself was a prisoner in Burma. He was ill treated by Japanese and as such he always felt the difficulties of a prisoner. It was through his kindness that I got vegetables added to my dal and bread. At times good guard commanders would come on duty and bring dry fruits stealthily in their pockets and give some to my orderlies. Sometimes the orderlies would give their small share to me. This was how I could taste dry fruits.

66. "In June 1948, Dr. Wanger of the International Red Cross Society visited me. The P. A. as well as Col. Jilani were accompanying him. I was sick at that time. He told me that I could write letters to my relatives. From now onward I was sending telegrams and letters. After this P. A. would once in a month visit my quarters and ask me about any difficulties. I had out down my needs and a such was not worrying them for ordinary things. He arranged milk for me and gave me some money from the balance of my pay to defray such expenses. He later on

showed great respects for me and sent a few peaches three or four times. It was now more than 8 months that I did not go for a walk. One day when he came to me I told him that I was tired of this life, as I was not allowed to go out of my four walled compound would it be unfair on my part if I ask for going out to the garden for a walk even only a hundred yards outside. He agreed to my request and I started walking, after about nine months stay inside the walls.

67. "One day in the evening the P. A. met me in the garden and asked if I play tennis. He was a keen tennis player. He prepared a tennis court and in the last month of my stay in Gilgit I played tennis with him for a month. Thus in the end we parted as friends and I owe gratitude to him for his nice behaviour especially in the latter part of my stay.

68. "It is pity however, that the civil employees of the Jammu and Kashmir State were not paid any sort of allowance during their stay in Gilgit, though I had made repeated requests both to the Jammu and Kashmir Government through Dr. Wanger and the P. A. Gilgit. A few converts, however, were getting maintenance allowance from the Pakistan Government. It may also be mentioned that some of the Hunza guard commanders were very lenient to my orderlies. Guard Commanders from Nagir Scouts considered my men as their enemies and would treat them most harshly. Behaviour of Scouts of other Rajas was quite fair. Officers and men of our own 6th J&K Infantry were most appalling. They would abuse our men, ill treat them and lodge complaints against Scouts guard commanders, if they would see any of my orderlies sitting outside or going to the Bazar to buy anything.

69. "In short Gilgit Scouts of Nagir and Mohammedans of J&K 6th Infantry, would not tolerate the sight of my men, whether on duty or off the duty.

70. "It was on the 7th of July, 1948 that seven planes of the R.I.A.F., appeared and surprised the population of Gilgit. As far as I could see, six planes started raiding the town and one kept flying up in the sky watching the result. The targets selected by the pilots were as follows.

(a) Scouts lines,

(b) Radio Station and,

(c) Aerodrome,

71. "The casualties of Gilgit Scouts and the Civilians were four or five killed and six or seven wounded. Pt. Vidh Lal, Head Clerk Scouts and Pt. Omkar Nath of Srinagar were among the victims. As it was a surprise raid, the whole population of the town was present, including the whole J&K State Civil establishment with families stationed in Scouts lines.

72. "Both heavy and small bombs were dropped and strafing also was done by the R.I.A.F. Two bombs fell in line of my quarters, one about 100 yards short and the other about 100 yards ahead.

73. "Gilgit is a small and congested town. Bazar, School and Scouts lines were in one sector. Similarly Political Agents House, Radio Station and Hospital were in the other sector. Therefore, the pilots were extremely cautious to avoid bombing the non-military objectives. The whole bazaar was safe, the school was safe and the populated area was safe.

74. "The Scouts opened a lot of rifle and machine guns fire from Scouts line, aerodrome and Political Agents vicinity, which is near Radio Station. In this air raid about 50 per cent bombs did not explode perhaps due to old ammunition, so the damage was confined only to the Scouts barracks.

75. "The Major chunk of population in Gilgit was very much harassed and people started running to the hills and countryside. The scouts and a few leaders of the town approached the Political Agent and told him to slaughter all the non-Muslims as they suspected some of us to have contact with Jammu and Kashmir authorities.

76. "The Political Agent (Khan Mohd. Alam) did not agree to the above request and so they dispersed.

77. After this raid the whole population deserted the town and only one company of the Scouts was in the area. After about ten days the men folk returned to their homes and gradually women also came back. Thus the confidence of the people was restored. Had there been any

move of troops from Gurez side thee was a great chance of success in that area but at the same time it is worth stating that all non-Muslims would have been killed and none would have survived to tell the tale. The plan of the enemy was that as soon as Indian Army appeared in Burzi area the non-Muslim elements be finished.

78. "After this air raid all necessary precautionary measures were taken by the authorities. Trenches were dug in, etc.

Second Air Raid

79. "After about 3 weeks, the second air aired took place in the afternoon. I could locate only two aeroplanes. These aeroplanes selected only two objectives scouts' lines and Radio Station.

80. "This was not a surprise attack. As soon as the aeroplanes reached Kamri pass, we got air alarm in Gilgit. Telephone message was passed from Kamri to Astore and thence to Gilgit. So we had to wait for about 10 minutes before the aeroplanes appeared. All civilians and locals had in the meantime run away from the town to the hills.

81. "The Radio station was close to the Gilgit hospital. After explosion of a bomb, one woman was hit by a stone and died. No other human life was lost. In this air raid most the bombs were picked up unexploded.

Third Air Raid

82. "This was the heaviest of all the air raids. As far as I could see there were eight aeroplanes, which took part. They came in two waves. The raid lasted for more than one hour. In this air raid the pilots selected the same military targets.

83. "One bomb fell in the kitchen of the Political Agent and it was removed from there. I did not hear about any casualty in the hospital locality. It was however said that there were a few additions due to the heavy shock of explosions. I do not know how for this news was correct.

84. "In this raid one house of the Raja of Punial was burnt by a bomb. I came to know that the Raja of Punial had brought with him a few men from Darel in connection with a murder case. They were armed. As soon as the planes appeared the Raja of Punial ran away, but these men came out with rifles from the houses. My assumption is that one of the pilots may have seen a few men with rifles near that building and dropped a bomb as otherwise thee was no occasion to release a bomb and that was the impression which an agent of the Raja related to the others in Gilgit.

85. "House of other Rajas of the Agency remained all-intact and were never touched by the pilots.

General

86. "After first air raid the morale of the people was very low. The authorities tried to keep it up by assisting that every rifleman can drop an aeroplane when on a low flight. Several shots were tried by gunners and rifleman in the first air raid but with no result.

96. In the second air raid a lot of selected shots were sent for from Darel to shoots the planes. This time also they failed to drop or hit the actual target.

87. "In the third raid also, some tactics were used with no result. People got more demoralized and upset, when they saw planes flying low and dropping bombs. To maintain their morale, authorities arranged for two anti-aircraft guns from Peshawar.

88. "They were dropped in Gilgit by a Dakota. One was kept in Scouts lines and the other in the Aerodrome.

89. "On the whole after seeing all the three air raids, I was convinced that the pilots of the R.T.A.F. who participated in the raids deserved high appreciation for the selection of their targets, in a small and congested town like Gilgit.

Communications

90. "Gilgit had one Telegraph office and one Radio Station. Radio Station belonged to the British Government and the Government of

Jammu and Kashmir was expected to purchase it. The State authorities failed to purchase it and bring the establishment on their state pay. The establishment was paid and maintained by Peshawar Station all along. Telegraph officer was originally a Kashmiri Pandit and in my time he was replaced by a Mohammedan.

91. "The Radio Station was controlled by a Parsi gentleman on pay of Pakistan and Telegraph office by a Mohammedan. It is doubtful whether they were transmitting my secret messages to the state authorities or not. The transfer was not effected through I had pointed out this fact to the State authorities, in time. The taking over of the Radio Station was one of the points given to General Scott for early decision, but nothing was done to effect transfer till my arrest.

92. "A new jeep road from Babusar was prepared by the Pakistani authorities.

Civil and Military Prisoners

93. "During the whole period of the detention of civil employees, they had to buy their own foodstuffs. The arrangements were made by the Political Agent through his civil authorities. The Civil employees had exhausted their own private money. At this critical juncture, one Lala Hans Raj of Amritsar, a shopkeeper in Gilgit came to their rescue. He gave liberal monetary help to all who needed money. Two Mohammedan Civil Officers Raja Noor Ali Khan, Revenue Assistant and Sultan Alam, Naib Tehsildar, remained most loyal. They were offered high posts and salaries but they refused to serve Pakistan. They were not paid anything, but managed to live independently like non-Muslim officials.

94. "A new jeep road from Babusar was prepared by the Pakistani authorities.

95. "As regards military prisoners, I had no occasion to see them except on my return to Babusar. Their condition was deplorable. They were mere skeletons. They had hardly any food or clothing. Dysentery became prevalent on account of bad food and shortage of clothing in

high altitudes. They were brought to Balakot and then to Attock. At Attock, Pakistan officers gave them full scale ration and clothing. As a result of this their health improved a bit. The treatment here was on the whole satisfactory.

96. "Gilgit people in the beginning were given the impression that they will rule Gilgit when Pakistan is established. They will be free from any foreign domination. On the establishment of Pakistan, people found that the governing machinery is Pathan government replaces all from Peshawar and the State Government. After comparing administration of both the Government they have realized their bounder in supporting the revolution and in this area we have still sympathizers for the State administration.

97. "On my arrest Scout guard was posted at my house and I had to vacate it. All my private arms and ammunition, kit and stores were retained in it.

98. "A few days after the arrival of Khan Mohammed Alam Khan. The Political Agent, Gilgit, my kit was returned to me but no arms, etc.

99. "Major Brown personally opened and searched my boxes in my room. He took all my secret records away. He also took the military pattern and one country made sword lying in the boxes.

100. "The stuff in two of my boxes was stolen away. I had following arms with me, which was taken away.

(a) One D.B.12 Bore gun manufactured by Churchill and Coy.

(b) One Rifle.

(c) One Service Revolver.

(d) One Pistol.

(e) Four thousand cartridges costing Rs.2400/- at @Rs.60/- per hundred.

(f) One brand new fishing rod superior type.

101. "After a few months, one enquiry from the P. A. I came to know that out of my private stuff, Major Brown had not handed over to the P.A. my service revolver, fishing rod and four thousand cartridges.

102. "I was asked to move on short scale, so I deposited my kit (seven boxes and one kit bag) with the P. A. Gilgit. It was for the Government about the return of my private arms and kit from Gigit and a proper action against Major Brown, especially when he was in J&K State Service.

103. "I was released on 15th January, 1949 at Suchetgarh.

104. "On arrival here, I reported to the Revenue Minister and submitted my joining report, but got no reply.

105. "During my activity, my family was given no allowance of any sort. After arrival, I had to wait for 6 months. After termination of a period of 21 months, I got my pay at the rate of Rs.1, 000/- instead of Rs.1, 700/- p.m. on 16th July 1949, i.e., 1st Sawan 2006 and nothing for the remaining period up to date.

106. "The main causes of the fall of Gilgit Agency were as follows:-

(a) After the conquest of Gilgit illaqa normally the protective units for this far flung mountainous area used to be a weal Brigade that consisted of Brigade Headquarters, one Infantry Battalion, one Mountain Battery and the Gilgit Scouts.

(b) In 1947 only two companies of 6th Infantry were sent, one Company commanded by Capt. Hussain of Gilgit, was a trained coy but the other Sikh coy consisted only of raw recruits. This instead of a weak Brigade, there was only one Mohammedan trained coy at the disposal of the Governor, but this coy commander had started Pakistan along with from Srinagar, well known to the State Army Headquarters Officers located in Srinagar.

(c) Two British officers Commanding Gilgit Scouts took active part in bringing about this revolution.

(d) Mirs of Hunza and Nagir, who were state guests in Srinagar, before return to Gilgit, had openly told the Chief Minister, that they would establish Pakistan in Gilgit, if the State opted for India.

(e) Mohammedan Officers of the State posted in Gilgit were very keen to establish Pakistan. They joined heads with the British Officers for the purpose.

(f) Promises made by General Scott to remove grievances of the Scout officers and civil employees were not considered in Srinagar, hence there was discontentment amongst the employees."

This original diary report of Governor in detention speaks volumes about the mala fide intention of the Government headed by Pt. Nehru vis-à-vis J&K. Many historians and intellectuals have been unnecessarily arguing that Gilgit-Baltistan was never a part of J&K.

The Supreme Court of POK held in a famous petition of Ammanullah Khan that Gilgit-Baltistan formed integral part of J&K. The petitioner had challenged the transfer of nearly 5000 sq. miles of J&K territory in Karakoram by Pakistan to China in 1963. Indian leadership failed to respond at home or in the United Nations while this was a grave violation of UN Resolutions on J&K directing Pakistan to withdraw from entire occupied territories of J&K. China has built its Highway connecting Beijing with Peshawar. China has recently built sixteen battle helipads in this sector threatening the national security of the country.

BLUNDERS 10

Fall of Mirpur November 25, 1947

Every year 25th November is remembered as Mirpur day. On November 25, 1947 a curse descended on Mirpur in POK (Pakistan Occupied Kashmir). Out of a total population of 25000 about 18000 were killed (primarily Sikhs) and about 3500 were wounded by the aggressors sponsored by Pakistan.

About 650 years ago, according to a legend, City of Mirpur was founded by two Saints, Mira Shah Gazi and Gosain Bodhpuri. The word, 'Mir' was taken from the name of the former while 'Pur' from the latter to give the name, 'Mirpur', which became the Hindu-Muslim unity and brotherhood. Simplicity, fair deal, integrity, hospitality and tolerance marked the character of its inhabitants. Not only were they imbued with the feelings of self-respect and qualities of hard-working, intelligence and God-fearing but were also brave and courageous, and ever-ready to sacrifice anything in the cause of their mother-land. Hospitality and courtesy are the inherited qualities of the people of Mirpur. They have their own sweet language known as Mirpuri.

Mirpur was under attack by the armed raiders' right from 1st week of November, 1947. Indian Army was not deputed on Jammu front for the reason stated extensively in this book. Indian Army was stationed in Kashmir only. Abdullah was the administrator and his writ ran alone.

The air strikes of the Indian Air Force against the enemy did not work. On November 22 and 23, the enemy used its full force and putting bullets into the city from all directions. This continued day and night without any break.

On November 24, came the final blow when a full battalion of the enemy strongly supported by artillery and 3" Mortar fire launched an attack on the south western part of the city. The post put up the most spirited resistance, but the enemy came in wave after wave and after six hours of ceaseless fighting, this portion of the defence was over run by the Pakistan army, units of which entered the city at mid-night. Alarmed by the most critical situation, the internal flying squads engaged themselves in hand to hand fighting with the invaders.

At this critical juncture, the administrative machinery at Mirpur clandestinely took the decision of retreating to Jammu leaving the civil population at the mercy of the enemy. The Wazir Wazarat and his officers decided to retreat after failed to receive any support from Jammu. This led to create panic, chaos and confusion among the civil population. Thousands of women committed suicide to save themselves from the clutches and rape of the cruel enemy let loose by the invaders.

According to an eyewitness in nineties for a moment, there appeared a hope when at midnight a fighter aircraft of the Indian Air Force buzzed appeared in the sky. But nothing happened. The enemy then greeted the people of Mirpur with showers of bullets from all sides and the whole town was witnessed blood and dead bodies of over 18000 residents mostly Sikhs. About 3500 wounded and half-dead were made prisoners while another group of about 3500, after walking miles and miles managed to run away towards Jammu.

Thus the curtain of that tragic scene of, **'the naked dance of death at Mirpur'** on 10 Maghar 2004 (25th November, 1947) dropped with grave silence where none was left to mourn even.

Had Indian Government chosen to defend Mirpur, this human tragedy would have been averted and Indian interest saved.

Maharaja regrets Fall of Mirpur

In his letter dated January 31, 1948 he told Sardar Patel that;

"In Mirpur district, at the time when the Indian forces arrived, we are still holding Mangla and our territory along the Jehlum Canal bank, but during the past two months we have lost Mangla, Alibeg, Gurudwara, and the town of Mirpur, the town of Bhimber and the villages of Deva and Battala, the town of Rajouri and the whole of the area adjoining Chhamb, Nowshera. Jhangar, a key-place both for Mirpur and Kotli, was lost after a defeat. These defeats have been a heavy blow for us and have also undermined the prestige of the Indian forces. Not a single town has so far been recovered by the Indian troops. The people judge an army from results and not from propaganda carried on about it. On the Kathua-Sialkot border attacks have been intensified. Everyday there is one raid after another. A number of villages have been burnt, people have been looted, women abducted and there have been killings also. The result has been that all the border villages have been vacated and we have about 70,000 to 80,000 refugees in the city of Jammu. Crops, houses and valuables have been lost. Most of the people are also vacating Jammu and its suburbs and are going to West Punjab. The situation, therefore, is worsening everyday."

BLUNDERS 11

Fall of Bagh (Poonch)

Poonch and Rajouri remained under the siege of Pak-troops for one year. It was great resistance, says Captain Dewan Singh who was serving in Poonch in J&K army in that sector during the defence of Poonch campaign. Brigadier Pritam Singh displayed a unique military strategy in defence of Poonch. Col. Hiranand Dubey made historic contributions to save town of Poonch and Rajouri from the siege of Pakistani Army. The role of local Muslim, Hindu and Sikh leaders was highly nationalist and historic.

However, Bagh, Rawalakote and other areas on the west of Poonch town were lost. This was one more blunder that the most strategic areas of J&K were allowed to break from J&K only because the Sheikh did not want them with Kashmir. Nehru was Sheikh's top supporter.

Delhi's Mischief

Earlier, N. Gopalaswami Ayyangar, an important Dominion Minister dealing J&K shot a letter to Maharaja Hari Singh on December 24, 1947 which reveals the mischief that was cooking up in Delhi against the Maharaja.

"I am most grateful to Your Highness for your letter of December 17, 1947. We have given anxious consideration to all the points mentioned in that letter and during the last two days we have had the advantage of further discussion of several of those points with Sheikh Abdullah.

2. I have set out below our considered conclusions. In our opinion they are in the best interests of the Jammu and Kashmir State, its Ruler

and its people. I earnestly hope that you will find yourself able to accept and give effect to all of them.

3. The Government of India does not desire that you should deviate from the Mysore model except in respect of matters which are considered minor and which are necessitated by the different conditions, which ordinarily, and particularly now, prevail in Kashmir. For the Interim Government which you are anxious to set up immediately, the model should undoubtedly be the Mysore one but, in adopting that model to the present situation in your State, its peculiar conditions and the provisions of its existing Constitution deserve to be taken into account. These have been kept fully in view by us.

4. You have laid stress on the reservation of subjects listed in Schedule-II of the Mysore Proclamation dated September 24, 1947 as being its most important essential. Most of the items in this schedule are reserved matters under the Jammu and Kashmir Constitution Act. Items 1, 2 and 4 are reserved from the cognizance of the Praja Sabha under Section 24 of the Jammu and Kashmir Constitution Act, 1896, though the description is not identical. They can be included in the list of subjects in the administration of which you are not bound to obtain the advice of your ministers. The powers of the Ruler under item 3 in regard to the High Court are to be found in Sections 48 and 49 of that Act. In addition, similar powers are reserved to the Ruler in Section 71 as regards the Board of Judicial Advisers. The Ruler's powers to summon and dissolve the Legislature (Item 6 of the Mysore model) are provided for in Section 15 of the Act. The residuary and emergency powers (Item 8 of the Mysore Schedule) are reserved to the Ruler and Sections 4 and 5 of the Jammu and Kashmir Act. The only matters in the Mysore Schedule which do not find specific mention in the Jammu and Kashmir Act are:

(a) protection of legitimate interests of minorities; and

(b) superintendence, direction and control of elections.

(a) may be reserved in the Proclamation to issue. It seems unnecessary to reserve (b) also. The matter referred to therein is one which could well be left to the Council of Ministers.

5. The Interim Ministry will, as suggested in your letter function as a Cabinet with a Prime Minister at its head, and with such number of other Ministers as may be fixed by you in accordance with the provisions of Section-6 of the Constitution Act.

6. There may be a Dewan in addition to the Council of Ministers It is desirable that he should have the right to attend meetings of the Cabinet, so that he may be closely associated with the work of the Cabinet, and might function as an effective Liaison Officer between the Cabinet and the Ruler, interpreting the one to the other and aiding and advising the Ruler in the transaction of business connected with reserved subjects. Not only does Section 6 of the Constitution Act require that the Prime Minister should preside over the Council of Ministers, but it is on the merits essential that he should do so. To direct that a person other than the Prime Minister should preside over the Cabinet would not make for that perfect understanding and intimate association between the Ruler and his Prime Minister, which are so essential for efficiency of administration.

7. I agree entirely that the person to be selected for the post of Dewan should be a man who enjoys your full confidence. It is, however, at the same time desirable that man should not be one to whom the leader of the Government has any violent objection The two have to get on with cordiality and good understanding if Your Highness' Government of the State is to achieve the maximum beneficial results for the people that it ought to achieve. There can be no question of anybody attempting to sabotage your selection of the proper man for the Dewan's post. I am in a position to assure you that Sheikh Abdullah himself is only too anxious to have, as liaison between him and you, a Dewan who enjoys your fullest confidence, so that his relations with you might be of the smoothest possible description. Should Your Highness so desire, I shall be glad to be of assistance in selecting a Dewan who will be the best possible choice from all points of view.

8. We and in 'we' I include myself, Pandit Jawahar Lal Nehru and Sardar Vallabhbhai Patel are convinced that it is not possible for Sheikh Abdullah and Mr. Mehr Chand Mahajan to work together in the same

Government hereafter and that it is best in the circumstances that Mr. Mahajan should be allowed to terminate his present connection with the State. I have already informed you that I have good reason to think that Mr. Mahajan would probably himself be glad to be relieved from the embarrassment of Your Highness asking him to say on in the State.

9. In ordinary circumstances I should certainly have agreed in your view that six Ministers should be adequate for a State like Kashmir. The State is, however, in great turmoil. The invader has to be expelled, rebellion has to be quelled, law and order have to be established and normal economic life revived. For a considerable time to come, the burden of Government in Kashmir will be much heavier than in ordinary times. I have discussed this question with Sheikh Abdullah. He considers that there is more than enough work for each of 12 or 14 Ministers and he urges that this number need not scare anybody, as the salaries that will be taken by them will be very much smaller than the salaries that you have been paying your Ministers hitherto the pitch of the salaries is not wholly relevant in this connection. It is desirable to avoid a crowd of Ministers. Responsibility will get too scattered and unity of policy and close collaboration in administration might not be fully achieved if the number of Ministers is too large. Taking all circumstances into consideration, I should recommend for the Interim Government, which will function only till the new Constitution is fashioned and comes into force, strength of nine Ministers. This would incidentally provide room for adequate representation, in the Ministry of Minorities and the different areas of the State. On this latter matter, namely, representation of Minorities and province, Sheikh Abdullah is as keen as you yourself are. His immediate object is so to constitute his Government that he will be able to rally to his support the maximum proportion of the population, especially in view of the threatened plebiscite.

10. On the question of the Army I though I had made it clear to Your Highness that there was no need to fix proportions for the recruitment of the different communities in the Army. I am glad that

you are prepared to take Kashmiris, both Hindus and Muslims, into the Army provided that suitable material offers for recruitment. For the rest, no more is necessary than to apprise all sections of population in the State of the policy of Your Highness and Your Government to provide opportunities of service, whether civil or military, to members of all creeds and communities in the State on their merits. I agree, and I am in a position to assure you that Sheikh Abdullah agrees, that, for sometime to come and until things have completely settled down and normal life has been in full swing for a considerable period, we should hardly think of recruiting any large number of Muslims from the Jammu Province (including the Poonch area) which has contributed the largest number to the rebel ranks in the present disturbances. The populations of these areas have first to be won over and their loyalty to the State proved beyond cavil before recruitment to the Army from their ranks can be safely allowed to take place. It is, however, important that, in order to win them over, they should have the expectation from now that, if they become and remain loyal to the State, opportunities for service to the State, whether in a civil or military capacity, will not be denied to them.

11. The Mysore Proclamation dated September 24, 1947 laid down the Dewan the duty of framing a Constitution Bill and directed that, in doing so, he should obtain the advice and counsel of a committee elected by the Legislature and of such other experts and expert bodies as might be found suitable and desirable. There was some controversy on this matter in Mysore State and, in the final understanding that was arrived at between the Dewan and the President of the Mysore Congress and embodied in the Mysore Maharaja's Proclamation dated 29th of October, the direction in this respect was that the Interim Ministry should set up a Constituent Assembly composed of elected representatives of the people and entrust to it the task of framing a Constitutional Bill providing for Responsible Government under the aegis of the Maharaja. I think that, so far as Kashmir is concerned, it would be sufficient if the Proclamation that will be issued by Your Highness gives the direction that the Interim

Ministry should submit to you, as soon as possible, proposals for bringing into existence a Constitution making body composed of elected representatives of the people for the purpose of framing, for your approval and promulgation, a Constitution for the J&K State. The Constitution of the present Praja Sabha provides for a large faction of nominated members and will therefore not be accepted either to the National Conference or even to other political bodies in the State. It would seem, therefore, best to ask the Indian Ministry itself to submit for your consideration proposals as regards the composition of the Constitution making body and the method of choosing the members.

12. This letter has become longer than I originally intended, I hope, however, I have met all the points raised in your letter.

13. With a view to saving time, the States Ministry is being asked to prepare a draft of the Proclamation and to send it on to you as early as possible for your consideration. If you desire, in the meantime, to give any instructions in connection with such drafting, will you kindly have them communicated to that Ministry direct by telegram or by letter?

14. The actual personnel of the Ministry have to be proposed by Sheikh Abdullah for your acceptance. If, in connection with this matter or for the purpose of further discussion of what I have said in this letter, my services should be required, they are always at your disposal."

BLUNDERS 12

PVC Denied to Kashmir Saviour

Unique heroic sacrifice of Brig. Rajinder Singh who met martyrdom being Chief of the Army Staff of J&K Forces at Uri sector on the day Maharaja signed Instrument of Accession did not touch the souls of Delhi rulers. He was denied Paramvir Chakra only because he defended his state and was a Dogra Rajput.

In October 1947, Pakistan supported raiders were pressing towards Srinagar. Brigadier Rajinder Singh on receiving a message for help from Camp Domel set out for Srinagar with two platoons and a mortar detachment. They were heavily outnumbered by the enemy who engaged them at Garhi. The Brigadier fell back and re-organized his forces. In a fierce confrontation that followed the Brigadier was struck on his right arm by a burst of machine gun fire. Realizing that his evacuation would hold up and even jeopardize his men's safety he ordered them to proceed without him.

The Brigadier's body was never recovered as he probably fell into enemy hands. But his act of sacrifice inspired his men to hold up the enemy advance for three days, thereby ensuring the safety of the entire Valley.

The great hero was deprived PVC, which shows the bias against the Dogras.

To remember Maharaja Hari Singh on the Day of Accession 27th October which is the day of Martyrdom of Brig Rajinder Singh who saved Kashmir for India on this Day by sacrificing his life on the Uri front on the night of 26/27th October, 1947. The aggression-plot was hatched by the British as the Chief of Pakistan Army was General Gracy and the overall Commander-in-Chief of both the Dominions of India and Pakistan was General Auchinleck under the command of Lord Mountbatten. No operations could be launched against another country without the knowledge of the Commander-in-Chief.

When he had exhausted all his resources he decided to be himself the last man with the last bullet in his hands as commanded by his Ruler, Maharaja Hari Singh dated October 23, 1947 when he was sent to Uri. "**Brigadier Rajinder Singh is commanded to hold the enemy at Uri at all costs and to the last man. Reinforcement is sent with Capt. Jawala Singh. If Brigadier Rajinder Singh is not contacted, Capt. Jawala Singh is commanded to hold the enemy at all costs and to the last man. He will do his best to contact Brigadier Rajinder Singh.**"

In letter and spirit, he sacrificed his life to save his motherland. He was awarded a gallantry award of Independent India only, Mahavir Chakra not PVC which he deserved most.

Brigadier Rajinder Singh was born on June 14, 1899 in a small village of Bagoona (since renamed Rajinderpura after him) 35 kms. East of Jammu in the family of Dalpatia Clan of Jamwals. The history of bravery and sacrifice ran in the family, his illustrious ancestor General Baj Singh having sacrificed himself almost a century earlier in the defence of Chitral. His grand father was a war veteran with seven battle scars on his body. His father Subedar Lakha Singh, whom Rajinder lost at an early age of six months, was a Junior Officer in the State Forces. Lt. Col. Govind Singh, an affectionate uncle brought him up. He was educated in Jammu and graduated from the Prince of Wales College now Govt. Gandhi Memorial Science College, in 1921. During his student days he was remembered as being unassuming, obedient and student who did well in his studies.

Denial of PVC was a great blunder of Nehru which shall not be forgotten by the Dogras.

BLUNDERS 13

Unilateral Ceasefire

The first test for the Indian armed forces came immediately after independence with the first Indo-Pakistani conflict (1947-48). The military was called upon to defend the borders of the state of Jammu and Kashmir when tribals—principally Pathans—attacked from the northwest reaches of Kashmir on October 22, 1947. India's 161st Infantry Brigade was deployed and thwarted the advance of the tribal forces. In early November 1947, the 161st counter-attacked and successfully broke through the enemy defenses. Despite early successes, the Indian army suffered a setback in December because of logistical problems. The problems enabled the forces of POK to retreat. In the spring of 1948, the Indian side mounted another offensive to retake some of the ground that it had lost. No doubt fearing that the war might move into Pakistan proper, regular units of the Pakistani army became actively involved. As the conflict escalated, the Indian leadership was quick to recognize that the war could not be brought to a close unless Pakistani support to the raiders was stopped. Accordingly, on the advice of Governor General Earl Louis Mountbatten (Britain's last viceroy in India in 1947 and Governor General of India, 1947-48). The Indian government sought United Nations (UN) mediation of the conflict on December 31, 1947. There was some opposition to this move within the cabinet by those who did not agree with referring the Kashmir dispute to the UN. The UN mediation process brought the war to a close on January 1, 1949. In all, 1,500 soldiers died on each side during the war. General Cariappa of the Indian Army sought clearance from Delhi to liberate occupied areas. Nehru Govt. refused and Delhi declared unilateral ceasefire before the UN asked for it. Even the Maharaja offered to lead Indian Army in J&K to liberate occupied areas. India's decision to go to United Nations seeking its intervention was another blunder rather a disaster.

The echelons of power in Delhi deliberately chose to command General Cariappa to stop liberation campaign after the Indian Army forced out the Pakistan Army from Uri town. They were stopped to proceed further and stop their liberation campaign at Teetwal with the result the Indian Army had to abandon their campaign to liberate highly sensitive zones in Uri as well as in Karnah, parts of which lie under Pak control between Uri and Karnah between Teetwal and Keran also between Poonch and Uri. On the other hand the Govt. of India allowed fall of entire Mirpur District including Kotli in POK sector and entire Baltistan and Gilgit regions in the after presence of Indian Army. The serving Governor of J&K, Brig. Ghansara Singh was kidnapped and detained from November 1 to 16 (1947) by half a dozen Muslim Scouts at Astore, Gilgit. The Maharaja's repeated reminders to the Govt. of India on the issue went to the dustbin of Pt. Jawahar Lal Nehru who was monitoring the Sheikh's mission in Kashmir. They betrayed. Sheikh did not want annexation of Punjabi Kashmir into the Valley. General Cariappa and the brave fighting Indian soldiers were turned into mute, stony, sculptures standing along the so-called ceasefire line as Delhi had announced unilateral ceasefire.

This author when called on ailing General Cariappa in Mysore Military Guest Hospital in 1981, the General told this author, "**You should have better asked these questions from Pandit ji**. You are son of a soldier and you must know that Army implemented orders and did not question. It is for the politicians to answer your questions because they are answerable to their electorates." The hint was clear that it were Nehru-Abdullah dictates to keep out the non-Kashmiris for J&K to enable Abdullah family to rule forever.

No sooner has this been done, the Army was called upon to defend J&K against an armed invasion first from Phatan rebels in October 1947 and then in 1948 from the Pakistan Army. Military operations in Jammu and Kashmir, in the most difficult terrain and at enormous heights raged from October 1947 to January 1949, ended in ceasefire. However, a ceasefire declared by India enabled Pakistan to hold nearly one-third of Jammu and Kashmir State. These areas under Pakistan's occupation are called Pak-occupied Kashmir (POK) and Gilgit-Baltistan.

This was a blunder that showed that the Govt. of India was interested to establish Sheikh Abdullah as Sultan of J&K minus non-Kashmiris. Gilgit-Baltistan, Mirpur, Kotli, Muzaffrabad etc. were deliberately axed out of the geographical and political boundaries of J&K to ensure that the Sheikh dynasty ruled comfortably. Sheikh never wanted Ladakh and Jammu which he took as headache. Delhi could not go that far.

BLUNDERS 14

UN Intervention Sought January 1, 1948

Indian Army was capable to liberate occupied territory which had acceded to the Union of India. The Indian Army which commanded from Delhi to stop while they were moving forward. India moved a petition in UN seeking intervention while one-third of J&K territory was still under the illegal occupation of the Pak Forces. Sardar Patel even Maharaja Hari Singh and many other central leaders were insisting that India should liberate its territory from Pak occupation and seek UN intervention. It was a blunder committed with knowledge of the consequences.

The Petition

"This letter of historic value though. This is the tragic tale of aggression against J&K by Pakistan which was taken lightly by the Indian leadership."

"1. Under Article 35 of the Charter of the United Nations, any Member may bring any situation whose continuance is likely to endanger the maintenance of international peace and security to the attention of the Security Council. Such a situation now exists between India and Pakistan owing to the aid which invaders, consisting of nationals of Pakistan and of tribesmen from the territory immediately adjoining Pakistan on the north-west, are drawing from Pakistan for operations against Jammu and Kashmir, a State which has acceded to the Dominion of India and is part of India. The circumstances of accession, the activities of the invaders which led the Government of

India to take military action against them, and the assistance which the attackers have received and are still receiving from Pakistan are explained later in this memorandum. The Government of India requests the Security Council to call upon Pakistan to put an end immediately to the giving of such assistance, which is an act of aggression against India. If Pakistan does not do so, the Government of India may be compelled, in self-defence, to enter Pakistan territory, in order to take military action against the invaders. The matter is, therefore, one of extreme urgency and calls for immediate action by the Security Council for avoiding a breach of international peace.

"2. From the middle of September 1947, the Government of India had received reports of the infiltration of armed raiders into the western parts of Jammu province of Jammu and Kashmir State; Jammu adjoins West Punjab, which is a part of the Dominion of Pakistan. These raiders had done a great deal of damage in that area and taken possession of part of the territory of the State. On 24th October, the Government of India heard of a major raid from the Frontier Province of the Dominion of Pakistan into the Valley of Kashmir. Some two thousand or more fully armed and equipped men came in motor transport, crossed over to the territory of the State of Jammu and Kashmir, sacked the town of Muzaffrabad, killing many people and proceeded along the Jhelum Valley road towards Srinagar, the summer capital of Jammu and Kashmir State. Intermediate towns and villages were sacked and burnt, and many people killed. These raiders were stopped by Kashmir State troops near Uri, a town some fifty miles from Srinagar, for some time, but the invaders got around them and burnt the power house at Mahora, which supplied electricity to the whole of Kashmir.

"3. The position, on the morning of 26th October, was that these raiders had been held by Kashmir State troops and part of the civil population, who had been armed, at a town called Baramulla. Beyond Baramulla there was no major obstruction up to Srinagar. There was immediate danger of these raiders reaching Srinagar, destroying and massacring large numbers of people, both Hindus and Muslims. The

State troops were spread out all over the State and most of them were deployed along the western border of Jammu province. They had been split up into small isolated groups and were incapable of offering effective resistance to the raiders. Most of the State officials had left the threatened areas and the civil administration had ceased to function. All that stood between Srinagar and the fate which had **overtaken the places** en route followed by the raiders was the determination of the inhabitants of Srinagar, of all communities and practically without arms, to defend themselves. At this time Srinagar had also a large population of Hindu and Sikh refugees who had fled there from West Punjab owing to communal disturbances in that area. There was little doubt that these refugees would be massacred if the raiders reached Srinagar.

"4. Immediately after the raids into Jammu and Kashmir State commenced, approaches were informally made to the Government of India for the acceptance of the accession of the State to the Indian Dominion. (It might be explained in parenthesis that Jammu and Kashmir from a State whose ruler, prior to the transfer of power by the United Kingdom to the Dominions of India and Pakistan, had been in treaty relations with the British Crown, which controlled its foreign relations ceased with the transfer of power on 15th August last, and Jammu and Kashmir like other States acquired the right to accede to either Dominion).

"5. Events moved with great rapidity, and the threat to the Valley of Kashmir became imminent. On 26th October, the ruler of the State, Maharaja Hari Singh, appealed urgently to the Government of India for military help. He also requested that the Jammu and Kashmir State should be allowed to accede to the Indian Dominion. The people in J&K strongly supported the move for the State's Accession to the Indian Dominion. The Government of India were thus approached not only officially by the State authorities, but also on behalf of the people of Kashmir, both for military aid and for the Accession of the State with the Union.

"6. The grave threat to the life and property of innocent people in the Kashmir Valley and to the security of the State of Jammu and Kashmir that had developed as a result of the invasion of the Valley demanded immediate decision by the Government of India on both the requests. It was imperative on account of the emergency that the responsibility for the defence of Jammu and Kashmir State should be taken over by a Government capable of discharging it. But, in order to avoid any possible suggestion that India had utilized the State's immediate peril for her own political advantage, the Government of India made it clear that once the soil of the State had been cleared of the invader and normal conditions restored, its people would be free to decide their future by the recognized democratic methods of a plebiscite or referendum which, in order to ensure complete impartiality, might be held under international auspices.

"7. The Government of Indian felt it their duty to respond to the appeal for armed assistance because:

"(1) They could not allow a neighbouring and friendly State to be compelled by force to determine either its internal affairs or its external relations;

"(2) The accession of Jammu and Kashmir State to the Dominion of India made India really responsible for the defence of the State.

"8. The intervention of the Government of India resulted in saving Srinagar. The raiders were driven back from Baramulla to Uri and are held there by Indian troops. Nearly 19,000 raiders face the Dominion forces in this area. Since operations in the Valley of Kashmir started, pressure by the raiders against the western and south-western border of Jammu and Kashmir State had been intensified. It is understood, however, that nearly 15,000 raiders are operating against this part of the State. State troops are besieged in certain areas. Incursions by the raiders into the State territory, involving murder, arson, loot, and the abduction of women continue. The booty is collected and carried over to the tribal areas to serve as an inducement to the further recruitment of tribesmen to the ranks of the raiders. In addition to those actively participating in the raid, tribesmen and others, estimated at 100,000 have been collected in different places in the districts of West Punjab bordering Jammu and Kashmir State, and many of them are receiving military training under Pakistani nationals, including officers of the Pakistan Army. They are looked after in Pakistan territory, fed, clothed, armed and otherwise equipped, and transported to the territory of Jammu and Kashmir State with the help, direct and indirect, of Pakistani officials, both military and civil.

"9. As already stated, the raiders who entered the Kashmir Valley in October came mainly from the tribal areas to the north-west of Pakistan and, in order to reach Kashmir, passed through Pakistan territory. The raids along the south-west border of the State, which had preceded the invasion of the valley proper, had actually been conducted from Pakistan territory, and Pakistan nationals had taken part in them. This process of transmission across Pakistan territory and utilization of that territory as a base of operations against Jammu and Kashmir State continues. Recently, military operations against the western and south-western borders of the State have been intensified, and the attackers consist of nationals of Pakistan as well as tribesmen. These invaders are armed with modern weapons, including mortars and medium machine-guns, wear the battle dress of regular soldiers and, in recent engagements, have fought in regular battle formation and are using the tactics of modern warfare. Man-pack wireless sets are in regular use and even mark V mines have been employed. For their transport the invaders have all along used motor vehicles. They are undoubtedly being trained and to some extent led by regular officers of the Pakistan Army. Their rations and other supplies are obtained from Pakistan territory.

"10. These facts point indisputably to the conclusion;

"(a) that the invaders are allowed transit across Pakistan territory;

"(b) that they are allowed to use Pakistan territory as a base of operations;

"(c) that they include Pakistan nationals;

"(d) that they draw much of their military equipment, transportation, and supplies (including petrol) from Pakistan; and "(e) that Pakistan officers are training, guiding, and otherwise actively helping them.

"There is no source other than Pakistan from which they could obtain such quantities of modern military equipment, training or guidance. More than once, the Government of India had asked the Pakistan Government to deny to the invaders facilities which constitute an act of aggression and hostility against India, but without any response. The last occasion on which this request was made was on 22nd December, when the Prime Minister of India handed over personally to the Prime Minister of Pakistan a letter in which the various forms of aid given by Pakistan to the invaders were briefly recounted and the Government of Pakistan were asked to put an end to such aid promptly; no reply to this letter has yet been received in spite of a telegraphic reminder sent on 26th December.

"11. It should be clear from the foregoing recital that the Government of Pakistan are unwilling to stop the assistance in material and men which the invaders are receiving from Pakistan territory and from Pakistan nationals, including Pakistan Government personnel, both military and civil. This attitude is not only un-neutral, but constitutes active aggression against India, of which the State of Jammu and Kashmir forms a part.

"12. The Government of India have exerted persuasion and exercised patience to bring about a change in the attitude of Pakistan. But they have failed, and are in consequence confronted with a situation in which their defence of Jammu and Kashmir State is hampered and their measures to drive the invaders from the territory of the State are greatly impeded by the support which the raiders derive from Pakistan. The invaders are still on the soil of Jammu and Kashmir and the inhabitants of the States are exposed to all the atrocities of which a barbarous foe is capable. The presence in large numbers of invaders in those portions of Pakistan territory, which adjoin parts of Indian Territory other than Jammu and Kashmir State, is a menace to the rest of India. Indefinite continuance of the present operations prolongs the agony of the people of Jammu and Kashmir, is a drain on

India's resources and a constant threat to the maintenance of peace between India and Pakistan. The Government of India have no option, therefore, but to take more effective military action in order to rid J&K State of the invader.

"13. In order that the objective of expelling the invader from Indian Territory and preventing him from launching attacks should be quickly achieved, Indian troops would have to enter Pakistan territory; only thus could the invader be denied the use of bases and cut off from his sources of supplies and reinforcements in Pakistan. Since the aid which the invaders are receiving from Pakistan is an act of aggression against India, the Government of India are entitled, under international law, to send their armed forces across Pakistan territory for dealing effectively with the invaders. However, as such action might involve armed conflict with Pakistan, the Government of India, ever anxious to proceed according to the principles and aims of the Charter of the United Nations, desire to report the situation to the Security Council under Article 35 of the Charter. They feel justified in requesting the Security Council to ask the Government of Pakistan.

"(1) to prevent Pakistan Government personnel, military and civil from participating or assisting in the invasion of Jammu and Kashmir State;

"(2) to call upon other Pakistani nationals to desist from taking any part in the fighting in Jammu and Kashmir State;

"(3) to deny to the invaders: (a) access to any use of its territory for operations against Kashmir, (b) military and other supplies, (c) all other kinds of aid that might tend to prolong the present struggle.

"14. The Government of India would stress the special urgency of the Security Council taking immediate action on their request. They desire to add that military operations in the invaded areas have, in the past few days, been developing so rapidly that they must, in self-defence, reserve to themselves the freedom to take, at any time when it may become necessary, such military action as they may consider the situation requires.

"15. The Government of India deeply regrets that a serious crisis should have been reached in their relation with Pakistan. Not only is Pakistan a neighbour but, in spite of the recent separation, India and Pakistan have many ties and many common interests. India desires nothing more earnestly than to live with her neighbour-state on terms of close and lasting friendship. Peace is to the interest of both States; indeed to the interests of the world. The Government of India's approach to the Security Council is inspired by the sincere hope that, through the prompt action of the Council, peace may be preserved."

The letter concluded the Security Council under the dictates of Anglo-American Bloc (China was represented by Farmosa, an American stooge) made India to dance to their tunes. It was 'USSR' direct intervention through its veto which avoided a 'disaster' that would have rocked entire South East Asia. Krishna Menon's logistic and factual speeches on the floors of the General Assembly of UN turned the table against Pak' bogus claims. This has been a continuing blunder of Nehru's era which needs to be rectified. It is time that India should withdraw its complaint from the Security Council and settle the status of 'LoC' with Pakistan in the light of the prevailing factors and changing cultural climate of POK.

BLUNDERS 15

Nehru's Lal Chowk Speech, 1948

Immediately after the accession, Nehru went to Srinagar and addressed a Kashmir crowd. It was an unforgivable blunder of the Indian Prime Minister, a Kashmiri himself when he declared in 'Lal Chowk' that the Maharaja was nobody to decide about the future of Kashmir. He asserted that the future of the state shall be decided by a referendum by the people of J&K. Pakistan as well as the agencies inimical to India have kept harping on the 'blunder speech' of Nehru though this speech had neither any legal nor political authenticity. Nehru's anger reflects his vengeance against Ram Chander Kak in 1946 for having arrested Nehru. While he was addressing a massive gathering in Ajaib Ghar, Jammu in 1948 some people shouted from the crowd Nehru demanding return of Maharaja. Nehru shouted back in his microphone, "**Hari Singh kabhi wapis nahin ayega, wapis nahin ayega.**" Nehru, perhaps, never visited Dogra land again, sowing the seedlings of hatred and conflict between the Kashmiris. The Kashmiri Pundits remained victims of this hatred for half a century till they were humiliated, disgraced and forced to vacate their homes in the Valley. This may need half a century to heal the wounds of hatred that Nehru and Sheikh had created.

BLUNDERS 16

India did not Liberate POK

Indian forces were strong enough to deal with Pak army in every respect of military offensive. Instead of liberating the occupied areas of Neelam, Muzaffrabad, the Indian Govt. allowed fall of Bhimber, Mirpur, Kotli, Sudan, Bagh now formed as part of POK (Azad Kashmir), which were captured by Pak-troops after the State's Accession with the Union and 28 days after the arrival of the Indian Army in Kashmir on October 27, 1947.

Sheikh Abdullah became the super boss on October 30, 1947 after his appointment by the Maharaja as administrator ignoring the Prime Minister, Mehr Chand Mahajan to please Nehru. As administrator he guided the Indian Army to liberate only the Kashmir Valley areas. Non-Kashmiri speaking areas now called 'Azad Kashmir' were allowed to slip out of J&K instead Abdullah being administrator and Nehru's favourite allowed non-Kashmiri territories of J&K to slip out of the State which was crated by the Dogras by shedding their blood for a century. This impression was given to me by Lord Mountbatten when I met him in UK in 1970 during my student days in London University. He did not want non-Kashmiri areas. This was the reason that Indian Army stood helpless and India had to loose Gilgit-Baltistan as well as POK. Kashmiris speaking population were only 21% in J&K. Sheikh wanted Kashmiri speaking population in majority.

Nehru's coercion had exhausted the Maharaja. The Congress President, Sardar Patel and Mahajan failed to use their good offices to manage ouster of the Maharaja. Nehru and Abdullah had one point programme to make the Maharaja to quit. Maharaja had no way except fixing Abdullah as Prime Minister. This was another blunder which

Nehru realized in 1953 when he got Abdullah dismissed and arrested through the warrants of Yuvraj Karan Singh, the son of the exiled Maharaja. Strange are the roads of destiny!

Note: Author's meeting with Mountbatten in UK, 1970: When this author called on Mountbatten in his Srinagar Palace, he took me in his boat. Cigar never came out of his mouth. To my several requests he refused to another one, when I asked him did not he fix a nail on the future relationship of India and Britain, he smiled. Looked funny! I was to act on the advice of the Dominion Government when I asked him, how could he justify the two armies (Indian Army and Pak-Army) fighting a battle of which Lord Mountbatten happened to be Commander-in-Chief. He dismissed question saying two armies never fought in 1947. He was flabbergasted when I asked him that who did you unilateral ceasefire declaration without giving General Cariappa '24' to liberate the area. 'Ceasefire' was done by two Prime Ministers of India and Kashmir; both were Kashmiris how they could lose their majority by holding hostile Punjabi Dogra Camp within Kashmir. He did not allow me to go further saying that you waited to know some facts, but added, since you are a young emerging young man in Indian politics, Prof. Gladhill has been talking high about you. I received you. But remember you being a Dogra shall find more magnetic closeness in Azad Kashmir than in Central Kashmir. Kashmir and Azad may with go together.

BLUNDERS 17

Maharaja's Advice to Patel Ignored January 31, 1948

Maharaja Hari Singh was highly pained and disheartened on the passive role that was being played by the Indian Army whose Commander-in-Chief was still Lord Mountbatten, the Governor-General of India. Lord Mountbatten was also the Commander-in-Chief of the Pakistan Army. The two armies headed by same commander were fighting against each other. The Maharaja who himself was the Commander-in-Chief of J&K Army holding a rank of Major General had been a member of the war cabinet during the second world war. The contents of his letter addressed to Sardar Vallabhbhai Patel on January 31, 1948 deserve attention of every Indian when he observed with anger and agony that;

"The name of the Indian Army is getting into the mud in spite of its brilliant record. I was a member of the War Cabinet. I travelled in war zones during the Great War. The name of the Indian Army was at its highest pitch and it pains me to see that the name of the Indian Army has become a topic of every tongue during these days and it is daily losing prestige. Some people think that it is not the fault of the Army but the fault of the policy that is being followed: others feel that it is the fault of the commanders who are quite new to the job. People who would have had to wait for 10 to 15 years to become generals have been put in charge of operations. Opinions differ, but the fact is that the name of the Army is in the mud. Sardar Baldev Singh was here for a day. He has heard from our politicians, members of the public and from me and my Prime Minister all that everyone had to say. He told me secretly that he had ordered certain actions to be taken. I told him that a mere order is nothing unless it is implemented. When you kindly spent two days with us here, a number of decisions were taken and you gave instructions in certain matters. Since your departure nothing has been done and, as I have said, we had more serious attacks. The effort on the part of Pakistan is gaining ground everyday. Their morale owing to success is going up. They loot property, they take away cattle and women and when they go back to Pakistan, they incite people and tell them how much loot and what benefits there are to raid our territory. On the other hand, our morale is rapidly going down. So far as the people are concerned, they are thoroughly demoralized and they start fleeing as soon as there is even a rumour of a raid. Even people living at distant places start fleeing when they see fire five or six miles from their villages. So far as the Indian forces are concerned, they do not leave their apportioned places to meet the raiders. There are no mobile columns to meet them. The work is felt to a few Home Guards or to a platoon or so of very tired state forces. How can it be possible for them to engage 500 or 1,000 raiders? Last time you ordered guerrillas to come into the state and take over this work. As far as I know, no guerrillas have arrived so far...

"In the situation, therefore, my position as Ruler has become very anomalous ant one of great perplexity. People in the State continue sending me telegrams and asking for help. Our civil administration is in the hands of the National Conference and military operations in the hands of the Indian Union. I have no voice or power either on the civil or military side. The State forces are under the Indian Army Commander. The result, therefore, is that I have just to watch the terrible situation in a helpless manner, to look on at the abduction of women, killing and loot of my people, without power to give them any redress whatever. People continue to approach me everyday and they still think that it lies in my power to give them relief and redress. You will realize that my position is getting most awkward every day, so long as the military situation is adverse to us and refugees continue pouring in the city and daily raids from Pakistan keep on coming without any reply from us." **Maharaja Hari Singh in his letter offered to lead the**

Indian Army along with the J&K Infantry to liberate the areas occupied by Pakistan. He thus wrote to Sardar Vallabhbhai Patel;

"I am prepared to takeover command of my own forces along with the forces of the Indian Army personally to help the State. I am prepared to lead the Army personally and to command if the Indian Union agrees, also their troops. I know my country much better than any of your generals will know it even during the next several months or years and I am prepared to take the venture boldly rather than merely keep on sitting here doing nothing. It is for you to consider whether the Indian Union will accept this in both the situations, whether after the withdrawal of the accession or even if the accession continues. I am tired of my present life and it is much better to die fighting than watch helplessly the heartbreaking misery of my people."

The Maharaja added a strong note to the Central leadership and even he threatened to find some other alternative to save the people of J&K from deaths and destruction. He concluded in his letter to Sardar Vallabhbhai Patel;

"The third alternative in the situation that has arisen is that the Indian Dominion discharges its duty on the military side effectively and makes an all-out effort to stop the raids from Pakistan and to drive out of the State not only the raiders but also all rebels. This can only be done if the Dominion really fights. It has avoided fighting so far. Two or three courageous battles will more or less end this situation, and, if it is delayed, there is bound to be a catastrophe. Pakistan is more organized against Kashmir than the Indian Dominion, and as soon as snow melts it will start attacking Kashmir on all sides and the province of Ladakh will also come into the hands of the enemy and the Valley and the whole border will be raided and even double the number of troops at present in Jammu and Kashmir will not be able to save the situation. What should have been done and achieved a month before can still be achieved during the next month, but if matters are delayed and if owing to the UNO reference and the attitude of compromise, the situation remains at a standstill, it would become terribly grave after the expiry of the month. Therefore, unless the Indian Union makes up its mind to fight fully and effectively, I may have to decide upon the two alternatives mentioned above."

All the protests lodged by the Maharaja remained unattended and uncared for by the echelons of power in Delhi. Sardar Patel failed to persuade Gandhi or Nehru on the sensitivities of the issues relating to J&K Maharaja's exit. The situation that was created by the mishandling of J&K Affairs in 1947 continues till day in 2010.

BLUNDERS 18

Abdullah Replaced Mahajan March 5, 1948

On March 5, 1948, the Maharaja announced the formation of an interim popular Government with Sheikh Mohammad Abdullah as the Prime Minister to address the Nehru wish.

"In accordance with the traditions of my dynasty I have, from time to time, provided for increasing association of my people with the administration of the State with the object of realizing the goal of full Responsible Government at as early a date as possible and in pursuance of that object have, by the Jammu and Kashmir Constitution Act of 1996 (xiv of 1996) established a Constitutional Government with a Council of Ministers, a Legislature with a majority of elected members and an independent judiciary.

I have noted with gratification and pride the progress so far made and the legitimate desire of my people for the immediate establishment of a fully democratic constitution based on adult franchise with a hereditary Ruler from my dynasty as the Constitutional Head of an Executive responsible to the legislature;

I have already appointed the popular leader of my people Sheikh Mohammad Abdullah as the Head of the Emergency Administration;

It is now my desire to replace the Emergency Administration by a Popular Interim Government and to provide for its powers, duties and functions, pending the formation of a fully democratic Constitution.

I accordingly hereby ordain as follows;

My Council of Ministers shall consist of the Prime Minister and such other Ministers as may be appointed on the advice of the Prime

Minister. I have by Royal Warrant appointed Sheikh Mohammad Abdullah as the Prime Minister with effect from today."

Sheikh started a campaign of vilification against the Maharaja. Sheikh managed to woo some disgruntled elements in Jammu province. The people who joined the Sheikh included Pt. Girdhari Lal Dogra of Hiranagar, Pt. Baiz Nath of Chenani, Pt. Motilal Baigra of Udhampur, Pt. Bhagat Ram, Advocate of Jammu whereas Jammu Muslims did not join the Sheikh bandwagon.

The prominent Muslim leaders of Jammu who enjoyed a status not less than the Sheikh namely Choudhary Ghulam Abbad were put in jail and got him deported in exchange of Brig. Ghansara Singh (Governor of Gilgit) to Pakistan though Choudhary Abbas was resident of Jammu. Mr. K.H. Khursheed, who was close to Mr. Jinnah and a prominent state leader, was also pushed to Pakistan. Later he was killed in a road accident in Pakistan. Maulana Massaudi, a foremost Muslim leader of Kashmir was sidelined by the Sheikh was killed in 1992 by the terrorists.

Sheikh started a tirade against the Maharaja a vilification campaign with the patronage of Nehru. He wanted Maharaja and the Maharani to quit not only Kashmir but the State. Both Nehru and Abdullah wanted all the flesh from the Maharaja's heart. Nehru vetoed every move of Sardar Vallabhbhai Patel and other Indian leaders which favoured Maharaja's stay in J&K. Even Maharani was forced out of the state. She had to stay in Kangra for the rest of her life.

The Maharaja left the State on June 9, 1948 for Delhi and stayed there till June 20, 1948. Maharaja tried to persuade the Dominion Home Minister Sardar Vallabhbhai Patel to intervene for the liberation of occupied areas of J&K which were under the illegal occupation of Pakistan. At times the Maharaja even threatened to reconsider his decision for having signed the Instrument of Accession. He made a daring offer to lead the Indian Army in J&K for the liberation of the occupied territories of his state.

The Maharaja abdicated in favour of Yuvraj Karan Singh and moved to Dehradun. History has been revealed that has been changed the Dogra

Maharaja in his words contained in his letters addressed to the President of India and Sardar Patel. These letters have not ever been noticed by general public, the government of India or by the Kashmiri Governors.

Maharaja to Sardar Patel January 31, 1948

Oppressed and suppressed by the prevailing circumstances, the Maharaja wrote to the Dominion Home Minister, Sardar Vallabhbhai Patel on 31st January, 1948 which remained hidden from pages of history. Thus wrote the Maharaja in anguish;

"The military situation as you know has been quite depressing since the arrival of the Indian troops. Except the first gains in the Kashmir Valley there has been a debt balance throughout so far as achievements are concerned.

"Apart from the military situation, the reference to the UNO and the proceedings that are hanging fire there are causing great uncertainty and perplexity not only to me but to every Hindu and Sikh in the State as well as to those who belong to the National Conference. The feeling is strongly gaining ground that the UN Security Council will take an adverse decision and that the State will eventually have to accede to Pakistan as a result of what the Security Council will decide. The Hindus and Sikhs have, therefore, started going away from the State, as they anticipate that the result of the UNO decision will be the same as what happened in West Punjab and therefore it is much better to clear out of the State before that eventuality arises. The National Conference leaders also feel that they may eventually be let down by accepting the decision of the Security Council and what would be disastrous for them.

"In the situation described above, a feeling comes to my mind as to the possible steps that I may take to make, so far as I am concerned, a clean state of the situation. Sometimes I feel that I should withdraw the accession that I have made to the Indian Union. The Union provisionally accepted the accession and if the Union cannot recover back our territory and is going eventually to agree to the decision of the Security Council which would result in handing us over to Pakistan then there is no point in sticking to the accession of the State to the Indian Union. For the time being, it may be possible to have better terms from Pakistan, but that is immaterial, because eventually it would mean an end of the dynasty and end of the Hindus and Sikhs in the State. There is an alternative possible for me and that is to withdraw the accession and that may kill the reference to the UNO, because the Indian Union will have no right to continue the proceedings before the Council, if the accession is withdrawn. The result may be return to the position the State held before the accession. The difficulty in that situation however, will be that the Indian troops .... have to work as volunteers to help the State.

"Another alternative that strikes me is that if I can do nothing, I should leave the State (short of abdication) and reside outside so that people do not think that I can do anything for them. For their grievances they can hold the civil administration responsible or the Indian forces who are in charge of the defence of the State. The responsibility will then clearly be either the Indian Union or of the administration of Sheikh Abdullah. If there is any criticism, those responsible can have it and the responsibility for the suffering of the people will not be mine. Of course, I well anticipate that, as people started saying when I left Kashmir only on Mr. Menon's advice that I had run away from Srinagar, they will say that I have left them in their hour of misery, but it is no use remaining in a position where one can do nothing merely to avoid criticism. Of course, if I go out of the State, I will have to take the public into confidence and tell them the reasons why I am going out."

"The Indian troops arrived in the Valley on 27th October, at that time we were in possession of about ¾th of Poonch and the whole of the Mirpur district. We had by then lost only small bits of Poonch and Muzaffrabad district. After the recapture of Baramulla and Uri, there has been a standstill. Two months have passed and the Indian troops are still at Uri. They attempted to venture to the town of Poonch and though they reached it, it was at a great cost and the road was eventually lost. In the Poonch Jagir, which was held by the state troops inch by inch, we had to withdraw and eventually lost the whole of the Jagir except the town itself, where about 40,000 people are besieged along with 4 battalions (3 State and 1 Indian). The situation is by no means satisfactory. I may mention that in the August disturbances, with two battalions of the state troops we cleared the whole of Poonch Jagir, peace was restored, the whole of the revenue was realized and the administration was functioning normally. It was only in the second week of October that trouble again began in Poonch and our troops resisted it till about the end of December. But as no help was given, they had eventually to fall back on Poonch town..." Signed by Maharaja Hari Singh on January 31, 1948.

Conspiracies in Delhi

The conspiracies in Delhi and Srinagar grew stronger day by day. It was Sheikh Abdullah started a similar campaign against not only the Maharaja but the Maharani also seeking their expulsion from the state. Dr. Karan Singh was under medical treatment in USA, may be 17. Mahatma Gandhi went to Srinagar to advice Maharaja to go on brief vacation and relieve Kak. Congress President, Mr. Kripalani had made similar advice earlier. Nehru was adamant to ensure exit of Maharaja Hari Singh and the Maharani too. The Sheikh and Nehru wanted the last drop of blood from Maharaja's heart. How much patience, perseverance, farsightedness the Maharaja must have accelerating can be read from the contents of his letters to the Sardar Patel, Pt. Nehru and an exercise one cannot imagine.

BLUNDERS 19

India's Failure at UN

The Resolution of the UNCIP of August 13, 1948 directed to withdraw from all occupied areas.

Having given careful consideration to the points of view expressed by the representatives of India and Pakistan regarding the situation in the State of Jammu and Kashmir; and

Being of the opinion that the prompt cessation of hostilities and the correction of conditions the continuance of which is likely to endanger international peace and security are essential to implementation of its endeavours to assist the Governments of India and Pakistan in effecting a final settlement of the situation;

Resolves to submit simultaneously to the Governments of India and Pakistan the following proposal.

Part II: Truce Agreement

Simultaneously with the acceptance of the proposal for the immediate cessation of hostilities as outlined in Part I, both Governments accept the following principles as a basis for the formulation of a truce agreement, the details of which shall be worked out in discussion between their representatives and the Commission.

1. As the presence of troops of Pakistan in the Territory of the State of Jammu and Kashmir constitutes a material change in the situation since it was represented by the Government of Pakistan before the Security Council, the Government of Pakistan agrees to withdraw its troops from that State.

2. The Government of Pakistan will use its best endeavour to secure the withdrawal from the State of Jammu and Kashmir of tribesmen and Pakistani nationals not normally resident therein who have entered the State for the purpose of fighting.

3. Pending a final solution, the territory evacuated by the Pakistani troops will be administered by the local authorities under the surveillance of the Commission.

B. When the Commission shall have notified the Government of India that the tribesmen and Pakistani nationals referred to in Part-II, A, 2 hereof have withdrawn, thereby terminating the situation which was represented by the Government of India to the Security Council as having occasioned the presence of Indian forces in the State of Jammu and Kashmir, and further, that the Pakistani forces are being withdrawn from the State of Jammu and Kashmir, the Government of India agrees to begin to withdraw the bulk of its forces from that State in stages to be agreed upon with the Commission.

2. Pending the acceptance of the conditions for a final settlement of the situation in the State of Jammu and Kashmir, the Indian Government will maintain within the lines existing at the moment of the ceasefire the minimum strength of its forces which in agreement with the Commission are considered necessary to assist local authorities in the observance of law and order The Commission will have observers stationed where it deems necessary.

3. The Government of India will undertake to ensure that the Government of the State of Jammu and Kashmir will take all measures within its powers to make it publicly known that peace, law and order will be safeguarded and that all human and political rights will be guaranteed.

Maharaja's Reaction on his Exit

After 'Patel' conveyed his help ness on the Nehru-Sheikh determined view that the Maharaja should quit J&K. Maharaja got a clear message from Patel as the purpose for which Maharaja was needed to appoint

(Sheikh as Prime Minister was accomplished on March 5, 1948. The Sheikh did not want the Dogra Maharaja to stay for a day in J&K. With total support of 'Nehru' the Sheikh had assumed all powers for himself. He started vilification campaign against the Maharaja which is mentioned by him in his letter that;

6th May, 1949
New Delhi

My dear Sardar Patel ji,

With reference to the discussions I had with you on 29th April and 1st May, 1949, I have been revolving the matters in my mind and am now in a position to let you have my settled reactions to the proposal in regard to my temporary absence from the State which you put to me.

I should like to say at the outset that I was completely taken aback by this proposal but coming as it did from you, in whom I have since the very beginning placed implicit trust and confidence and whose advice I have throughout followed on the many questions affecting my personally and my State both in the present and in future, I have been able somehow to adjust myself to it. I would not, however, be human if I did not express my sense of keen disappointment and bewilderment at having been called upon to make such a sacrifice of personal prestige, honour and position when all along I have been content to follow, sometimes even against my own judgment and conscience, the advice in regard to the constitutional position in the State which I have been receiving from the Prime Minister of India or yourself, some times even against arrangements which were agreed to only a few months before. Now would it be fair on my part to conceal from you my own feeling that while Sheikh Abdullah has been allowed to depart from time to time as suited his inclination from the pledged and written word, to act consistently in breach of the loyalty which he professed to me prior to his release from jail and the oath of allegiance which he took when he assumed office, and to indulge openly along with his colleagues in a campaign of vilifications and foul calumny against me, both inside the

State and outside, I should have had to be driven from position to position each of which I thought I held on the advice of the States Ministry.

The contrast naturally fills me with poignant feelings. However, once again putting my complete trust in your judgment and benevolent intentions towards me, I might be prepared to fall in with your wishes and to absent myself from the State for a period of three or four months in consideration of the fact as emphasized by you namely complications created by the reference to UNO and the plebiscite issue.

There are, however, certain questions arising out of this proposal on which I would venture to make my position clear to you and on which I would be grateful to have your assurance. I hope you will kindly appreciate the necessity or my seeking these assurances. I have to think of the immediate future in the light of my bitter experiences of the last several months and I owe it to myself, my family and my dynasty to procure a clear declaration in respect of these matters:-

1. I should like to be assured that this step is not a prelude to any idea of abdication. I should like to make it clear now that I cannot entertain the latter idea even for a moment and am fully prepared to take the consequences. I regard such a demand from my Prime Minister and his colleagues as a clear breach of the many understandings on which constitutional arrangements have been based from time to time and a position act of his disloyalty, treachery and deception.

2. Sheikh Abdullah should be clearly told to stop the campaign of vilification against me and to abandon all activities, both on his part and that of his followers, aimed at securing my abdication. I feel that the sacrifice which I am being called upon to make would be in vain if I continued to be the target of their public or private attacks.

3. There should be a clear assurance of protection of myself and my adherents against my victimization. In this connection, I should like especially to draw your attention to the facts that have been reported to me about persons having been detained in jail for their future to sign for my abdication.

4. The question that I should remain out of the State for three or four months for reasons of health, will, I am afraid, not be believed by anybody and is likely to give rise to many misgivings and speculations within and outside the State as:-

(i) everybody knows that I am not in such a state of health as would necessitate a long rest outside the State. I have on your advice been recently touring parts of the Jammu Province in the heat of April.

(ii) For everybody in bad health Kashmir is considered to be the best health resort and it will certainly look strange if I went outside the State giving out that I am doing so for reasons of health.

(iii) wherever I take my temporary residence I cannot confine myself to the four walls of the house. I am bound to meet people, who, when they meet me, will never believe that I am staying there for reasons of health;

(iv) some other reasons which may be plausible and may also at the same time not compromise my dignity and position, should be given out. The best thing would be that the Government of India should find a suitable position for me in Delhi where my services may be utilized in a fitting manner during the above period of three or four months.

5. It is a matter of paramount necessity that Her Highness should remain with the Yuvraj in the State during the period of my absence. He is young and impressionable and requires paternal guidance and personal supervision of at least one of his parents. I can see no reason either of political expediency or justice in insisting on the separation of a mother from her only child whom she is seeing after thirteen months of absence abroad. Considerations of humanity alone should suffice to rule out this altogether.

6. My private estates, houses and other property should be protected against the aggressive acts of Sheikh Abdullah's party. They will attempt to take possession of my houses, gardens, lands and other property. The Indian Dominion should guarantee against that act of

aggression. While I am there they dare not do these things but in my absence they will attempt this. I have received information that even during the last few days, after I left Jammu for Delhi, encroachments have been made on my lands at Srinagar.

7. No change should be made without my consent in the present arrangements regarding the State Forces or the constitutional position, Prerogatives etc. of the Ruler as now subsisting. Arrangements will continue for me to draw my staff (both State and private Deptts.) from amongst Officers of my Forces, Guards mounted by my forces at my Palaces will also continue as at present as per agreement reached vide my letter of 30th August and Mr. Menon's reply of 3rd September thereto. I shall also take whatever staff etc. I require with me outside.

8. I should be entitled during my stay in India to suitable strength of military guards wherever I stay.

9. Yuvraj's safety and protection should be the concern of the Indian Dominion. State and Indian Military should guard his person.

10. Outstanding matters with the States Military, Civil Lists, Hazur Departments etc. should be decided with me immediately.

Yours very sincerely,

Sd/-
Hari Singh

BLUNDERS 20
The Maharaja Humiliated

Camp Doon Court
Dehradun
May 23, 1949

My dear Maharaja Sahib,

Thank you for your letter dated the 6th May, 1949.

2. I am very glad to know that Your Highness has reconciled yourself to the proposal which I put forward at my discussion with you. It was with no light heart that I did so. No one can be more cognizant than myself of the attitude which Your Highness has adopted ever since you signed the Instrument of Accession. I am grateful to Your Highness for the spirit of cooperation and understanding which you have always extended to me and also for the kind sentiments which you have expressed. I can assure Your Highness that, before putting forward my proposal, I had, after careful consideration, come to the conclusion that the interests alike of Your Highness, the dynasty and the country demanded the step which you have now agreed to take. I know full well the personal sacrifice involved in it, but, I am sure, along with so many other changes to which Your Highness has accustomed yourself, you will undertake this step also with a sense of duty to your country and in a spirit of calm resignation to the superior dictates of events.

3. Regarding the points which Your Highness has referred to me, I should like to state that the question of Your Highness's abdication does not arise. We have made the position quite plain

to Sheikh Mohammad Abdullah, and we hope there will be an end to the public controversies centering round this matter as well as to the derogatory references to Your Highness in the press and on the platform in the State. Your Highness will of course, appreciate that the future constitution of the State would be determined by the duly **elected Constituent Assembly**. I am afraid, in the absence of any specific instances of victimization to which Your Highness refers in paragraph 4, it may not be possible for me to give any assurance, but I can tell Your Highness that, if any such instances are brought to our notice, we shall look into them and try to see that justice is done.

4. I appreciate what Your Highness says in regards to the reasons for your remaining outside the State, but I feel that it would be best just to say that Your Highness has decided, after the strain of the last so many months and continued ill-health, to say out of the State for a few months. The actual period need not be stated.
5. We have carefully considered the question of Her Highness staying with the Yuvraj during your absence, but you a variety of reasons, we feel that it would be best, for the present, for her also to stay away for a while. Later, she can certainly visit the Yuvraj from time to time, and the Yuvraj can also visit Your Highness and Her Highness occasionally.
6. We would be grateful if Your Highness would let me have a list of the private estates, houses and other property belonging to Your Highness and referred to in para 6 of you letter. On receipt of the list we shall take up the matter with your Ministry. In the meantime, I hope that, with the understanding that has been reached with Sheikh Abdullah on the various controversial issues, he will himself take steps to safeguard Your Highness's property against encroachments. In particular, I hope that the feelings which he entertains for the Yuvraj will succeed in closing the chapter of the past several months and in introducing a healthy change in the approach of both the Government and the National Conference workers to these and other problems affecting Your

Highness and the family personally and the dynasty in general. I hope that no need for a change in the arrangements to which Your Highness has referred in paragraph 7 would arise, but should any such need arise, we would of course consult Your Highness. We would also make necessary arrangements for guarding you during your stay in India, and we take full responsibility for the Yuvraj's safety and protection.

7. As regards outstanding matters, we have already informed Your Highness separately that your Civil List has been fixed at Rs.15 lacs, out of which Rs.6 lacs would be paid by the State and Rs.9 lacs by the Government of India during the period of the emergency. Out of this sum, Your Highness will have to make allotment to Her Highness and the Yuvraj. The latter's expenses would, of course, be larger than before on account of his being Regent. I hope Your Highness will agree to make a suitable allowance for him, bearing in mind his needs. I should be glad to know your suggestion in this respect. Similarly, I should welcome Your Highness's proposal regarding Her Highness's allowance. As regards Hazur Departments, Sheikh Sahib has already agreed to our suggestion that an allowance of Rs. 5 lacs should be made to Your Highness for this purpose. A list of items, which will be controlled by Your Highness, and during your absence, by the Yuvraj as Regent, has been furnished to Sheikh Sahib, and he has promised to let us have his comments as soon as possible. After his comments are received, we shall finalize the whole matter, but in the meantime, Your Highness can make suitable allocations to major and other heads of the expenditure on State Departments from our of the allotment of Rs. 5 lacs.

With kindest regards,

Yours sincerely,
Sd/-
Vallabhbhai Patel

The issues were settled. The Maharaja named Yuvraj Karan Singh as the 'Regent' on June 20, 1949 entrusting all his powers in his 18 years old son. It was first victory for Kashmir leaders. First part of the 'Quit Kashmir' movement was accomplished by 'NC' with the active support of the Congress leaders from Delhi. The second part of the movement was against India which continues in one form or the other.

BLUNDERS 21

A Maharaja's Tragic Exile May 23, 1949

Pakistan aggression continued in silence. India stood as mute spectator. Conspiracies continued their game plans up in Delhi against the Maharaja who stood firm as an Indian. Even Sardar Patel could not help it. Sheikh Abdullah and Nehru were the might and their writ alone could run. It was May 1, 1949 that Sardar Patel advised Hari Singh for a temporary exit from the State in a meeting at Delhi. He was asked that Yuvraj Karan Singh be appointed as Regent in his absence. Maharaja was left with no alternative but to accept the same. He communicated his consent while he was staying in Imperial Hotel New Delhi. Sardar Patel, the Union Home Minister assured Maharaja on May 23, 1949 of the security of Yuvraj Karan Singh as Regent and representative of Maharaja in Kashmir. Yuvraj Karan Singh went to J&K on June 20, 1949 for the first time as Regent. The temporary exit of Hari Singh from J&K became his permanent exit there after. He left J&K and settled in Bombay. He remained unattended, uncared and completely ignored by the tall national leaders. He died in Bombay in May, 1961 at the age of 65 after spending 12 years in his loneliness exile. Some of Maharaja's letters to the national leaders deserve attention of the intellectuals, nationalists and historians and the present and the next generation.

Correspondence of the Maharaja with Mountbatten, Nehru, Patel and President of India is reproduced to the satisfaction of the critics, who have fallen prey to the cooked propaganda against the nationalist Maharaja who fought for his people in exile, the way Maharana Pratap fought for the glory of Chittaur, Gandhi, Nehru and Sheikh were responsible for the exile of the great nationalist Maharaja. This is the judgment of the history.

Sardar Patel wrote to the Maharaja on February 9, 1948 that, "I fully realize what an anxious time you must be having. I can assure you that I am no less anxious about the Kashmir situation and what is happening in the UNO, but whatever the present situation may be, counsel of despair is entirely out of place."

On June 20, 1949 when Maharaja Hari Singh had to leave the State under pressure from Delhi, he appointed Yuvraj Karan Singh, his only son, as Regent through a Royal Proclamation.

On January 26, 1950, when India became a Republic, Article 370 of the Constitution of India conferred a special status on the State of Jammu and Kashmir. There was no reason to insert Article 370. Its introduction indicated that the Congress had hidden understanding with the Sheikh on Kashmir. Congress did not intend to integrate J&K.

Blunders 22

Article 370 vis-à-vis J&K

Nehru led Congress was satisfied by the Accession. Nehru intended to gift Kashmir to Sheikh Abdullah. They did not want J&K to integrate with the Union. Sheikh Abdullah and his men were nominated to the Constituent Assembly against all norms and rules only to curb Maharaja's powers within the State. A constitutional device to make Sheikh Abdullah and his party legal heir to the Maharaja was adopted through a temporary provision in the guise of Article 370. The Constituent Assembly was dominated by the Nehru-led Congress. Gandhi ji was no more. Jinnah had reluctantly chosen his separation and opted for a theocratic State. The Chairman of the Constituent Assembly, Dr. Ambedkar's reservations was dumped into the dustbin. 'Nehru-Sheikh' kept a Pandora's Box shut for the country. In order to curb the Maharaja's nationalist strategy, he was brought under the control of Sheikh Abdullah. Parliament was disarmed to legislate vis-à-vis J&K even in respect of the subjects Maharaja had included in Instrument of Accession.

Article 370 in the Indian Constitution

Temporary provisions with respect to the State of Jammu and Kashmir

1. Notwithstanding anything in this Constitution,
    (a) The provisions of Article 238 shall not apply in relation to the State of Jammu and Kashmir;
    (b) The power of Parliament to make laws for the said State shall be limited to,

(i) those matters in the Union List and the Concurrent List which, in consultation with the Government of the State are declared by the President to correspond to matters specified in the Instrument of Accession governing the accession of the State to the Dominion of India as the matters with respect to which the Dominion Legislature may make laws far that State; and

(ii) Such other matters in the said Lists as, with the concurrence of the Government of the State, the President may by order specify.

Explanation For the purposes of this article, the Government of the State means the person for the time being recognized by the President as the Maharaja of Jammu and Kashmir acting on the advice of the Council of Ministers for the time being in office under the Maharaja's Proclamation on 5th March, 1948;

(c) the provisions of article 1 and of this article shall apply in relation to that State;

(d) such of the other provisions of this Constitution shall apply in relation to that State subject to such exceptions and modifications as the President may by order specify:

Provided that no such order which relates to the matters specified in the Instrument of Accession of the State referred to in paragraph (i) of sub-clause (b) shall be issued except in consultation with the Government of the State:

Provided further that no such order which relates to matters other than those referred in the last preceding proviso shall be issued except with the concurrence of that Government.

2. If the concurrence of the Government of the State referred to in paragraph (ii) of sub-clause (b) of clause (1) or in the second proviso to sub-clause (d) of that clause be given before the Constituent Assembly for the purpose of framing the Constitution of the State is convened, it shall be placed before such Assembly for such decision as it may take thereon.

3. Notwithstanding anything in the foregoing provisions of this article, the President may. by public notification, declare that this article shall cease to be operative or shall be operative only with such exceptions and modifications and from such date as he may specify:

Provided that the recommendation of the Constituent Assembly of the State referred to in clause (2) shall be necessary before the President issues such a notification.

In exercise of the powers conferred by Article 370 the President, on the recommendation of the Constituent Assembly of the State of Jammu and Kashmir, declared that as from the 17th day of November, 1952, the said Article 370 shall be operative with the modification that for the Explanation in Cl. (1) thereof, the following explanation is substituted namely.

"**Explanation**: For the purpose of this article, the Government of the State means the person for the time being recognized by the President on the recommendation of the Legislative Assembly of the State as the Sadar-i-Riyasat (now Governor) of Jammu and Kashmir, acting on the advice of the Council of Ministers of the State for the time being in office."

BLUNDERS 23

Dixon Plan

US Conspiracy

Owen Dixon submitted his report to United Nations Security Council on September 15, 1950.

Anglo-American plot to fix their military base in Gilgit-Baltistan was revived by sending Sir Graham and Justice Owen Dixon, a Jewish Judge of the Australia to Kashmir as UN Observer to find the 'working situation' to resolute J&K for Pakistan had refused to withdraw its armies and civilian settlers from POK and Gilgit. Pakistan did not implement the Resolution because it knew that Pakistan may not get even 6% of voters of Muslims in Kashmir. The Anglo-American Bloc wanted to bail out Pakistan from this 'charge of violation of UNCIP' Resolution. The Security Council which was a 'stooge' of US managed to dispatch Dixon to Kashmir whose recommendations were not only treacherous but dangerous to the newly established Nation—India which was trying to recover from the wounds of partition. Dixon Plan was a 'CIA' plot to divide J&K on communal lines and establish a buffer state of Greater Kashmir. His proposal suggested to carve out Greater Kashmir comprising Kashmir Valley and the Muslim majority areas of Jammu province namely falling in the North of Chenab. Entire country rejected it. Congress could not dare support that.

The so-called Dixon Plan, a Jewish plot to destabilize India suggested that, "It assigned Ladakh to India, the Northern Areas and Pakistan-Occupied Kashmir (POK) to Pakistan, split Jammu between the two, and envisaged a plebiscite in the Kashmir Valley. Pakistan demurred at first, but agreed. It fell through because Nehru did not accept the conditions in which the plebiscite could be held; precisely the issue on which the United Nations Commission for India and Pakistan (UNCIP) and Graham failed".

BLUNDERS 24

Usurping Land Sans Compensation, 1951

Confiscation of Landed Properties of the land owners restricting limit to 23 acres, along without a penny's compensation was another 'revengeful' act of the nominated National Conference government headed by Sheikh Abdullah to suck the blood from every person who did not agree with him. 23 acres of kanals of land in Jammu or Kupwara sector did not yield grass for the cattle even. 12000 families of the Dogra soldiers who perished during the Pak-sponsored invasion disappeared, unattended, uncared and treated as enemy agents by the government. On the other hands those who opposed the Maharaja, joined 'Quit Kashmir' movement were decorated as 'freedom fighters', which remained permanent and competent.

Sheikh Abdullah's 'Quit Kashmir' movement started with the exit of the Maharaja. His second target was the landlords and middle class land-holders in 1951 without any popular government Sheikh Abdullah through an Ordinance forcibly usurped land without any prescribed rules or law without compensation at all. The limit was 23 acres only irrespective of the nature of land. Thousands of the families suffered and starved. He did not want any stint of fundamental right. That is why he had proposed so-called 'Delhi Agreement' that fundamental rights should be kept out of the Chapter of the J&K Constitution. The fundamental rights in J&K have entered by the intervention of the Supreme Court from time to time. The NC landlords and the bureaucrats' government their land converted into Orchards which were kept out the scope of the so-called 'Land Reforms Ordinance'.

Maharaja to K. N. Katju
Nehru's Vengeance!

Pune
June 29, 1952

Dear Dr. Katju,

With reference to the statements made by the Prime Minister of India at a recent Press Conference and in the House of the People regarding the decisions taken by the Constituent Assembly of the State of Jammu and Kashmir with respect to the Headship of the State in the proposed Constitution which vitally affects my position and that of my dynasty. I am constrained to communicate to you my feelings in the matter.

2. The statement regarding the attitude of the Government of India in this matter seems to have been arrived at without regard to the assurances repeatedly given to me that nothing would be done in the matter unless my interests and the interests of my dynasty were affectively secured by appropriate agreement.

3. I must confess that the reported attitude of the Government of India ignores integral aspects of the question which affect me and my dynasty and is not in conformity with the assurances and the understanding between the Government of India and myself when at the insistent advice of the Government of India accompanied by their definite assurances I permitted the Yuvraj to sign the Proclamation setting up the Constituent Assembly.

4. The Ministry of State is fully aware of the circumstances and the political context in which I agreed to raise the ban put by me on the Yuvraj from signing the Proclamation setting up the Constituent Assembly. At the time of the setting up of the Constituent Assembly I had certain apprehensions which I communicated to the then Minister for State, Shri Gopalaswami Ayyangar. In his letter dated the 5th April, 1951 in reply to my letter the Minister for States (Shri Gopalaswami Ayyangar) stated:

"On neither of the two matters about which I can understand your entertaining apprehensions, namely the continuance of the accession of the Jammu and Kashmir State or part thereof to India and the connection of the Headship of the State or part thereof to India and the connection of the Headship of the State with your dynasty no final decision could be taken by the Constituent Assembly to be convened. They are essential matters which could be decided only as a matter of agreement between the Government of India and Parliament on the one side and the Government of Jammu and Kashmir State, Constituent Assembly or Legislature on the other. The Government of India will, no doubt, at the proper time take the decision on these matters which, I need hardly assure you, would be essentially just from the standpoint both from dynasty and the people of the State. You have obviously to put your trust in the people of the State and the Government of India in respect of this matter. I hope, therefore, you will immediately lift the ban which you have placed on Shri Yuvraj affixing his signature to the Proclamation and which naturally has placed him in great embarrassment."

5. It was on this assurance and promise of the Government of India through the Minister for States that I authorized the Yuvraj to affix his signature to the Proclamation setting up the Constituent Assembly.

6. On the basis of such assurance and promise I all the while believed that the question of the connection of the Headship of the State with my dynasty will not be dealt with by the Constituent Assembly without an agreement between the Government of India and Parliament on the one side and the Government of Jammu and Kashmir on the other. I believed that such agreement would make adequate and affective provision for the Privy Purse and all other matters affectively securing my interests, rights and privileges and those of dynasty.

7. With this background you will appreciate with what feeling of surprise and resentment I read the following passage in the report

of the Press Conference held by the Prime Minister on 21st June, 1952 as appearing in the Time of India;

"In his first public reference to the Kashmir Constituent Assembly's decisions to abolish hereditary ruler ship and have an elected head, Mr. Nehru said that the principle of abolishing dynastic rule in Kashmir had been stated repeatedly by the Kashmir Government and the Government of India had accepted it. The question that arose now was what to do in the present circumstances, so that it may be in keeping with the Indian Constitution and at the same time give affect to the wishes of the people of Kashmir."

8. The Ministry of States is fully aware of the circumstances under which I acceded to the Dominion of India on 26th October, 1947 and the circumstances and the reasons and the purposes for which I agreed to stay out of the State and appoint the Yuvraj as the Regent. Fully appreciating the political situation in the context and having regard to the larger interests of the State as well as of India in the larger context, I agreed to and carried out the suggestions made by the Government of India from time to time, with a view to create a situation which would secure full accession of the State of Jammu and Kashmir to the Indian Union and would facilitate the process of complete integration of the State of Jammu and Kashmir with India. Fully appreciating the internal situation in the State and the necessity of strengthening politically the hands of the Government of India at the UNO and to facilitate a favourable verdict in case plebiscite is taken in the State I readily cooperated with the Government of India in all the necessary steps which were required to be taken to achieve the double object on the assurances given by the Government of India from time to time that in the ultimate decision my interests and the interests of my dynasty would be safeguarded while giving affect to the wishes of the people of the State. Realizing the necessity of establishing responsible Government to meet the criticism at the UNO to prepare a ground for a favourable

plebiscite to move with the progressive trends and to establish a Government in accordance with the wishes of the people and to enable the people of Jammu and Kashmir to draw up their own Constitution. I have all the while followed the policy and the suggestions made by the Government of India, who were mostly instrumental in my decision for the establishment of responsible Government in the State and the Constituent Assembly to achieve the desired objects. I did not stick to the legal aspects of the various steps which were taken, I realized that the occasion was not for indulging in legal niceties, but for facing the inevitable pressure of events and making adjustments accordingly.

9. Having regard to the provision contained in Article 370 of the Constitution, I naturally assumed that my Headship of the State could not be altered unilaterally by the Constituent Assembly without amending the said Article, and without making adequate provisions for my Privy Purse and other rights and privileges in the Constitution itself. I feel that the significance of the fundamental law of the Union of which the State of Jammu and Kashmir is an integral part is not fully appreciated by the Constituent Assembly. I am greatly worried as I feel that the attitude disclosed renders the assurances and promises of the Government and even the provision of the Constitution of very little significance.

10. I wonder if it is realized that implementing the reported decision would mean giving a go by not only to the promises and assurances given to me but also to a specific provision of the Constitution of India.

11. May I therefore have a definite assurance and a clear statement as to how my rights are to be safeguarded.

Yours sincerely,

Sd/-
Hari Singh

Nehru to Maharaja
Undesirable, impolite!

(*This is only letter that Nehru addressed a great nationalist Maharaja a few days before terminating Monarchy).* Events will take their natural course'. Nehru tells the Maharaja.

New Delhi
July 5, 1952

Dear Maharaja Sahib,

Our Minister of States, Dr. Katju, has shown me your letter on June 29, 1952 which you sent him.

In this letter you refer to certain statements made by me at a Press Conference and in the House of the People and also to assurances given to you by or on behalf of the Government of India. At the end of the letter you ask for a definite assurance and a clear statement as to how your rights are to be safeguarded.

The Minister of States will, no doubt, reply to your letter. But as this letter of yours has been occasioned chiefly by what I said, I think that I should also write to you and make it clear what our basic position is in this matter.

You are, no doubt, aware that the whole Constitution of India is based on and is derived from the people of India. In the final analysis, it is the people and their wishes that count and all private and personal interests must give way to the larger interests of the people. In so far as the old States are concerned, it was our position, repeatedly stated, that, wherever necessary, the wishes of their people will be consulted and will prevail. This was in regard to the accession to India. In the great majority of these States the wishes of the people were will known and obvious and, therefore no question arose of a separate consultation with them. In regard to the Jammu and Kashmir State, we felt that the people there would prefer accession to India, but the matter was delicate and not beyond dispute. Hence, even before Partition, and when large numbers of other States were acceding to India, we did not press for the accession of Jammu and Kashmir State. We suggested that this matter should be considered at a large stage when the people's whishes could be ascertained in some form or other. Our then suggestion was that some kind of a Constituent Assembly might be constituted in Jammu and Kashmir State to decide the question of accession as well as other questions. Meanwhile Standstill Agreements were proposed.

On the invasion of the State by tribal raiders and others late in October 1947, a crisis arose there. **At the time of that crisis you left Srinagar at the dead of night for Jammu.** Many of your officers followed your example and the State was left without leadership or means of defence, in so far as official authority was concerned. You asked us then for help and proposed accession of the State to India so that that help could be more easily given. At the same time the leading poplar organization of the State, the National Conference, also sent us an urgent request for help in their hour of danger. It was suggested by them also that the State should accede to India. After long and anxious consideration we accepted these requests and took immediate steps to tender assistance **to the people of Kashmir** against the ruthless invaders who were bringing arson, loot and murder in their train. In accepting accession, however, we repeated our policy that the wishes of the people must prevail in the end. It was, indeed because your request had been powerfully supported by the National Conference, representing the people of Kashmir that we decided to accept accession. Nevertheless, we stated even at that moment that the people of Jammu and Kashmir State would finally decide the fate of their State.

War developed in the State and India became more and more involved in it. There was danger of this war spreading to other areas. In order to avoid this danger and in pursuance of our general policy to pursue peaceful methods, we referred this matter to the United Nations. Again we laid stress on our policy and our desire that the people of Kashmir should decide about their future, whenever a suitable opportunity for this was given to them.

In the Security Council of the United Nations, it was later proposed that a plebiscite should be held in the State after a number of other steps had been taken and conditions created for the proper holding of such a plebiscite. We accepted that resolution. That has been our position in the Security Council ever since. The plebiscite has been delayed because of Pakistan's insistence on certain conditions which we could not agree to. The mater is still pending before the United Nations where our position has been clearly stated on many occasions.

You will observe that in this basic picture of the crisis of Kashmir **you do not come in at all**. The fact that emerges is that the people of Kashmir must decide their own future. We have pledged ourselves to this not only in the Security Council but directly to the people of Jammu and Kashmir State. If, as a result of the plebiscite, it was decided that Kashmir should not accede to India, we would naturally have to accept that decision. And, in that event, it is clear that your personal interests in the State would automatically disappear. If the people of Kashmir decided in favour of India, as we hoped and believed they would, then also it would be for them to say what, if any your position should be in future. India went to the help of Kashmir on the invitation of the people of Kashmir. We did not go there, as Pakistan falsely asserts, as an invading army to suppress the people. We do not propose to continue there for a day when we are no longer wanted by the people of the State.

It has been our policy all over India to settle the problems of the old States peacefully and with goodwill and the consent of the parties concerned. We were fortunate to gain that consent in a very large number of cases and so the radical changes that were brought about were done in a spirit of cooperation. But it is always to be remembered that those changes were necessitated by the fierce pressure of changing time and the demands of a revolutionary situation. Those changes would have taken place, whether consent came or did not come, because the will of the people has to prevail and no vested interests could come in its way. The Government of India softened the change and made generous settlement with the Princes. But the main thing was the demand from people and the vital necessity of that change. It was because you did not sense the spirit of the times and the revolutionary changes that were coming over India and the world that you and your then advisors pursued a mistaken policy that led to the grievous development of subsequent days. You will remember how you discarded our advice, repeatedly given in 1946 and 1947. We saw a situation developing there which was full of danger. But your advisors then led you along a wrong path, which undoubtedly, would have led to complete disaster for you and your dynasty if the Government of India had not come to your help. They came to your help, but on that major conditions that the people's will must prevail.

It surprises me that even after all these terrible experiences you still fail to understand the true nature of events in Jammu and Kashmir State, in India and the world. Those Princes in India, who had some understanding of these events and the new forces at work, adapted themselves to them and thereby, though they lost power and authority they secured an honourable place for themselves. Kashmir was rent by war in which India poured her blood and treasure. The people of Kashmir suffered greatly. In this crisis, you still imagined that your personal claim had first importance. The Government of India sought to help you **in spite of you**, but they had to face on many occasions difficulty and obstruction from you. Your refer to your permitting the Yuvraj to sign the Proclamation setting up the Constituent Assembly. Even in doing so you delayed matters considerably and obstructed, to some extent, the natural course of events. You did not appreciate then, as you do no seem to appreciate now, that Constituent Assemblies do not ultimately derive their authority from a Ruler but base their sanctions on the People. Certain forms are observed and it is desirable to observe them where possible. But if those forms are not available, they are done away with and matters take their course. The Constituent Assembly would have met whether you agreed to it or not.

In view of the assurances given by us to the United Nations we made it clear that we would not consider a decision of the Constituent Assembly as binding upon us, if it went against those assurances. Even so, we could not come in the way of the Constituent Assembly in deciding in regard to accession or other matters. Indeed, it was made clear that they had full authority, derived from the people to draw up their internal Constitution. Naturally that Constitution had to be in keeping with the Constitution of India, if the accession to India was to endure.

In your letter to Dr. Katju you refer repeatedly to what you consider your rights and the rights of your dynasty. There is little mention in their letter of the rights of the people. That is the basic difference between your outlook and that of the Government of India. We have tried here and elsewhere to adjust rights, as far as possible but there can be no doubt that no right can prevail if it comes in conflict with the right of the people. For our part we would welcome any decision taken by the people of the Jammu and Kashmir State which acknowledges any right of yours but it would be against our policy as well as against the dominating facts of the situation, for us to consider your rights as overriding public rights, whatever your theoretical position might be, you have no authority of position left now to influence the future of Kashmir. Because of various considerations, however, we have tried to maintain for you an honourable position, though that is devoid of authority. But if you claim rights which in reality you do not possess and if you come in the way of changes which are inevitable, then even that formal place that you occupy will be endangered. That place would intimately be made secure only if you had the confidence and the affection of your people. Since you have lost this confidence and affection, the right also goes.

You will have appreciated that the people of Kashmir have gone through fire and suffering during these past four and a half years. I have seen no evidence of any great sympathy on your part for these people, no desire to help them in their distress. Kashmir became an international problem and the people there lived in fear and doubt, facing day-to-day perils, but you only laid stress from time to time on what you called your rights and privileges, on your Privy Purse and the like. You can imagine that this did not enhance your prestige or lead your people towards you.

You ask for a definite assurance and a clear statement as to how **your rights are to be safeguarded.** The only assurance I can give you is that the first place will be given always **to the rights of the people and to the wishes of the people. If you fall in with those rights and wishes, then we shall endeavour to help you to the best of our ability. If you do not do so, then events will take their natural course.**

Yours sincerely,

Sd/-
Jawahar Lal Nehru

Sensing the mood of the Prime Minister of India and guessing the future dark clouds hovering in the skies of J&K, Maharaja dashed a detailed memorandum to the first President of India, Dr. Rajendra Prasad from Pune.

Maharaja's Protest to President of India

16/17th August, 1952
Pune

Dr. Rajendra Prasad
President of India
New Delhi

Sir,

I am making a direct approach to you in the matter of the affairs of the State of Jammu and Kashmir and its Ruler as the situation has become acute owing to the rapid developments that are taking place and the further steps which are being taken in the next few days as these will vitally affect me personally apart from the repercussions they will have on the subjects of the State.

2. It is necessary to set out very briefly the events that have happened so far as the State of Jammu and Kashmir is concerned since my accession to the Gaddi.

3. I became the Ruler of the State in 1925. I then found that the British had strengthened their hold on the State by taking advantage of certain circumstances because, it being a border State of great strategic and political importance, they wanted it to be completely in their grip. The British created in the myth of paramountcy without any historical or political sanctions and exploited the State as a set of against the fast approaching political awakening and urge for freedom in what was then known as British India.

4. Realizing what was coming. I took it upon myself to shake off the British yoke by insisting that the relations of the State with the British should be governed by the Treaty and all other strings which had been attached to such relationship with a view to gain domination over the State should be removed. I succeeded in my efforts to a large extent but incurred the wrath of the British who thenceforth became openly hostile to me.

5. Simultaneously with this, I started taking measures to ameliorate the condition of my people and to organize my Government on progressively democratic lines. I enacted laws to relieve rural indebtedness and to impose generally the lot of the agriculturist and the economic and social condition of my people. Some of three enactments were resented by my Hindu subjects who thought that their interests were being sacrificed in the cause of Muslim uplift. I established industries and made provisions for education and medical relief far in advance of any other State. Special provision was made for the educational advancement of Muslims who were then considered backward. I was even more enthusiastic as regards the better organization of my Government. In this, I had the assistance of men of unquestionable integrity and ability from British India as my Prime Ministers and other Ministers and heads of the various Departments. It

will not be out of place to name a few of them, such as, Raja Harikrishen Kaul, Mirza Sir Zaffar Ali, Mr. V.N. Mehta, Mr Vijahat Husein, Sir Burjor Dalal, Sir Abdus Samad Khan, Sir Lal Gopal Rau. As a result, the administration of the State in the mater of efficiency and organization was better than even in some of the Provinces of British India. One further fact to which I wish to draw your attention in this connection is that I invariably acted on the advice of such Ministers and did not interfere or overrule their directions. It therefore, follows that if any fault is now to be found with the administration of the State and/or the policies then pursued, the blame cannot be laid at my door alone. It is significant that for six year (1938 to 1943) Shri N. Gopalaswami Ayyangar was the Prime Minister of the State and he will bear me out that I never interfered with his policies and decisions adopted and taken from time to time. Consequently, with my desire to give to the people of the State complete self government, I discussed in 1945 with my Prime Minister, Sir B.N. Rau, in the presence of Sir Tej Bahadur Sapru and Sir Kailash N. Haskar, the inauguration in the State of Full Responsible Government with Provincial Autonomy and a Central Government comprised of Representatives of the Provinces and a Board of Judicial Advisers with myself as the Constitutional Head. I was prepared to do this even with the knowledge that it would not be relished by the British. Sir B.N. Rau wanted this to be put into execution within the next fortnight. I was of opinion that it should be done in about six months so as to enable us to complete the scheme. The news leaked out, there were intrigues, position became very difficult and Sir B.N. Rau left shortly thereafter.

6. The finances of the State were governed on modern principles. My expenditure was strictly limited and kept separate and distinct from the State finances and proper and well defined limits were laid down as between my personal and private matters and matters of the state. Thus, I had a well organized and efficient Executive, a democratically elected Legislature, an independent judiciary, definite policies for expansion of education, medial relief and all other essential features of a

progressive state. The eminent administrators and judges who worked for the State from time to time will bear testimony to this.

7. All that I did aggravated the hostility of the British towards me as they were not sincerely inclined towards ameliorating the conditions of the people or for the freedom of the country.

8. In other days, the Rulers of Indian States were judged by the condition and feelings of their subjects and I can say, without fear of contradiction, that the people of my State were content and had no cause for grievances against me or the administration of the State.

9. It is not unknown that trouble started in the State in 1931 and what has on occasions been described by so-called 'national leaders' of the State as 'the Freedom Movement' was engineered by elements outside the State under the instigation of the British. The movement in the beginning was a religious movement with slogans like 'Down with Hindu Raj' and 'Islam in danger'. The leaders of the movement were men who now figure as Ministers and Administrators in Azad Kashmir under Pakistan such as, Chaudhary Ghulam Abbas and Mauli Yousuf Shah and some others. To gain sympathy and cooperation from those fighting for freedom from the British yoke in British India, 'National Conference'. The name was adopted also to fall into line with the movement carried on in other States in the name of the 'State People Conference' and to take advantage of the declining prestige of the British. The movement thus gained the sympathy of the Indian National Congress. It became known in British India as the National Movement in the Jammu and Kashmir State.

10. These facts clearly showed that my people had no grievance against me, that the movement was started by disgruntled people with the British behind them and that those in charge of the movement gained the confidence and sympathy of the Indian National Congress by adopting the name of the 'National Conference'.

11. I have been accused by the Prime Minister of not listening to the advice of the Congress leaders during the fateful period 1946-47. I deny that charge. In 1946 when the leaders of the Indian National Congress formed the Viceroy's Cabinet for the Interim Government, I

had occasion to meet Mahatma Gandhi and Shri J.B. Kripalani, the then President of the Indian National Congress, when they both visited the State. Mahatma Gandhi suggested that I should have the backing of the people in whatever I did, Shri J.B. Kripalani suggested the immediate release of Sheikh Abdullah because the nominees of the National Conference who were in the Government had resigned. I pointed to them that I had already set up a Constitutional government which included two nominees of the National Conference and that it was not then possible to entrust the Government entirely in the hands of one group, viz, the National Conference. I said to them that I was willing to make such further changes as might be suggested towards making it a completely population Government in consonance with the safety of the State and to keep the balance between the divergent views of different parts of the State. The matter rested there for the time being.

12. Then came the development of 1947 and the question of accession. The position of my State was very difficult, situated as it was in contiguity to India and Pakistan as also to Afghanistan, Tibet and Russia. The situation therefore required to be dealt with more tact and foresight than in the case of other states. Mahatma Gandhi and the Prime Minister were anxious that I should not make a declaration of Independence and the Prime Minister was anxious to secure the release from prison of Sheikh Abdullah. Having regard to what my Government had done when the Prime Minister visited the State in 1946, Lord Mountbatten chose to visit the State in June 1947 and we had several talks. Lord Mountbatten then urged me and my Prime Minister, Kak, not to make any declaration of Independence but to find out in one way or another, the will of the people of Kashmir as soon as possible and to announce our intention by the 14th August to send representatives accordingly to one Constituent Assembly or the other. Lord Mountbatten further told us that the newly created States Department was prepared to give an assurance that if Kashmir went to Pakistan, it would not be regarded as an unfriendly act by the Government of India. Lord Mountbatten stressed the dangerous

situation in which Kashmir would find itself if it lacked the support of one of the two Dominions by the date of the transfer of power. The impression which I gathered from my talks with Lord Mountbatten who explained the situation with plans and maps was that, in his opinion, it was advisable for me to accede to Pakistan. I thought that in the circumstances it was advisable to have Standstill Agreements with India and Pakistan and get breathing time to decide which accession would be in the interests of the State. Pakistan very quickly and willingly agreed to a Standstill arrangement, perhaps with mental reservations, as appears from their subsequent conduct. On the other hand, the Government of India did not make up their mind and, if I may be permitted to say so, dealt with the situation in a half-hearted and desultory manner; thus, giving an opportunity Pakistan to do mischief, as they did. This gave rise to misunderstandings on both sides resulting in dissatisfaction and delay in coming to an understanding. The results have been detrimental to both the State and India. Pakistan became impatient and, having failed to force accession, started with blockading the supplies to the State and ended by invading the State. Lord Mountbatten realizing the uncertain and dangerously unstable position of the State, asked Lord Ismay to approach me and get me to decide on accession without further delay to whichever Dominion I and my people desired. This was at the end of August, 1947.

My difficulties were as follows:

1. The People of the State were divided in several groups, each group having its own ideas about accession;
2. The Border Feudatory Territories such as Hunza, Nagar and Chitral and the District of Gilgit, where British influence was supreme were definitely for accession to Pakistan and were pressing me to accede to Pakistan without delay and threatening me with dire consequences if I did not act according to their suggestion;
3. The Muslim population of the State was also divided into groups with divergent views. Muslims from parts of Jammu such as, Mirpur, Poonch, Muzaffrabad, were for accession to Pakistan because of Pakistan propaganda inside the State. Muslims of

Kashmir and some Muslims of Jammu who were led by Sheikh Abdullah and the leaders of the National Conference did not want the question of accession to be decided at that stage but wanted me to part with power in their favour so that they could decide the question independently of me. They made no secret of their views and obstructed me in deciding the question of accession instead of helping me to accede to India;

4. Hindus of Jammu and all the people of Ladakh were for affiliation with or accession of India;
5. A portion of the population of Kashmir was also for accession to Pakistan.

Thus, there was a sharp division of opinion. The Partition aggravated the situation and unhinged and unbalanced the minds of the people with the result that the people of the State were not in a position to give any considered opinion if chose to consult them.

13. In September 1947, it was suggested to me that it would be a wise move on my part to appoint Shri Mehr Chand Mahajan as my Prime Minister as he would be able to handle the affairs of the State in the then critical period firmly and in a statesmanlike manner. Before Shri Mehr Chand Mahajan took up his appointment he discussed with Sardar Patel about immediate requirements of the State and Sardar Patel promised him full support and cooperation on behalf of the Government of India. Sardar Patel also wrote to me stating this and adding that the Government of India fully realized how difficult the situation in the State was and assured me that the Government of India would do their best to help the State in the critical period. I then wrote to Sardar Patel that a little further elucidation of the points of view regarding the essential requirements of the movement would result in a satisfactory solution. Sardar Patel replied on the October 2, 1947 that he had a further talk with Shri Mahajan and understood that Shri Mahajan was joining my service very shortly. As by that time I had proclaimed a general amnesty, Sardar Patel expressed his pleasure at the step I had taken and stated that this would rally round me the men who might otherwise have been a thorn in my side. He also stated that he

was expediting as much as possible the linking up of the State with the Indian Dominion. Shri Mahajan then received Sardar Patel's letter of the October 21, 1947 in which he said that he had further discussion with Sheikh Abdullah, that Sheikh Abdullah seemed to him genuinely anxious to cooperate and sincerely desirous of assisting the State in dealing with the external dangers and the internal troubles with which the State was threatened. He further said that at the same time Sheikh Abdullah, as was natural, felt that unless something was done and done immediately, to strengthen his hands, both in popular eyes and in dealing with the dangers, it would be impossible for him to do anything substantial. He said he felt that the position which Sheikh Abdullah took up was understandable and reasonable, that in the mounting demands for the introduction of a Responsible Government in the State, such as was witnessed in Travancore and Mysore, it was impossible for me to isolate myself, that the upsurge was bound to affect me sooner or later, that the Government of India on their part had pledged to give me the maximum support and would do so, but without some measure of popular backing, particularly from amongst the community which represented such an overwhelming majority in Kashmir, it would be difficult to make such support go to the farthest limit that was necessary if the disruptive forces which were being raised and organized, were to be crushed. He advised me in the circumstances to make a substantial gesture to win Sheikh Abdullah's support. He said he had no desire to suggest that I should do so in a manner which would be completely revolutionary in character, that such a step might undermine the loyal and willing support which the State had commanded from strong elements of the body politics.

14. Shri Mahajan also received the Prime Minister's letter dated October 20, 1947 in which he referred to the friendliest feelings the Government of India had towards Kashmir and its people and their desire to help to the best of their ability in providing Kashmir with the commodities it needed. He said the Government of India would like to do so for humanitarian reasons as well because of their deep interest in the future of the people of Jammu and Kashmir State. That the self

interest of India also demanded that and that Government of India were strongly of the opinion that no coercion should be exercised on Kashmir and its people and that they should be allowed to function in their own way and to make such decision as they thought fit and proper and that in the furtherance of this policy the Government of India would direct their efforts. The Prime Minister in his letter dated October 21, 1947 to Shri Mahajan said that the future of Kashmir was of the most urgent importance to the Government of India and for him, it was both a personal and a public matter that it would be a tragedy so far as he was concerned, if Kashmir went to Pakistan. The Prime Minister referred to the urgent need of Pakistan to get Kashmir's accession to Pakistan and that they were threatening every now and then to that end and that everything else that they did was an accessory to the same, that the top ranking leaders of Pakistan were continually approaching the Kashmir National Conference leaders, that they assured to them for their best behaviour and promised them something approaching independence if only they would agree to Kashmir acceding to Pakistan. They were even prepared to give the right of secession. The Prime Minister then suggested the urgency of taking some step like the formation of a Provincial Government and that Sheikh Abdullah, who was obviously the most popular person in Kashmir, might be asked to form such a Government. The Prime Minister further added that in view of all the circumstances he felt that it would probably be undesirable to make any declaration of adhesion to the Indian Union at that stage that this should come later when a popular Interim Government was functioning.

15. After the amnesty proclaimed by me, Sheikh Abdullah wrote to me on September 26, 1947 in which, after referring to his incarceration for about a year and a half, he said as follows:

In spite of what has happened in the past I assure Your Highness that myself and my Party have never harboured any sentiment of disloyalty towards Your Highness' person, throne or dynasty. The development of this beautiful country and the betterment of its people is our common aid and interest and I assure Your Highness the fullest and loyal support of myself and my organization.

He added:

> In order to achieve the common aim set forth above, mutual trust and confidence must be the main step. Without this it would not be possible to face successfully the great difficulties that upset our State on all sides at present.

He concluded:

> Before I close this letter, I beg to assure Your Highness once again of my steadfast loyalty and pray that God may grant me opportunity enough to make this country attain under Your Highness' aegis such an era of peace, prosperity and good Government that it may be second to none and be an ideal for others to copy.

16. I wrote to Lord Mountbatten on the 26th October, 1947 informing him of the situation in the State. I received his letter dated 27th October, 1947 stating as follows:

In the special circumstances mentioned by Your Highness my Government have decided to accept the accession of Kashmir State to the Dominion of India

> It is my Government's wish that as soon as law and order has been restored in Kashmir and her soil cleared of the invaders the question of the State's accession should be settled by a reference to the people

My Government and I note with satisfaction that Your Highness has decided to invite Sheikh Abdullah to form an interim Government to work as your Prime Minister.

The Prime Minister also wrote to me on the 26th October, 1947 stating as follows:

Shri V.P Menon returned from Jammu this morning and informed me of his talks there. He gave me the Instrument of Accession and the

Standstill Agreement which you had signed and I saw also your letter to the Governor General of India. Allow me to congratulate you on the wise decision that you have taken. I earnestly hope and they will lead not only to the effective protection of Kashmir State in the present but also to the freedom and well-being of Kashmir and India as a whole.

I then acceded to India.

17. The Prime Minister in his letter dated 13th November, 1947 pointed out to me that the only person who could deliver the goods in Kashmir was Sheikh Abdullah, that he was obviously the leading and popular personality in Kashmir, that the way he had risen to grapple with the crisis had shown the nature of the man, that the Prime Minister had a high opinion of his integrity and his general balance of mind and that he was likely to be right in regard to major decisions.

18. Shri Gopalaswami, who was then a Minister without a portfolio, wrote to me on the 9th December, 1947 indicating for my consideration his views on the changes which in the critical situation of the State, were immediately called for in the then existing constitutional and administrative set up in the State.

19. A draft of the Proclamation which I was intended to issue was sent to me by the Government of India. It was seen by Sheikh Abdullah. Sheikh Abdullah also saw the correspondence which had passed between Sardar Patel and myself. Shri Gopalaswami wrote to me on 1st March, 1948 as follows:

1st March, 1948

My dear Maharaja Sahib,

Messrs. V. P. Menon and Mahajan are going to Jammu this afternoon to discuss and finalize with you the draft of the Proclamation which Your Highness has to issue for appointing Abdullah as Prime Minister and others on his advice The draft has been very carefully considered by myself, Pandit ji and Sardar ji, and we are of the opinion that the whole of it should be accepted by you. Anything less would not satisfy the requirements of the present situation.

2. As a friend of yours, I consider it most important that Your Highness must make a very big gesture in order to rally the maximum percentage of the population of the State behind you with the help of Abdullah. Things are moving very fast and we have yet to fight a great battle at Lake Success. I have already stated during the discussions at Lake Success that Your Highness had only been waiting for Sheikh Abdullah to return from America to convert the Emergency Administration into an Interim Council of Ministers with Abdullah as Prime Minister. I am leaving Delhi for Lake Success the day after tomorrow, and it would be a great strength to the cause I have to plead there on behalf of Kashmir if this Proclamation is issued before I leave. I have not the slightest doubt that the issue of this Proclamation at this juncture, is, in the circumstances that confront us at present, in the best interests of yourself and your people.

3. It is further very important that everything that has happened in the past should be forgotten and forgiven and that Your Highness should take Sheikh Abdullah into your fullest confidence In fact, I was almost going to suggest that you should give up your usual reserve, come out in the open and put yourself at the head of your people, both Muslims and non-Muslims, for the purpose of consolidating and strengthening the large volume of support for preserving the integrity of the State and maintaining its accession to India, which thanks to Sheikh Abdullah and the Indian Army, you have already behind you.

With kind regards,

Yours sincerely,

Sd/-
N. Gopalaswami

Sheikh Abdullah in his letter dated 24th March, 1948 stated as follows:

The situation in Jammu and Kashmir State is, as you are well aware, a difficult one and requires the most careful handling. The emergency continues and has to be dealt with as such till normal conditions are restored. The burden of a Prime Minister in these circumstances will be a heavy one. He cannot function effectively without the fullest cooperation of his colleagues and the people as well as, of course, Your Highness. I have consulted some of my colleagues, who were available and have come to the conclusion that it is my duty in these circumstances to undertake this burden. I trust that in the heavy work ahead I shall have Your Highness' full help and cooperation. I appreciate the spirit in which you have made the offer of the Prime Minister to me and on my part I assure Your Highness that I shall fully reciprocate it.

20. Then came the Proclamation dated 5th March, 1948 which was drafted by Shri Gopalaswami and approved by the Government of India and Sheikh Abdullah. It has been referred to in Article 370 of the Constitution of India and the State of Jammu and Kashmir has to far been governed under the constitutional set up for that Proclamation.

21. It is necessary to set out briefly what happened in the State and between the Government of India and Sheikh Abdullah in relation to the State after the Proclamation of 5th March, 1948 and my leaving the State at the end of April 1949. Sheikh Abdullah and the men of his party took all power to themselves, ignored my existence and where they felt necessary, they got the consent of the Government of India to do what they liked in the State disregarding me and my wishes. This gradually led to a deterioration and to the outside world, the State and Sheikh Abdullah became convertible terms. The people of Kashmir were utterly ignored and everything that Sheikh Abdullah desired to do was done in the name of the State with the express or tacit consent of the Government of India. He approached the Government of India with the result that I was asked to stay out of the State for a few months. I accepted the advice of Sardar Patel and agreed to stay out. The Yuvraj was appointed Regent. It need hardly be pointed out that the Yuvraj became a figurehead and had to take orders from Sheikh Abdullah. In this connection it may also be pointed out that although my Proclamation of 5th March, 1948 was based on the Mysore

Constitution, which stipulated the appointment of a Dewan and reserved subjects yet gradually Sheikh Abdullah succeeded in getting the approval of the Government of India to making changes in the Constitution of the State, so as to make it very different from what was expressly intended to be. This mischief began with Sheikh Abdullah going direct to the Government of India on certain points over my head and the Government of India countenancing him and giving the desired directions and then informing me of what they had done at the instance of Sheikh Abdullah. The correspondence on the subject and the events following on each change bear testimony to what Sheikh Abdullah was trying to achieve in breach of the solemn promises and assurances given by him and also by the Government of India on his behalf. After my leaving the State things went from bad to worse. Sheikh Abdullah was not satisfied with what he had achieved and aspired to absolute control of the State. He became openly inimical and hostile to me. He even interfered with my private properties and personal belongings, issued order to humiliate me and even interfered with the administration of the Dharmarth Trust, a Trust created by my forefathers of which I am the Trustee and which is being administered from day to day by the President of the Dharmarth Council appointed by me. The charities and institutions maintained from the revenues of Trust are starved. Even the routine expenses of the Trust, such as, for Puja in temples and Devasthans cannot be met because it pleases Sheikh Abdullah to prevent the income of the Trust coming to my hands or to the hands of President of the Dharmarth Council. The Jammu branch of the Imperial Bank of India refused to pay even to me the amounts of the fixed deposits to the Bombay Office of the Imperial Bank of India with the result that I had to renew the deposits to avoid loss of interest to the Trust. It would be interesting to know under whose order the Jammu branch of the Bank acted in the manner it did. As will be apparent from my correspondence with the States Ministry my complaints as regards both my personal properties and the Dharmarth Trust have been galore and none of them has been remedied either by Sheikh Abdullah or by the States Ministry. Leaving aside for the moment my grievances as regards what is being done with reference to my personal properties in Jammu and Kashmir how can Sheikh Abdullah's attitude towards the administration of the Dharmarth Trust be reconciled with secularism and impartiality?

22. I may now refer to Mr. V.P. Menon's letter to Shri Mahajan dated 30th January, 1948 in which he stated as follows:

As I told you, I have already contradicted the news that the Maharaja fled from Srinagar to Jammu. I propose again to take up this question with the Ministry of Information and have asked Sharma, our Publicity Coordination Officer, to get into touch with foreign correspondents and give them the correct picture. I hope, this canard will stop once for all.

This gives a direct lie to the report set afloat both inside and outside the State by Sheikh Abdullah and this party that I had run away from my State in October 1947 leaving the State in chaos and the people at the tender mercies of the invaders. It appears that the Prime Minister was deliberately misinformed as to what I then did and he was also misinformed that my officers had deserted their posts and runaway. In third week of October 1947 Lord Mountbatten was of opinion that it would be dangerous to send any Indian troops to the help of the State unless the State first offered to accede particularly as such accession would be temporary, being prior to a plebiscite. No final decision was, however, taken on these vital questions by 25th October, 1947 but Mr. V.P. Menon was asked to fly to Srinagar to find out the true position there. He met me at Srinagar and I made him realize the urgency of the situation and that unless India helped immediately, all would be lost. It was then that on the strong advice of Mr. V.P. Menon who said it would be foolhardy for me to stay in Srinagar when raiders were as near as Baramulla then, I left Srinagar with my wife and son. I also ignored the Letter of Accession which Mr. V.P. Menon took back with him.

None of my officers fled. The families of some of the officers left for Jammu as the Government used to move to Jammu at the end of October and open at Jammu on the first Monday in November.

On the other hand, it was Sheikh Abdullah who fled from Srinagar and did not return till the Indian troops had started coming into Srinagar.

23. Regarding my leaving the State, I may refer to my letter dated 6th May, 1949 to Sardar Patel and Sardar Patel's letter to me dated 23rd May, 1949. I may also refer to my letter dated 1st June, 1949 to Sardar Patel and Sardar Patel's letter dated 9th June 1949 to me. I attach herewith copies of the letters. In June, 1949 I issued a Proclamation appointing the Yuvraj as my Regent during my stay outside the State.

24. This was in compliance with the wishes of the Government of India.

25. In November 1950 I received from Mr. Vishnu Sahay his letter dated 30th November 1950 wherein he drew my attention to the resolution passed by the Council of the National Conference asking that a Constituent Assembly be set up for the State and to my Proclamation of 5th March, 1948 wherein the setting up of such an Assembly was foreshadowed and stated that it appeared to the States Ministry that the time had come to reduce the uncertainty in Kashmir by going ahead with this proposal. He sent a copy of draft Proclamation to set up the Constituent Assembly, for my comments. I took exception to the proposed manner and method of setting up the Constituent Assembly. I summarized my objection to it as follows:

1. That the Proclamation with the object and spirit of which I wholeheartedly agree be issued by me as Ruler who is the properly constituted authority in law to promulgate it and not by my Regent.
2. The powers and functions of the body intended to be constituted should be express, well defined and accurately worded and should exclude from the purview of their enquiry and consideration matters not expressly entrusted to them;
3. They should report to the authority that constitutes it, i.e. the Ruler who shall seek the advice of the Parliament of India in the matter.

I refer to the correspondence that took place, the interview which Mr. Menon had with me in Bombay in February 1951 under the instructions of the Prime Minister and the subsequent negotiations which ended with my giving consent to the Yuvraj for setting up the Constituent Assembly. I also refer to the assurance given to me by the Minister of States (Shri N. Gopalaswami Ayyangar) in the course of the negotiations as to the position of myself and my dynasty and other important matters. I am constrained to refer to the relevant portions of his letter which, I quote below.

5th April, 1951

Developments have, however, since taken place both in the State and at Lake Success which make it imperative that the issue of this proclamation is not delayed any longer. The Government of India are committed to the convening of a Constituent Assembly, the preparations for which are in active progress in the State. That Assembly will be held whether the formal Proclamation issues or not. In the view of the Government of India it must be convened, if both their commitments to the people of Kashmir and their stand at Lake Success are to be implemented in spirit and in the letter. From the beginning they have held that this Constituent Assembly should be called under the provisions of the Constitution of India and that this should be done from both a tactical and constitutional point of view, on the authority of Proclamation issued by the Head of the State. The draft of the Proclamation has been agreed between the Government of India and the Government of Jammu and Kashmir. No purpose will, therefore, be served by any act of Your Highness which holds up the signing and issue of this Proclamation by Shri Yuvraj.

On their of the two matters about which I can understand your entertaining apprehensions, namely, the continuance of the accession of the Jammu and Kashmir State or of part thereof to India and the connection of the Headship of the State with your dynasty, no final decision could be taken by the Constituent Assembly to be convened.

They are essentially matters which could be decided only as a matter of agreement between the Government of India and the Parliament on the one side and the Government of Jammu and Kashmir and the State Constituent Assembly or Legislature on the other. The Government of India will, no doubt at the proper time take the decision on these matters, which, I need hardly assure you, will be essentially be just from the standpoint both of your dynasty and the people of State and the government of India in respect of this matter. I hope, therefore, you will immediately lift the ban which you have placed on Shri Yuvraj affixing his signature to the agreed Proclamation and which naturally has placed him in great embarrassment.

26. Apprehending what was coming and in order not to embarrass the Government of India and the Yuvraj, I have been prepared to abdicate provided that a satisfactory arrangement was to come with me by the States Ministry and provided also that the Yuvraj's position as the Head of the State was assured. The negotiations in this behalf which were carried on with Shri Gopalaswami as the States Minister were left in an indecisive state because of Shri Gopalaswami having been succeeded as the States Minister by Dr. K. N. Katju. Having regard to the trend of events I wrote to Dr. Katju on the 29th June, 1952. I waited for Dr. Katju's reply as foreshadowed in the Prime Minister's letter. I then received Dr. Katju's reply dated 30th July, 1952. I replied to Dr. Katju by my letter dated 8th August, 1952. I enclose copies of these letters as they have an important bearing on the situation.

27. These letters speak for themselves Dr. Katju's reply is not a reply at all. The legal position, it appears to me, has not been considered and it further appears that it is being taken for granted by the Prime Minister and Dr. Katju that the relevant Articles, particularly Article 370, of the Constitution of India can be altered and/or amended to suit the present attitude of Sheikh Abdullah. It would not be out of place to point out that Article 370 refers specifically to my Proclamation of 5th March, 1948. That is the law which governs the State of Jammu and Kashmir until a new Constitution is framed, approved and adopted not only by the Constituent Assembly of the State but also approved by me

and then by you and yet, I learn that the Prime Minister has asked the Yuvraj (who is acting only as my Regent and represents me) to agree to be the elected Head of the State forthwith, that is to say, even before the Constitution of the State is framed much less approved and adopted thus throwing over not only me but also the dynasty. I do not know what reply Dr. Katju proposes to make to me but it appears that the Prime Minister is dealing with the matter. (Vide his letter dated 5th July, 1952). I have, therefore to specifically deal with the charges made in the Prime Minister's letter.

28. The Prime Minister in para 4 of his letter refers to the Constitution of India as having been based on and derived from the people of India and says with regard to the Jammu and Kashmir State that the Government of India felt that the people would prefer accession to India but the matter was delicate and not beyond dispute and, therefore, the Government of India did not press for the Accession of Jammu and Kashmir State but suggested that the matter should be considered at a large stage when the people's wishes could be ascertained in some form or the other and the suggestion was that some kind of a Constituent Assembly might be set up in the State to decide the question of accession as well as other questions. I grant all this but how can the Government of India take all these steps over my head on whose authority they entered the State and are continuing there and who was the Chief Author of the Proclamation on which is based the future construction of political set up in the country? In para 5, the Prime Minister says that on the invasion of the State by tribal raiders and others late in October 1947 the crisis arose and at that time I left Srinagar at the dead of night for Jammu and many of my officers followed me and the State was left without leadership or means of defence in so far as official authority was concerned. This is in fact, untrue as pointed out above. I left Srinagar for Jammu on the advice of the Government of India conveyed to me through Mr. Menon. The Prime Minister says further that in the basic picture of the crisis of Kashmir I do not come in at all. That statement amounts to *suppresio veri* and *suggestion falsi.* I have acted all throughout from September

1947 under the advice of the Government of India, Lord Mountbatten, the Prime Minister, Sardar Vallabhbhai Patel and Shri Gopalaswami and, as pointed out herein above, Sheikh Abdullah himself made promises and gave assurances, which he is now backing out. Even in the book called New Kashmir published by the Kashmir Information Bureau, New Delhi, in 1950 and which is the political Bible of Sheikh Abdullah, Sheikh Abdullah has based his case for a Responsible Government in the State under the aegis of the Maharaja and even gone to the length of setting out what functions the Maharaja was no perform. The Prime Minister in his letter says that the people of Kashmir must decide their own future. I may well ask whether Sheikh Abdullah is a synonymous term with the people of Kashmir. The people of Kashmir have not been consulted. According to Sheikh Abdullah, the people of Kashmir have changed their mind to such an extent that they are determined to get rid of the idea of a hereditary ruler of the State. The Constituency Assembly has not yet come to a decision nor has it framed any constitution providing for the functions of the Head of the State either hereditary or elected and what one would like to know is where is the reason for this frightful hurry to elect the Head of the State thus doing away with me and my dynasty before the Constitution is framed and before the fate of the State is determined in the fight that is raging before the UNO between India and Pakistan. Are myself and my dynasty to be pawns in the game which Sheikh Abdullah is playing with the Government of India on the representation that he is actively helping India in the case before the UN Security Council? The Prime Minister says that he has seen no evidence of any sympathy on my part for the people of Kashmir who have gone through fire and suffering during the past four and a half years. May I ask who is responsible for his state of affairs? Have the Government of India given any choice of action to me during the last four and a half years? Have they at any time pulled up Sheikh Abdullah knowing as they did, on what promises and assurances Sheikh Abdullah became the Prime Minister? May I again point out that even before I left the State under the advice of Sardar Patel, I and my wife had started on a tour of the State as Sardar Patel had told me that I should see more of my people and they should see more of me. Sheikh Abdullah did not like this tour and approached and Government of India with the result that I was called at Delhi and asked to desist from returning to the State and finally to leave it. The Prime Minister says at the end of this letter that the only assurances he can give to me is that the first place will be given always to the rights of the people and to the wishes of the people and that if I fall in with those rights and wishes, the Government will endeavour to help me to the best of their ability. I am prepared to take up the challenge. Let the people of Jammu and Kashmir freely decide between me and Sheikh Abdullah without interference from the Government of India. Let me point out what has been happening. The world has been given to understand that the march of events, the changed political values have brought about rapid and inevitable changes and we must accept them no matter what the obligation of the Government of India, Government of Jammu and Kashmir, the assurance of both the Governments to me and their duties under certain legal and constitutional arrangements may be. With all due deference to this opinion, I must say that I emphatically challenge the contention that whatever has happened is an accordance with the will of the people and that the sovereignty has effectively and really passed to the people as it should and that they are consciously exercising their will and ask for the changes which are being brought about by an oligarchy backed by Government of India. I cannot conscientiously recognize the changes in the Proclamation of 5th March, 1948 which governs the relations of the State with India. But if the Government of India and you, Sir, feel that in the present stage of negotiations with Dr. Graham it would be inconvenient for the Government of India to allow this matter to be raked up, then at least, the Government of India should not succumb entirely to the wishes of Sheikh Abdullah but hold the balance equally between him and me and at least preserve the status quo as regards the headship of the State until the field is clear for the necessary steps to be taken to determine the will of the people of Kashmir.

29. Copies of the following documents are attached for your ready reference:

1. Note given to Prime Minister of Kashmir by Prime Minister of India on 26th October, 1947;
2. Letter dated 26th October, 1947 from the Prime Minister of India to the Prime Minister of Kashmir;
3. Letter dated 27th October, 1947 from Prime Minister of India to the Prime Minister of Kashmir;
4. Letter dated 27th October, 1947 from Prime Minister of India to me;
5. Letter dated 26th October, 1947 from me to Lord Mountbatten;
6. Letter dated 27th October, 1947 from Lord Mountbatten to me;
7. Letter dated 24th December, 1947 from Shri N. Gopalaswami to me.

30. Secure in the knowledge that I was out of the picture and could not reply I was, by a series of false statements and speeches intended to humiliate and malign me, painted black and unpatriotic. The Government of India who had assured me that I would be protected against such onslaughts remained an unconcerned spectator. Not only that, it is most distressing to know and feel that whenever Sheikh Abdullah and his party talked of me in disparaging and spiteful terms, the highest authority in the Government of India immediately endorsed it. If Sheikh Abdullah said I could not return to the State, the Prime Minister with all the authority, prestige and might at his back, endorsed it. If Sheikh Abdullah said I had lost the confidence of the people the Prime Minister referred to my alleged wrong-headed and mistaken policies, without saying what exactly they were and said the people had suffered on account of these. This no doubt had the effect of suppressing what is said to be the will of the people. Being placed as I was, I was absolutely unable to answer any of these accusations. I feel grievously wronged in that the Government of India whom I looked up to as the ultimate authority I could go to for redress, instead of stopping such malicious and false propaganda, not only went on countenancing it but endorsing it disregarding their solemn assurances.

Having eliminated me in a manner which had neither the sanction of law nor political morality, it was the duty of the Government of India to protect me. But that was not done and the matter did not end there. My properties and privileges etc., were attempted to be interfered with. I protested and asked for redress but never got it.

As I have said above, I was eliminated by a process which was neither fair nor honourable. It was not and it has never been due to the will of the people. It was due entirely to the machinations of Sheikh Abdullah and his party. They got themselves appointed on the definite assurance and later, with the connivance of the Government of India, systematically ignored all their legal and moral obligations and ultimately without rhyme or reason but to suit the books of Sheikh Abdullah successfully got me out of the State. Talking advantage of my absence and helplessness, started a campaign of vilification and harassment and thus created conditions wherein they could tell an unknowing world that they were doing what the people desired. I have taken the responsibility of making these statements and I earnestly request you, Sir, to ascertain the views of your Government about them and then come to an independent opinion as to whether I have not been seriously wronged and to redress the wrong.

31. I may be permitted to summarize the position:

1. The Government of the State of Jammu and Kashmir was more advanced and enlightened than that of my other Indian State in the pre-Partition days;
2. I employed men of undoubted ability and standing to be my Ministers from time to time;
3. In August 1947 Lord Mountbatten gave me the impression that I should accede to Pakistan, Government of India was undecided about the matter, wanted every step by me endorsed by Sheikh Abdullah, the people of Jammu and Kashmir were divided in their opinion and I decided to enter into Standstill Agreement with both India and Pakistan in order to have time for things to settle down;

4. Pakistan did not act up to the Standstill Agreements, blocked supplied to the State and aided and abetted the raiders;
5. I released Sheikh Abdullah as advised by Sardar Patel and relied on the assurance given by Sheikh Abdullah backed up by assurances given by the Government of India;
6. I took Sheikh Abdullah in my Government;
7. I issued the Proclamation of 5th March, 1948;
8. Sheikh Abdullah with the connivance of the Government of India started tinkering with the Constitution of 5th March, 1948;
9. Sheikh Abdullah persuaded the Government of India to drive me out of the State;
10. I left the State and appointed the Yuvraj, my Regent;
11. My rights of personal property and the affairs of the Dharmarth Trust were interfered with by Sheikh Abdullah;
12. Sheikh Abdullah by maligning me created an impression that the people of Kashmir were against me;
13. The Constituent Assembly was set up;
14. The will of the people of Jammu and Kashmir is now judged by the whims and caprices of Sheikh Abdullah;
15. Sheikh Abdullah having made up his mind to get rid of the Ruler and his dynasty, persuaded the Government of India to see eye to eye with him and to lay down that this could be done even before the new Constitution was framed much less approved by you on behalf of India;
16. I get no redress and am told that I am in the wrong, the will of the people is all that counts and I must abide by such will;
17. The Press carries reports from day to day creating feelings against me. False reports are not contradicted;
18. The Prime Minister got angry as evidenced by his letter dated 5th July, 1952 because I stated facts;
19. The States Minister avoids giving a proper reply to me and yet the Press says I have been asked and have not replied;

20. The Yuvraj is being coerced by the Prime Minister and Sheikh Abdullah to accede to their suggestions.

32. Finally, I have to say that I had my range of controversy with Sheikh Abdullah and the Prime Minister and I am bitter about the fact that the Government of India have been unable to afford me protection and safeguard my rights in spite of the fact that throughout these four and a half years, I have given full cooperation and the fact that my pre-1947 conduct did not compare unfavourably with that of the other Rulers who at present enjoy Government of India's protection and favour. During the last three years of my enforced absence from the State I have given them no cause for grievance and at the most, I have been charged with delay in permitting the Yuvraj to take action which having regard to the consideration involved and my better experience, was natural and understandable. Even in this matter ultimately I did fall in line with the Government of India. If the result of all this in the final stage has again to be a betrayal by the Government of India of their assurances and promises etc. and is to result not only in my final removal from the State but also of the sacrifice of the Yuvraj whom I had entrusted to the Government of India's protection. I can only say that it would be an ill return for the faith which I and the Yuvraj placed in the Government and the help and cooperation to the extent of self effacement that we rendered to it. Only history and posterity will be able to do justice to our respective points of view.

33. In these circumstances, I appeal to you to consider the matter impartially in all its aspects with your sagacity and wisdom and guide me as to what would be in the bet interests of the State.

Yours sincerely,
Sd/-
Hari Singh

This correspondence between the Maharaja and Pt. Nehru hastened the process that led to the termination of monarchy on August 20, 1952.

BLUNDERS 25
Termination of Monarchy

J&K became integral part of India. This made the integration complete as the Maharaja's stipulated conditions came to an end. Moment Maharaja's monarchy was terminated.

Interestingly a century old monarchy was abolished through a resolution of the nominated Constituent Assembly on August 20, 1952. Mr. D.P. Dhar was used to pilot the resolution which suffered from many legal discrepancies and lacuna. No permission was taken from the Raj Pramukh, the Regent of the State, Yuvraj Karan Singh though. The resolution was implemented without exercising the principles of the natural justice. The Head of the State never signed it. Anyhow, with the end of Monarch in 1952, all the powers retained by the ruler came to an end. The integration with the Union became absolute.

After effects of Termination of Monarchy

The Resolution adopted by an unelected Constituent Assembly terminating the well-recognized Monarchy suffered from several illegalities. The National Conference leaders stuck to their guns holding it to be just and appropriate. The universal opinion is that the Monarchy ended with the passing of the resolution on 20th August, 1952. With the termination of Monarchy, all the conditions attached by the Maharaja came to an end. The 'Accession' was legitimized as integration. This led the Constituent Assembly to insert Section-3 in the Constitution of J&K affirming that, "J&K is and shall be an integral part of India." With the imposition of Presidential Order, 1954 and later the word 'Maharaja' was replaced by 'Governor' in Article 370 which put a seal of full integration of J&K with the rest of the country. This legal position is supported by Article 1, First Schedule with Item 15.

BLUNDERS 26

Arrest of Dr. Shyama Prasad Mukherjee on his Entry to J&K 1953

Dr. Shyama Prasad Mukherjee, one of the tallest national leaders and Supremo of Jan Sangh was arrested by Abdullah backed by Nehru on May 11, 1953 at Lakhanpur on his entry to the State without an entry. He was taken to Srinagar Jail after 12 hours drive. Nehru could have intervened when he (Nehru) entered J&K from Kohala in 1946 in a similar situation when J&K was having independent status Maharaja stationed him honourably in a Guest House. Nehru was flown back to Delhi after four hours. Nehru was Prime Minister of India, he did not care for equally placed national leader, Dr. Shyama Prasad Mukherjee, who was a Cabinet Minister earlier in Nehru's Cabinet. Rather encourages Abdullah to teach 'Mukherjee' a lesson. Dr. Shyama Prasad Mukherjee was 'killed' in Srinagar prison on May 23, 1953. His 'arrest' was an unforgivable blunder. A request of the mother of Dr. Shyama Prasad Mukherjee to appoint an enquiry committee was ignored by Nehru. Atal Bihari government under BJP stalwarts also failed to fulfill their commitment to set up enquiry committee to seek the truth about the mysterious death of Jansangh Founder in a prison cell. This was a difference of Maharaja's rule and Abdullah's government. Nehru broke the international law by trespassing into J&K in July 1946 via Kohala to support 'Quit Kashmir' movement. Nehru was respectfully detained for couple of hours and flown back to Delhi. On the other hand Dr. Shyama Prasad Mukherjee, Founder of Jansangh entered J&K, part of Indian Union in May 1953. He was arrested by Sheikh Abdullah detained in Srinagar. His dead body was flown back.

BLUNDERS 27

Dismissal of Abdullah, 1953

Appointed Prime Minister by Maharaja Hari Singh on March 5, 1949, Sheikh Abdullah was dismissed by Maharaja's son Sadar-e-Riyasat, Dr. Karan Singh on August 9, 1953 on the direction of Pt. Nehru. What a U-turn in the cycle of history. Sheikh's speech of August 8, 1953 in R.S. Pura challenging State's relationship with the rest of the country had alarmed Pt. Nehru.

On May 18, 1953, members of the working committee of the National Conference (NC) appointed an eight-member committee to explore avenues of a settlement. Its members were Sheikh Abdullah, G.M. Sadiq, Maulana Mohamed Saeed Masoodi, Sardar Budh Singh, Mirza Mohammed Afzal Beg, Pt. Girdharilal Dogra, Bakshi Ghulam Mohammed and Pt. Sham Lal Saraf. Dr. Shyama Prasad Mukherjee died on May 23, 1953, allegedly killed in jail. Nehru might have gone to boost up morale of Abdullah.

Nehru, who was in Kashmir from May 23 to 25, 1953 was fully informed about the deliberations. Here is an extract from the minutes of the committee's final session held on June 9, 1953. "As a result of the discussions held in the course of various meetings, the following proposals only emerge as possible alternatives for an honourable and peaceful solution of [the] Kashmir dispute between India and Pakistan:

(a) Overall plebiscite with conditions as detailed in the minutes of the meeting dated 4th June, 1953 (this, apparently, was a reference to Maulana Masoodi's suggestion that the choice of independence be offered in the plebiscite);
(b) Independence of the whole State;
(c) Independence of the whole State with joint control of foreign affairs;

(d) Dixon Plan with independence for the plebiscite area (region-wise disposition of the State).

"Bakshi Ghulam Mohd. was emphatically of the opinion that the proposal (d) above should be put up as first and the only practicable, advantageous and honourable solution of the dispute. Maulana Saeed, however, opined that the order of preference as given above should be adhered to."

What G.M. Sadiq suggested that an agency consisting of India, Pakistan, Afghanistan, Soviet Russia and China to supervise and conduct the plebiscite? He was close to the Communist Party of India (CPI) and wanted the Union of Soviet Socialist Republics to be represented on the commission.

In June 1953, Maulana Abul Kalam Azad visited Kashmir and was apprised of these developments.

Nehru read the minutes and was greatly disturbed by the Sheikh's attitude. If Bakshi and Sadiq did not worry him with their "emphatic" support for plebiscite, it was because he knew they were dissimulating and playing for time.

A letter which Azad wrote to Abdullah on July 9, 1953, reveals that the Sheikh's fears were not unfounded after all. He offered to make Article 370 permanent, as if it was not meant to be so, until replaced by a final accord. The Sheikh's reply of July 16, pointed out that any final settlement required both a Union-Kashmir accord on autonomy and an India-Pakistan accord on the State's future. "I hope you are not unaware of the fact that even after Delhi Agreement responsible spokesmen of the Government of India declared that their ultimate objective was to secure complete merger of State with India and that they waited for appropriate time and conditions to bring that about.

Tragically, on July 31, 1953, Nehru took the fateful step. Mullik wrote in his memoirs My Years with Nehru: "On 31st July Mehra (D.W. Mehra, Mullik's Deputy) and I met the Prime Minister ... he came to the point that there was no other alternative but to remove Sheikh Abdullah and install Bakshi Ghulam Mohammed in his place ... he warned that we must be prepared for the worst, because the Sheikh undoubtedly had a large following in the Valley." Mehra should "assume control" of the State police, even become Chief Executive if need be.

On the same day, July 31, he prepared a statement which M.O. Mathai recorded. It contained his written instructions for the Sheikh's dismissal, outlining the very steps that were taken later: "A brief memorandum might be prepared and placed before the [State] Cabinet." The Head of the State (Yuvraj Karan Singh) should ask for the resignation of those who disagreed.

"If the resignations are not forthcoming, he should have an order ready for the dismissal of the government."

Also, "such assistance as may be considered necessary for the maintenance of law and order should be available"—from Delhi, of course.

What a tragic story of 'rise of fall' of Sheikh Abdullah on the lap of Nehru. Anyhow, Nehru might have realized that National Security was more important that mere friendship.

Sheikh's fall came 70 days after the mysterious death of Dr. Shyama Prasad Mukherjee.

Sheikh Arrest

Ajit Prasad Jain carried the memo and other papers to Srinagar and presented to Dr. Karan Singh. Sheikh was arrested at Gulmarg on August 9 with an order of dismissal. Bakshi Ghulam Mohd. was sworn in as Prime Minister at Yuvraj Karan Singh's residence, Karan Mahal at the midnight in Srinagar.

To one and all, Nehru flatly denied that he was responsible for the Sheikh's dismissal, let alone his arrest. He told the President on August 9 that, "We did not wish to interfere in any way with these internal happenings.... The Sadar-i-Riyasat (Karan Singh) has acted on his own responsibility in this matter." Parliament was given the same line on August 10 that, "Our advice was neither sought nor given." This is how Nehru failed to speak truth.

Nehru's Admission

Finally, Sheikh Abdullah wrote to Nehru on March 18, 1955, asking to be informed what sins he had committed. Nehru's reply of April 8 harked back to his Note of August 25, 1952: "You had decided to pursue a line of action which appeared to me to be very harmful for the future of Jammu and Kashmir" He was being punished for taking Nehru at his word and asking him to fulfill the pledges he had made publicly and repeatedly to the people of Kashmir.

On January 6, 1958, the Sheikh was released from jail. On April 11, 1958, he wrote to Nehru: "In spite of all that has happened since August 1953, I still believe that the key of the solution lies in your hands and I appeal to you not to be deceived by Bakshi Ghulam Mohammed and his other supporters in pursuing a policy which, in the end, is bound to prove disastrous for all." He was re-arrested on April 29, 1958, by D.W. Mehra, then Inspector-General of Police, J&K.

The cases against the Sheikh were withdrawn and Sheikh Abdullah, Mirza Afzal Beg and others were released on April 8, 1964. Nehru invited the Sheikh to be his guest. With Nehru's approval, he went to Pakistan on May 24, 1964, and met President Ayub Khan in Rawalpindi on May 26, 1964. He announced that Ayub Khan had accepted Nehru's invitation to visit Delhi for talks in June. The next day, on May 27, Jawahar Lal Nehru died of cardiac arrest while the Parliament was in session. May be due to heavy criticism for having sent Sheikh Abdullah to Pakistan. Parliament adjourned and the Flag went half-mast.

* *This author with his team was sitting on hunger strike in front of Parliament on May 27, 1964 demanding equitable share to the youth and student to end discrimination with Jammu and Ladakh. Nehru's sudden death caused shock to the Nation. Whole nation woke up for mourning the death of the first Prime Minister of India. Shastri ji came and requested us to end our hunger strike. The prominent youth leaders who were sitting on hunger strike included Thakur Rachhpal Singh, Advocate, Mr. Raj Kumar Sehgal, Mr. Durga Das Abrol, Mr. Suresh Anadi, Pt. Balbhadra Pathak and several other youth of Jammu. Abdullah returned from Pakistan and we returned to Jammu.*

Blunders 28

J&K Constitution Sans Civil Rights, 1957

In 1957, the so-called Constituent Assembly had 75 nominated Members. This Constituent Assembly promulgated Constitution of J&K with no induction of 'secularism', socialism or fundamental rights. In Section 3 of the Constitution, however affirmed that J&K is and shall remain integral part of India. This closed any scope to challenge State's Integration with the Union.

Its preamble says, "We, the people of the State of Jammu and Kashmir, having solemnly resolved, in the presence of the accession of this State of India which took place on the twenty-sixth day of October, 1947, to further define the existing relationship of the State with the Union of India as an integral part thereof."

BLUNDERS 29

Kashmiri Pundits Ignored

Blunder was committed by the framers of the J&K Constitution in omitting the legitimate and political representation of the Kashmri Pundits in the Legislature who formed a thin minority with their distinct culture and ethnic heritage. Scheduled Castes in Jammu region were granted reservation in proportion to their population. The same constitutional principle should have been applied to the Kashmir Pundits to preserve their cultural heritage and provide them their due share in political power. This was possible through constitutional safeguards by reservation in the State Assembly. Nehru himself was a Kashmiri Pundit from a most distinguished family. He could have taken care of political interest of Kashmiri Pundits who formed 4.5% the State population in 1957. Maharaja's Praja Sabha had political representation for Kashmiri Pundits from 1934-1947.

N.B: The process of Accession was complete on October 27, 1947, as it was accepted on October 27, 1947 only whereas integration of the State became absolute when the Monarchy was abolished on August 20, 1952 by the Constituent Assembly.

BLUNDERS 30

Arrest of Bakshi Ghulam Mohd.

Bakshi Ghulam Mohd. was arrested by G.M. Sadiq newly appointed Prime Minister on October 11, 1964 at Srinagar only to defeat the 'no confidence motion' moved by Bakshi Ghulam Mohd. against G.M Sadiq. To humiliate an undaunted nationalist leader whom Mrs. Indira Gandhi described as 'Himalaya Ka Sher' Tiger of the Himalayas in 1963 when I met Indira ji during Youth Festival at Talkatora.

Bakshi's arrest was another blunder committed with the permission of Central leaders. It was a wrong message of the Centre which created trust deficit. The deficit went on increasing. Any Kashmiri ruler who got the 'power-chair' applied all kind of methods of dirty tricks to down his rival. This trends remains in vogue till this day.

Anyhow, Enquiry Commission against Bakshi Ghulam Mohd. had failed to find any substantial material against him. Bakshi was humiliated by rigging polls in Lok Sabha elections. Lion of 'Himalaya' died a frustrated death in 1972 in his Sringar Flat.

After my release after 17 months detention in J&K I got admission in Aligarh Muslim University (AMU). I passed out Graduation as a private candidate (as a teacher in Convent School, Jammu), joined Law in Aligarh Muslim University. Bakshi Ghulam Mohd., who met me at Pathankote Railway Station inside Jammu Mail, gave me a letter for AMU, Vice Chancellor Mr. Badaruddin Tyabjee (ICS) which helped me get an admission, though I was late by two months. Bakshi Ghulam Mohd. had detained me in Jammu, Kathua and Reasi jails for having lowered the 'State Flag' half-mast in honour of Maharaja Hari Singh who died in Bombay in 1961. I was selected in AMU team representing AMU for Talkatora National Youth Festival (1963). I was the only one from J&K. I stood up and questioned Nehru, moment he finished his inaugural speech, "Mr. Prime Minister, why J&K is missing in* *the festival? Is J&K not part of India? There was a heavy applaud from the participants who must have been shared my concern. Nehru asked me about my university. I replied that, "I am from J&K but representing AMU." Nehru smiled and told me,* **"So you represent J&K." *Sensing that I might create further embarrassment; he asked Mrs. Indira Gandhi who was standing beside her father.* **"Kindly listen to this angry student from J&K."** *Mrs. Indira Gandhi took me aside and talked to me very comfortably while walking on the sideline of the festival lawn. When I accused Bakshi for not sending students from J&K to participate in the Youth Festival, she reacted mildly saying, Bakshi Sahib to Himalayan Tiger Hain. I shall tell him about this mistake."*

Bakshi Ghulam Mohd's arrest was condemned even by Sheikh Abdullah. This was the chain of events which got continuous support of Delhi. This was one more blunder to the credit of Central leadership.

This was nothing new in J&K. In 1984, this author and Shri (Late) Abdul Ghani Lone were carried away by the police like gunny bags while entering the gates of the Assembly. Both of us were elected MLAs. This was done to defeat the vote of no-confidence in the G.M. Shah's government which was to be voted the same day, 31st July, 1984.

BLUNDERS 31

Return of Haji Peer, 1965

Pakistan dropped its parachutes in Poonch and Kupwara sectors. India repulsed the attack and liberated several strategic occupied areas along LoC. Indian liberated Haji Peer, thus clearing the road from Poonch to Uri a distance of only 35 kms. It was a great strategic victory of India. India army won the battle in the field but lost on the table at Tashkent. This shock took the life of Shastri ji, the Prime Minister of India, in Tashkent. It is widely accepted that the war began with the infiltration of Pakistani guerrillas into Jammu and Kashmir on about August 5, 1965, which flashed into a war. The next day, Indian forces scored a major victory after a prolonged artillery barrage and captured three important mountain positions in the Kashmir sector. Later in the month, the Pakistanis counterattacked moving concentrations near Teetwal, Uri, and Poonch. Their move, in turn, provoked a powerful Indian thrust into POK. Other Indian forces captured a number of strategic mountain positions and eventually took the key Haji Peer Pass, a strategic point in the sector.

UN Security Council unanimously passed a resolution on September 20 calling for a ceasefire. New Delhi accepted the ceasefire resolution on September 21 and Islamabad on September 22, and the war ended on September 23. The Soviet-brokered Tashkent Declaration was signed on January 10, 1966. It required that both sides withdraw by February 26, 1966, to positions they held prior to August 5, 1965. Lal Bahadur Shastri and Ayub Khan met in Tashkent. Tashkent Declaration was signed on January 11, 1966. Lal Bahadur Shastri died in Tashkent under mysterious circumstances immediately after signing the Agreement. He could not comment on the agreement.

The Prime Minister of India and the President of Pakistan agreed that both sides will exert all efforts to create good neighborly relations between India and Pakistan in accordance with the Charter of the United Nations. They reaffirmed their obligation under the Charter not to have recourse to force and to settle their disputes through peaceful means. They considered that the interests of peace in their region and particularly in the Indo-Pakistan sub-continent and indeed, the interests of the peoples of India ad Pakistan were not served by the continuance of tension between the two countries. The return of Haji Peer may be recorded a blunder though under Soviet pressure.

The Tashkent Agreement

(a) The Prime Minister of India and the President of Pakistan have agreed that all armed personnel of the two countries shall be withdrawn not later than 25th February, 1966 to the positions they held prior to 5th August, 1965, and both sides shall observe the ceasefire terms on the ceasefire line.

(b) The Prime Minister of India and the President of Pakistan have agreed that relations between India and Pakistan shall be based on the principle of non-interference in the internal affairs of each other.

(c) The Prime Minister of India and the President of Pakistan have agreed that both sides will discourage any propaganda directed against the other country and will encourage propaganda which promotes the development of friendly relations between the two countries.

(d) The Prime Minister of India and the President of Pakistan have agreed that the High Commissioner of India to Pakistan and the High Commissioner of Pakistan of India will return to their posts and that the normal functioning of diplomatic missions of both countries will be restored. Both Governments shall observe the Vienna Convention of 1961 on Diplomatic Intercourse.

Trade Relations

(e) The Prime Minister of India and the President of Pakistan have agreed to consider measures towards the restoration of economic and trade relations, communications as well as cultural exchanges between India and Pakistan, and to take measures to implement the existing agreement between India and Pakistan.

(f) The Prime Minister of India and the President of Pakistan have agreed that they will give instructions to their respective authorities to carry out the repatriation of the prisoners of war.

(g) The Prime Minister of India and the President of Pakistan have agreed that the two sides will continue the discussions of questions relating to the problems of refugees and eviction of illegal immigrations. They also agreed that both sides will create conditions which will prevent the exodus of people. They further agree to discuss the return of the property and assets taken over by either side in connection with the conflict.

Soviet Leaders Thanked

(h) The Prime Minister of India and the President of Pakistan have agreed that the two sides will continue meetings both at highest and at other levels of matters of direct concern to both countries. Both sides have recognized the need to set up joint Indian-Pakistani bodies which will report to their Governments in order to decide what further steps should be taken.

(i) The Prime Minister of India and the President of Pakistan record their feelings, deep appreciation and gratitude to the leaders of the Soviet Union, the Soviet Government and personally to the Chairman of the Council of Ministers of the USSR for their constructive, friendly and noble part in bringing about the present meeting which has resulted in mutually satisfactory results. They also express to the Government and friendly people of Uzbekistan their sincere thankfulness for their overwhelming reception and generous hospitality.

They invite the Chairman of the Council of Ministers of the USSR to witness this declaration.

Sd/-	Sd/-
Prime Minister of India	President of Pakistan
Lal Bahadur Shastri	Mohammed Ayub Khan

Shastri ji's Death in Tashkent

India's unique war hero and Prime Minister, Shri Lal Bahadur Shastri ji died on January 11, 1966 under mysterious circumstances immediately, after signing of the Tashkent Agreement.

His reaction on the agreement died in him. This author was the Chief Organizer of J&K Students Congress and had launched a movement against the 'anti-India' propaganda taught in school books published by the government saying that, "J&K is Independent State etc." "It situates to the North of India." It was Congress government in J&K.

This author set tons of history books on 'bonfire'. Mr. Sat Sawhney's wrote front page story in the Times of India which brought the Sadiq government on the defensive. This author called on Shastri ji in Delhi and submitted memorandum against J&K government. Shastri ji was leaving for Tashkent. He fixed my stay with an MP in the South Avenue and asked me to wait in Delhi till his return. He never returned. His death was a great personal shock. I returned to Jammu and was detained under NSA in the Special Jail, Canal Road, which was made for Sheikh Abdullah and Mr. Mirza Afzal Beg. It was released only on the direction of the Supreme Court. Shri Gopal Sachar wrote a powerful story on my memorandum in the 'Current' weekly published from Bombay. Had Shastri ji lived longer, the history of J&K would have been written otherwise.

Drama of Sheikh's detentions and releases continued. NC was wound up by communist lobby lead of Shri Ghulam Mohd. Sadiq and the nomenclature of Prime Minister and Sadar-e-Riyasat were changed to Chief Minister and Governor. The State was brought on 'harmonious' line with the Centre. It was great success. The Kashmiris forgot the bitter memories of the past. The spirit and gains of Bakshi era showed their seedling. Mir Asim took over the Congress command after Sadiq's death with the break off of East Pakistan from West Pakistan, all the international combinations and permutations changed. Mrs. Indira Gandhi emerged as world's undisputed leader. Pakistan's humiliating defeat in East Bengal made Pakistan defensive. Mrs. Indira Gandhi was in the field but lost on the table at Simla. Her advisors to be blamed. Surrender of Chhamb was a grave blunder. India won abroad but lost at home.

BLUNDERS 32

Chhamb Surrender, 1971

Cornering India Pakistan attacked soft border in Akhnoor sector in J&K. On the evening of December 3, 1971 the Pakistani army launched ground operations in J&K and Punjab. It also started an armoured operation in Rajasthan. In Jammu, the operations were concentrated on two key points, Poonch and Chhamb. The Chhamb area witnessed a particularly intense battle where the Pakistanis forced the Indians to withdraw from their positions. In other parts of J&K, the Indians made some small gains along the ceasefire line. The major Indian counteroffensive came in the Sialkot-Shakargarh area south and west of Chhamb. There, two Pakistani tank regiments, equipped with US-made Patton tanks, confronted the Indian First Armoured Corps.

The role of the Indian Air Force was both extensive and daring. Command conducted 4,000 sorties in 14 days.

In spite of the India's dominant role and presence in the region, India surrendered Deva and Chhamb (across Manawar Tawi river) strategic areas in Jammu region. It proved to be a grave blunder in India's defence strategy. Exodus of the residents from Chhamb caused a grave situation. Displaced by unmindful act of the Central government, nearly one lac refugees have not been settled till day. The Govt. of India offered to rehabilitate them in Rajasthan or outside J&K for the reason to reduce the population of the nationalist citizens. They rejected the offer and chose to live in tattered tents and starvation.

It is surprising that country's national leadership in the opposition also failed to find out the 'truth' about this shameful surrender. The migrants have not been granted status of refugees. The population of the migrants from POK must have reached a million. 63 years have passed and they have not been recognized as refugees even though their properties in POK have already been consumed by the occupiers.

Neglect of Refugees

There lies an obligation for comprehensive settlements of all the refugees from Pakistan (about 85,000) by granting them civil and political rights to respect their human rights on the other hand, Jammu province has nearly a million migrants of 1947, 1965, 1971 from POK who have not been given even refugee status. Their permanent and comprehensive settlement according to the national and international law is an important issue.

BLUNDERS 33

Simla Agreement, July 1975

War mongering campaign continued from Pakistan side unabated. The result of the election to the National Assembly favoured East Pakistan when Sheikh Mujibur Rehman won majority in the National Assembly. Zulfiqar Ali Bhutto did not intend to surrender Prime Ministership of Pakistan to the Bengali leader. The Punjabi lobby in the National Assembly supported Zulfiqar Ali Bhutto. East Bengal under the leadership of Sheikh Mujibur Rehman revolted against the domination of West Pakistan. The conflict took the turn of a war between India and Pakistan.

India's military might showed its strength and the wishes of the people of East Pakistan were fulfilled. 98,000 Pakistani soldiers including their Generals surrendered. The unnatural union of Pakistan came to an end. Mrs. Indira Gandhi has been called as creator of Bangladesh. Pakistan was in disarray. Mrs. Gandhi demonstrated her magnanimity and invited Zulfiqar Ali Bhutto the Prime Minister of Pakistan to Simla.

Mrs. Gandhi signed six clauses of India's agreement with the Islamic Republic of Pakistan on July 2, 1972. This was a blunder to be added in the list of Kashmir blunders by the Indian leadership that India failed to settle the final status of LoC with Pakistan. Pakistan for survival would have been forced to vacate all occupied areas of J&K.

The intriguing situation which has never been investigated to was that under what circumstances Mr. D. P. Dhar, the Union Minister was asked to leave Simla during the dialogue. This author tried to find out the truth from Mr. B. K. Nehru and Mr. T. N. Seshan who were the last advisors around Mrs. Gandhi at the time of signing Simla Agreement. India released 98,000 Pakistani soldiers without any condition or without settling Jammu and Kashmir.

The only paragraph 6 of the Agreement made a passing reference to the extent, "Both Governments agree that their respective Heads will meet again at a mutually convenient time in the future and that, in the meanwhile, the representatives of the two sides will meet to discuss further the modalities and arrangements for the establishment of durable peace and normalization of relations, including the questions of repatriation of prisoners of war and civilians interests, a final settlement of Jammu and Kashmir and the resumption of diplomatic relations."

During this author's participation in discussion with General Musharraf, the President of Pakistan in March 2007 when I made this reference of Simla Agreement, the General quickly responded in the presence of about 100 representatives of both sides of Jammu and Kashmir saying that he was ready to sit with Dr. Manmohan Singh, the Prime Minister of India and settle out all the issues relating to Jammu and Kashmir. He was so fast in declaring that it would take only couple of hours to settle the J&K problem. The General had hinted for the acceptance of LoC with minor adjustments with India. Any way, Mrs. Indira Gandhi would have also realized the blunder later.

Simla Agreement, 1972

1. The Government of India and the Government of Pakistan are resolved that the two countries put an end to the conflict and confrontation that have hitherto marred their relations and work for the promotion of a friendly and harmonious relationship and the establishment of durable peace in the subcontinent, so that both countries may henceforth devote their resources and energies to the pressing task of advancing the welfare of their peoples.

In order to achieve this objective, the Government of India and the Government of Pakistan have agreed as follows:

(i) That the principles and purposes of the Charter of the United Nations shall govern the relations between the two countries;

(ii) That the two countries are resolved to settle their differences by peaceful means through bilateral negotiations or by any other peaceful means mutually agreed upon between them. Pending the final settlement of any of the problems between the two countries neither side shall unilaterally alter the situation and both shall prevent the organization, assistance of encouragement of any acts detrimental to the maintenance of peaceful and harmonious relations;

(iii) That the prerequisite for reconciliation, good neighborliness and durable peace between them is a commitment by both the countries to peaceful co-existence, respect for each other's territorial integrity and sovereignty and non-interference in each other's internal affairs, on the basis of equality and mutual benefit;

(iv) That the basic issues and causes of conflict which have bedeviled the relations between the two countries for the last 25 years shall be resolved by peaceful means;

(v) That there shall always respect each other's national unity, territorial integrity, political independence and sovereign equality;

(vi) That in accordance with the Charter of the United Nations they will refrain from the threat of use of force against the territorial integrity or political independence of each other.

2. Both Governments will take steps within their power to prevent hostile propaganda directed against each other. Both countries will encourage the dissemination of such information as would promote the development of friendly relations between them.

3. In order progressively to restore and normalize relations between the two countries step by step, it was agreed that:

(i) Steps shall be taken to resume communications, postal, telegraphic, sea, land including border posts, and air links including over flights.

(ii) Appropriate steps shall be taken to promote travel facilities for the nationals of the other country.

(iii) Trade and cooperation in economic and other agreed fields will be resumed as far as possible.

(iv) Exchange in the fields of science and culture will be promoted.

In this connection delegations from the two countries will meet from time to time to work out the necessary details.

4. In order to initiate the process of establishment of durable peace, both the Governments agree that:

(i) Indian and Pakistani forces shall be withdrawn to their side of the international border.

(ii) In Jammu and Kashmir, the line of control resulting from the ceasefire of December 17, 1971 shall be respected by both sides without prejudice to the recognized position of either side. Neither side shall seek to alter it unilaterally, irrespective of mutual differences and legal interpretations. Both sides further undertake to refrain from the threat or the use of force in violation of this Line.

(iii) The withdrawals shall commence upon entry into force of this Agreement and shall be completed within a period of 30 days thereof.

5. This Agreement will be subject to ratification by both countries in accordance with their respective constitutional procedures and will come into force with effect from the date on which the Instruments of ratification are exchanged.

6. Both Governments agree that their respective Heads will meet again at a mutually convenient time in the future and that, in the meanwhile, the representatives of the two sides will meet to discuss further the modalities and arrangements for the establishment of durable peace and normalization of relations, including the questions of repatriation of prisoners of war and civilian interests, a final settlement of Jammu and Kashmir and the resumption of diplomatic relations.

Sd/-
(Indira Gandhi)
Prime Minister
Republic of India

Sd/-
(Zulfikar Ali Bhutto)
President
Islamic Republic of Pakistan

Simla, the 2nd July, 1972

BLUNDERS 34

Sheikh-Indira Accord, 1975

Sheikh Abdullah realized that the situation had changed. He was also released by Mrs. Indira Gandhi from prison. He had tried his political position in Kashmir. Having realized the situation and the circumstances, Sheikh agreed to 'surrender for power'. Finally his second in command Mirza Afzal Beg signed an Accord with Mr. G. Parthasarthy, sole representative of Mrs. Indira Gandhi. The existing constitutional arrangement was accepted. The Congress with majority of 46 MLAs out of 75 surrendered power to the Sheikh, who returned to power after 22 years of wandering in darkness and jails. Abdullah took over as Chief Minister on February 25, 1975 with Mr. Beg as his number-II who had toiled and suffered all his life for promoting Abdullah. Got an award at the end of his life.

Sheikh Abdullah and his companions were set at liberty by Mrs. Indira Gandhi. The Sheikh realized after the division of Pakistan that his dream to become Sultan of Kashmir was a bad dream. Mrs. Indira Gandhi had soft-corner for the Sheikh and she deputed an experienced diplomat Mr. G. Parthasarthy to discuss the situation with Sheikh Abdullah and his most trusted Mirza Mohammad Afzal Beg. After a long discussion, dialogue and on the ground and underground talks Sheikh Mohd. Abdullah agreed to accept the ground reality that Jammu and Kashmir had already become integral part of India. His much debated proposition to become Prime Minister of J&K was rejected by Mrs. Indira Gandhi. This author happened to be a General Secretary of the Indian Youth Congress and was in close contacts with Mrs. Indira Gandhi and her emissaries.

There was a strong opposition within the Congress to grant any concession to Sheikh Abdullah. The National Conference had merged into Congress in 1965 when Mr. G.M. Sadiq was Prime Minister of J&K. It was during Mr. Sadiq's tenure when National Conference merged into Congress and nomenclatures Sadar-e-Riyasat and Prime Minister were changed to Governor and the Chief Minister. In fact, Sadiq himself assumed the title of Chief Minister relinquishing his title of Prime Minister of J&K. This was a great contribution of Sadiq that harmonious relations developed between the Union and J&K. The integration of J&K with the rest of India had, though, matured on August 20, 1952 on the termination of the monarchy in the state. The last straw was removed by the Legislature in 1965.

Sheikh Abdullah accepted this constitutional relationship without any hesitation. He agreed to take over the reigns of power. The fact was that sitting and elected Chief Minister, Syed Mir Qasim resigned and Sheikh Mohd. Abdullah took over as Chief Minister in 1975 following full and comprehensive agreement known as Sheikh-Indira Accord of 1975. This is also interesting to observe that Sheikh Mohd. Abdullah who used to plead for the implementation of the so-called Delhi Agreement, 1952 gave up this slogan and agreed to work as Chief Minister within the framework of the Constitution of J&K and Constitution of India. This was one more blunder by the leadership that Sheikh Mohd. Abdullah was imposed on the people of J&K against the will of the people. The Congress had 46 sitting MLAs out of 75.

Mufti Mohd. Sayeed had opposed this surrender. In 1977 the Congress withdrew support to Sheikh Mohd. Abdullah when the Sheikh publicly denounced Congress describing Congressmen as 'worms of the gutter'. The 1997 elections were fought during the Janata regime. The then Prime Minister, Morarji Desai publicly vetoed any manipulation or rigging. Sheikh one hands down. This author was also elected as Member of the Legislative Assembly from Chenani, Udhampur. The story of blunder after blunders never ceased.

Agreed conclusions which led to Sheikh Mohammad Abdullah's accord with Mrs. Indira Gandhi, Prime Minister, and his subsequent assumption of office as Chief Minister in February 1975:

1. The State of Jammu and Kashmir which is a constituent unit of the Union of India, shall, in its relation with the Union, continue to be governed by Article 370 of the Constitution of India.

2. The residuary powers of legislation shall remain with the State; however, Parliament will continue to have power to make laws relating to the prevention of activities directed towards disclaiming, questioning or disrupting the sovereignty and territorial integrity of India or bringing about secession of a part of the territory of India from the Union or causing insult to the Indian National Flag, the Indian National Anthem and the Constitution.

3. Where any provision of the Constitution of India had been applied to the State of J&K with adaptations and modifications, such adaptations and modifications can be altered or repealed by an order of the President under Article 370, each individual proposal in this behalf being considered on its merits; but provisions of the Constitution of India already applied to the State of Jammu and Kashmir without adaptation or modification are unalterable.

4. With a view to assuring freedom to the State of Jammu and Kashmir to have its own legislation on matters like welfare measures cultural matters, social security, personal law and procedural laws, in a manner suited to the special conditions in the State, it is agreed that the State Government can review the laws made by Parliament or extended to the State after 1953 on any matter relatable to the Concurrent List and may decide which of them, in its opinion, needs amendment or repeal. Thereafter, appropriate steps may be taken under Article 254 of the Constitution of India. The grant of President's assent to such legislation would be sympathetically considered. The same approach would be adopted in regard to laws to be made by Parliament in future under the Proviso to clause 2 of the Article. The State Government shall be consulted regarding the application of any such law to the State and

the views of the State Government shall receive the fullest consideration

5. As an arrangement reciprocal to what has been provided under Article 368, a suitable modification of that Article as applied to the State should be made by Presidential Order to the effect that no law made by the Legislature of the State of Jammu and Kashmir, seeking to make any change in or in the effect of any provision of Constitution of the State of Jammu and Kashmir relating to any of he under mentioned matters, shall take effect unless the Bill, having been reserved for the consideration of the President, receives his assent; the matters are:

(a) the appointment, powers, functions, duties, privileges and immunities of the Governor, and
(b) the following matters relating to Elections namely, the superintendence, direction and control of Elections by the Election Commission of India, eligibility for inclusion in the electoral rolls without discrimination, adult suffrage and composition of the legislative Council, being matters specified in sections 138, 139 140 and 50 of the Constitution of the State of Jammu and Kashmir.

6. No agreement was possible on the question of nomenclature of the Governor and the Chief Minister and the matter is therefore, remitted to the Principals.

Sd/-
Mirza Mohammad Afzal Beg

Sd/-
G. Parthasarathy
New Delhi, November 13, 1974

BLUNDERS 35

Resettlement Act, 1982

This author was forced under the circumstances to quit Congress when Sheikh Mohd. Abdullah enacted the so-called Resettlement Act in 1982 opening the doors of return and rehabilitation of those who had migrated in 1947 to Pakistan with their descendents. The Congress had no leadership who could dare oppose the mighty Sheikh for many reasons. This author was the only Congress MLA who opposed the draconian Act and the Sheikh inside and outside the Legislature earning wrath of the Congress leadership in Delhi and National Conference government in Kashmir. In spite of harassment, jails, mental and physical tortures this author continued the battle against the anti-people policies of the National Conference. The Panthers Party filed a writ petition in the Supreme Court for quashing the Resettlement Act. The Supreme Court had stayed the implementation of this Act. It is still pending since 2002. The Congress could not afford to annoy NC. They have been interested more in sharing power than serving national interest and its security.

The blunders of leadership in Delhi are unforgivable. The Govt. of India has been supporting the Govt. of J&K in the Supreme Court. This is a tragedy.

Before his death the Sheikh kept Pandora's boxes fixed in Srinagar in the name of 'Resettlement Act' to exploit the innocent Kashmiris. Mrs. Indira Gandhi used this weapon in Jammu during 1983 election to woe Hindu voters and succeeded in securing 26 seats in Jammu. BJP was 'zeroes' whereas Panthers Party from Chanani (Udhampur).

Mirza Afzal Beg who acted all his life as 'faithful' comrade of Sheikh Abdullah, was shunted out by Abdullah from his Cabinet in 1982. The reason was that Mr. Beg set up his son-in-law a candidate for the election for Legislative Council. He was with the support of the opposition MLAs. I and Sardar Parduman Singh (both were Congress MLAs) voted for the Beg's candidate, who won hands down defeating official candidate of NC Abdullah could not digest this humiliation. He fired Afzal Beg from the Cabinet and party on September 29, 1978. He died a humiliated death on June 11, 1982. Sheikh died on September 8, 1982 in less than 90 days from the death of Mr. Beg.

Abdullah continued his tirade to browbeat India and exploit innocent Kashmiris. The NC continued that practice for political power.

Sheikh Mohd. Abdullah died on September 8, 1982. His son Dr. Farooq Abdullah was installed as his successor by Mrs. Indira Gandhi, the Prime Minister of India. Assembly elections were held in 1983.

BLUNDERS 36

Farooq's Dismissal, 1984

After the death of Sheikh Abdullah, the National Conference stuck to their anti-national and anti-India campaign. The National Conference had a strong handle to exploit the innocent Kashmiris in the name of Rehabilitation of nearly half a million Muslims back in J&K who had migrated to Pakistan in 1947. National Conference declared that their descendents shall also be allowed to return to J&K. The Congress overplayed and Rajiv Gandhi led the campaign in Jammu region. This time hijacking Panthers Party slogan, the party was founded in 1982 by this author after resigning from the Assembly and the party against the Resettlement Act. Congress won 26 Assembly seats in Jammu province for opposing Resettlement Act whereas National Conference won almost all seats in the Valley for riding the anti-national wave created in the name of Resettlement Act. The Janata Party had 17 sitting Members in the Assembly and they lost all. This author was the only Panthers Party candidate who retained his seat in Chenani, Udhampur in spite of Mrs. Indira Gandhi's strongest campaign against this author and Rajiv Gandhi's personal tour of the area.

Dr. Farooq Abdullah with huge majority became the Chief Minister. When he refused to share power and loot with the Congress party, he was removed unceremoniously while he was riding a motorcycle somewhere around Gulmarg with his guest. Mrs. Indira Gandhi had invited this author and offered position number two in the government with G.M. Shah, brother-in-law of Dr. Farooq Abdullah. Mrs. Gandhi literally dismissed this author from her drawing room at Safdarjung Road when he raised the questions of democracy.

This was a turning point of restoration of much maligned leadership of National Conference. Dr. Farooq Abdullah emerged as a leader without credentials or credibility. A blunder committed by Prime Minister, Indira Gandhi in haste and on the advice of inexperienced and non-political leaders.

20 months of G.M. Shah's rule was a golden era for the Congress and the NC leaders to continue their loot by suppressing any legitimate movement of the people. This author and Mr. Abdul Ghani Lone were sitting MLAs. They were never allowed to enter the Assembly complex in Srinagar. In July, 1984 when the Chief Minister was directed by the Governor, Mr. Jagmohan, to show his majority in the Assembly, Mr. Lone and this author were not allowed to enter the Assembly, instead they were taken to Central Jail, Srinagar. Mrs. Jay Mala, wife of this author moved a habeas corpus petition in the Supreme Court against the illegal arrest.

Bhim Singh's Illegal Detention

The Supreme Court in his historic judgment awarded a compensation of Rs.50,000 to this author. This was exposures of the Congress leadership which has been ruling through its agencies for decades. The mentioning of this famous judgment may be a source of information on the working of the governments in J&K and the existence of the rule of law, the judgment of the Supreme Court dated 22.11.1985 stated under;

"1. Shri Bhim Singh, a Member of the Legislative Assembly of Jammu & Kashmir, incurred the wrath of the powers that be. They were bent upon preventing him from attending the session of the Legislative Assembly of J&K, which was to meet on 11th September, 1985. That appears to be the only inference that we can draw from the circumstances of the case to which we shall now refer. On August 17, 1985, the opening day of the Budget Session of the Legislative Assembly, Shri Bhim Singh was suspended from the Assembly. He questioned the suspension in the High Court of J&K. The order of suspension was stayed by the High Court on 9th September, 1985.

On the intervening night of 9th-10th September, 1985, he was proceeding from Jammu to Srinagar. En route, at about 3.00 A.M (on 10th), he was arrested at a place called Qazi Kund about 70 kms. from Srinagar. He was taken away by the police. As it was not known where he had been taken away and as the efforts to trace him proved futile, his wife Smt. Jayamala, acting on his behalf, filed the present application for the issue of a writ to direct the respondents to produce Shri Bhim Singh before the court, to declare his detention illegal and to set him at liberty. She impleaded the State of Jammu & Kashmir through the Chief Secretary as the first respondent, the Chief Minister, the Deputy Chief Minister and the Inspector General of Police, J&K as respondents 2, 3 & 4. On September 13, 1985, we directed notice to be issued to the respondents and we also directed the Inspector General of Police to inform Smt. Jayamala where Shri Bhim Singh was kept in custody. On September 16, 1985, Shri Bhim Singh was released on bail by the learned Additional Sessions Judge of Jammu before whom he was produced. Shri Bhim Singh filed a supplementary affidavit on 20th September, 1985 stating more facts in addition to what had already been stated by Smt. Jayamala in the petition. He categorically asserted that he was kept in police lock up from 10th to 14lh and that he was produced before a Magistrate for the first time only on the 14th. Thereafter on 24th September, 1985, we issued notice to the Director General of Police, State of Jammu & Kashmir, Mr. Mir, Superintendent of Police, Anantnag, Mohd. Shafi Rajguru, Inspector of Police, Amin Amjun, Deputy Superintendent of Police, Udhampur, Gupta, Deputy Superintendent of Police, Jhajar Kotli and the Officer-in-charge of Police Station Satwari. A counter affidavit has been filed on behalf of the State of Jammu & Kashmir by Abdul Qadir Parrey. Affidavits have also been filed by M.M. Khajuria, Inspector General of Police, M.A. Mir, Superintendent of Police, Anantnag, Mohd. Shafi Laigroo, Inspector of Police, District Police Lines, Anantnag, Mohd. Amin Anjum, Deputy Superintendent of Police Headquarters. Udhampur and Rajinder Gupta, Probationary Deputy Superintendent of Police, Udhampur. Shri Bhim Singh has also filed a rejoinder affidavit.

2. From the affidavits filed by the several police officers, it transpires that an FIR Under Section 153-A of the Ranbir Penal Code was registered against Shri Bhim Singh on September 9, 1985 at Police Station Pacca Danga, Jammu on the allegation that he had delivered an inflammatory speech at a public meeting held near Parade Ground, Jammu at 7.00 P.M. on September 8, 1985. The office-in-charge of Police Station Pacca Danga brought the matter to the notice of the Senior Superintendent of Police, Jammu, who in turn informed the Deputy Inspector General of Police of Jammu range. On 10th September, 1985, requisition for the arrest of Shri Bhim Singh was sent to the Superintendent of Police, Anantnag through the Police Control Room, Srinagar. This fact is sworn to by Shri M.M. Khajuria, Inspector General of Police, Jammu & Kashmir. Shri M.A. Mir, Superintendent of Police, Anantnag has, however, stated in his affidavit that on September 9, 1985 at about 11.30 P.M, he was informed by the Police Control Room, Srinagar that Shri Bhim Singh, MLA was required to be apprehended as he was wanted in a case registered U/s. 153-A of Ranbir Penal Code. According to him, he immediately directed the Office-in-charge of Police Station Qazi Kund that Shri Bhim Singh may be apprehended as and when he reached his jurisdiction. He further instructed him that he should be brought to the District Headquarters, Anantnag after his arrest. These statements are obviously untrue in view of the affidavit of Shri Khajuria, Inspector General of Police that the information, to the Superintendent of Police Anantnag was conveyed through the Police Control Room, Srinagar on 10th September, 1985. Shri Mir has not chosen to explain why he expected Shri Bhim Singh to pass through Qazi Kund that night. Quite obviously even before he had received any information from the Police Control Room about the alleged case registered against Shri Bhim Singh, Shri Mir had instructed the Officer-in-charge Police Station Qazi Kund to arrest Shri Bhim Singh if he came within his jurisdiction. Whether he did it on his own and if so, for what reason or whether he did it on other instructions received by him is a matter which requires our consideration. At about 3,00 AM, according to Shri Mir, Shri Bhim Singh was arrested at Qazi Kund by the Officer-in-charge of Police

Station Qazi Kund and brought to the District Headquarters where it appears Shri Bhim Singh was provided with facilities for rest, wash, breakfast, etc. It is necessary to mention here that no affidavit has been filed before us by the Officer-in-charge of Police Station Qazi Kund, the officer who arrested Shri Bhim Singh. It appears that under the orders of the Superintendent of Police, Anantnag, Shri Bhim Singh was taken from Anantnag by Shafi Laigroo, Inspector of Police, District Police Lines, Anantnag in a Matador at about 7.30 AM on 10th September, 1985. They reached, according to Mohd. Shafi Laigroo, Batota at 2.00 PM where Bhim Singh was provided with lunch. They reached Udhampur at 5.00 PM where Bhim Singh was provided with lea and finally they reached Jammu city Police Station at 7.30 PM. There they learnt that Bhim Singh was wanted in connection with a case registered by the police of Pacca Danga Station. He was, therefore, taken to Pacca Danga Police Station and handed over to the Officer-in-charge of Pacca Danga Police Station. Mohd. Amin Anjum, Deputy Superintendent of Police Headquarters, Udhampnr and Shri Rajender Gupta, Probationary Deputy Superintendent of Police, Udhampur were directed by the Senior Superintendent of Police, Udhampur to see to the safe passage of Bhim Singh through Udhampur District. They were informed that Bhim Singh was taken from Anantnag to Jammu in a Matador. So they followed the Matador in which Bhim Singh was being taken from Chenani Police Station to Jammu and thereafter returned to their respective stations. According to the Inspector General of Police, Shri Bhim Singh was taken to Police Station Pacca Danga at about 9.30 PM. On 11th September, 1985, a remand to police custody for two days was obtained from an Executive Magistrate First Class. A copy of the application for remand made in Urdu with the endorsement of the Executive Magistrate First Class has been filed as an annexure to the affidavit of Shri Khajuria. The endorsement says, "Remanded for two days with effect from 11th instant." It is signed by the Magistrate and dated 11th 'September, 1985. Neither the application nor the endorsement shows that Shri Bhim Singh was produced before the Magistrate when remand was sought. Shri Bhim Singh expressly denied that he was produced before any

Magistrate on 11th. With reference to the remand obtained on 11th September, 1985, Shri Khajuria does not state in his affidavit that Shri Bhim Singh was produced before the Executive Magistrate First Class on 11th September, 1985. But in very careful and guarded language he says, "A remand to police custody for two days was obtained by Pacca Danga Police Station from Executive Magistrate First Class on 11th September, 1985". The Officer-in-charge Police Station, Pacca Danga has not filed any affidavit. It has to be mentioned here that Shri Bhim Singh moved an application before the Executive Magistrate on 24th October, 1985 to be informed as to the time when remand was obtained from the Magistrate. The Magistrate made the following endorsement on the application of Shri Bhim Singh:

Returned in original to the applicant with the remarks that the remand application was moved before me by the SHO Pacca Danga Jammu on 11th September, 1985 after office hours in the evening at my residence and the (illegible) remanded the applicant in police custody for a period of two days alone.

On the expiry of the remand of two days granted by the Executive Magistrate, a further remand was obtained for one day, this time, not from the Executive Magistrate First Class, but, from the Sub-Judge. It was probably thought not wise to go before the same Magistrate and ask for a second remand. The application made in Urdu to the Sub-Judge with the endorsement of the Sub Judge has also been filed as an annexure to the Affidavit of Shri Khajuria. The endorsement of the Sub Judge reads:

Application for police remand has been moved by Shri Bansi Lal (illegible) S.H.O. P/S Pacca Danga with the submission that the accused Shri Bhim Singh is sick (Medical Certificate attached) and he be removed to the Police lock up as the investigation in the case is still in progress.

Perused the police diaries with the SHO and also promised the medical (illegible) examination slip. The accused is authorized to be left in police lock up for one day. The accused be produced in the court by tomorrow for further necessary remand orders.

The endorsement is signed by the Sub-Judge and is dated 13th September, 1985. We have again to mention here that Shri Bhim Singh requested the Magistrate to give him a copy of the Medical certificate purported to have been submitted by the S.H.O. Pacca Danga. On this application, the Sub Judge made the following endorsement:

Shri Bhim Singh has moved an application requesting this court to certify the time when the police remand application was moved before me by police P/S Pacca Danga on 13.09.1985. The application is also accompanied with a photostat copy of the remand order passed by me on 13.09.1985 as a duty Magistrate. The application in original was forwarded to the I/C Police Station Pacca Danga for report and production of case diaries of the case for perusal, but it has been reported that the case diaries are with SHO who is out on law and order duty.

From the perusal of the photostat copies of the remand order and from my recollection, it is certified that the remand application was moved before me at my residence after court hours in the evening.

Shri Bhim Singh swears in his rejoinder affidavit that he was not produced before the Sub-Judge on 13th, nor was he examined at any time by any doctor. Shri Khajuria in his affidavit again uses very careful language and says, "On the expiry of this remand, an application for further remand was submitted before the Sub-Judge (Judicial Magistrate First class) on 13th September, 1985, who extended the remand by one day." Shri Khajuria does not say a word about Shri Bhim Singh having been examined by any doctor. He makes no reference to the production of any medical certificate before the Sub Judge. As already mentioned, the officer-in-charge of the Pacca Danga police Station has not filed any affidavit before us. Thereafter on 14th September, 1985, Shri Bhim Singh was produced before the Sub Judge and was remanded to judicial custody for two days with a direction to produce him before the Sessions Judge, Jammu on 16th September, 1985. He was accordingly taken to the court of the Sessions Judge on 16th September, 1985, but as the Sessions Judge was absent, he was produced before the Additional Sessions Judge. He was released on bail on his personal bond by the Additional Sessions Judge. That he was produced before the Magistrate on 14th, remanded to judicial custody for two days, produced before the Additional Sessions Judge on 16th and released on bail are facts which are not disputed by Shri Bhim Singh. In his affidavit when he reference to the events of 14th and 16th September, 1985, Shri Khajuria takes good care to use the words "produced before the Sub-Judge" and "produced before the Additional Sessions Judge." As mentioned by us earlier, with reference to the events of 11th and 13th September, 1985, Shri Khajuria very carefully refrained from using the word "produced." He merely said 'remand was obtained'. Shri Bhim Singh in his supplemental and rejoinder affidavits has stated certain facts relating to alleged further harassment by the police. We are not concerned with those further facts for the purposes of this case. We are only concerned with the detention of Shri Bhim Singh from 3.00 A.M. on 10th September, 1985 until he was produced before the Sub Judge on 14th September, 1985. The two remand orders said to have been made by the Executive Magistrate First Class and Sub-Judge on 11th and 13th September, 1985 respectively do not contain any statement that Shri Bhim Singh was produced either before the Executive Magistrate First Class or before the Sub Judge. The applications for remand also do not contain any statement that Shri Bhim Singh was being produced before the Magistrate or the Sub-Judge. Shri. Khajuria, the Inspector General of Police has very carefully chosen his words and stated in the affidavit that remand orders were obtained. He refrained from stating that Shri Bhim Singh was produced before the Magistrate or the Sub Judge on 11th and 13th. The Medical Certificate referred to in the application dated 13th September, 1985 has also not been produced and Shri Khajuria makes no reference to it in his affidavit. In addition we have the important circumstance that no affidavit of the officer in charge of the Police Station Pacca Danga has been filed before us. Nor has the affidavit of the officer, who arrested Shri Bhim Singh been filed before us. At the time of hearing the petition on 19th November, 1985, Shri E.C. Aggarwal stated to us that the affidavits of the two police officers had been got ready but were mislaid. He tried to show us some photo-stat copies of the alleged affidavits and prayed that the case might be adjourned for filing the affidavits of the two police officers. We refused to accede to the request. There was ample time for the respondents to file the affidavits of the two police officers after we issued notice to the respondents. It is not disputed that right from the beginning, they were aware of the writ petition filed in this court. The affidavits of Shri Khajuria and others were filed as far back as 16th October, 1985 and there was no reason whatsoever for not filing the affidavits of the two police officers at that the time. When the complaint was of illegal arrest and detention, the least one would expect the respondents to do is to file the affidavits of the officer who arrested the petitioner and the officer who produced him before the Magistrate for the purpose of obtaining orders of remand. Instead of filing their affidavits, several inconsequential affidavits were filed perhaps only to confuse the issue. Shri Khajuria, the Inspector General of police filed a lengthy affidavit containing statements of fact, most of which he could not be personally aware. However, he chose to use careful language, as pointed out by us, whenever he referred to the remand of Shri Bhim Singh or his production before a Magistrate or Sub Judge. We are convinced that the failure to file the affidavits of the officers, who arrested Shri Bhim Singh and the Sub-Inspector, incharge of Pacca Danga Police Station was deliberate. They were to be kept back until there was dire necessity. We do not have the slightest hesitation in holding that Shri Bhim Singh was not produced before the Executive Magistrate First Class on 11th and was not produced before the Sub Judge on 13th. Orders of remand were obtained from the Executive Magistrate and the Sub Judge on the application of the police officers without the production of Shri Bhim Singh before them. The manner in which the orders were obtained, i.e., at the residence of the Magistrate and the Sub-Judge after office hours, indicates the surreptitious nature of the conduct of the police. The Executive Magistrate and the Sub-judge do not at all seen to have been concerned that the person whom they were remanding to custody had not been produced before them. They acted in a very casual way and we consider it a great pity that they acted without any sense of responsibility or genuine concern for the liberty of the subject. The police officers, of course, acted deliberately and mala fide and the Magistrate and the Sub-Judge aided them either by colluding with them or by their casual attitude. We do not have any doubt that Shri Bhim Singh was not produced either before the Magistrate on 11th or before the Sub-Judge on 13th, though he has arrested in the early hours of the morning of 10th. There certainly was a gross violation of Shri Bhim Singh's constitutional rights under Articles 21 and 22(2). Earlier we referred to the circumstance that though Shri Khajuria, Inspector General of Police stated that information was sent to Superintendent of Police, Anantnag through the Police Control Room, Srinagar on 10th September, 1985, Shri Mir, the Superintendent of Police, Anantnag stated that on 9th September, 1985 at 11.30 P.M. he was informed by the Police Control Room, Srinagar that Shri Bhim Singh was required to be apprehended as he was wanted in a case registered Under Section 153-A of the Ranbir Penal Code. Nobody cared to explain why it was thought that Bhim Singh would pass through Qazi Kund in Anantnag District on the night of September 9-10. Nobody thought fit to explain how and why the Senior Superintendent of Police, Udhampur came to direct his officers to escort Bhim Singh. It has not been explained how and when the Senior Superintendent of Police, Udhampur came to know of the arrest of Bhim Singh and who required him to arrange for the 'safe passage' of Bhim Singh through Udhampur District. To our minds, it appears as if it was expected that Bhim Singh would proceed from Jammu to Srinagar on the intervening night of 9-10 September, 1985 as there was a meeting of the Assembly on 11th September and the police were alerted to arrest him when sighted en route to Srinagar and take him back to prevent him from proceeding to Srinagar to attend the session of the Legislative Assembly. We can only say that the Police Officers acted in a most high-handed way. We do not wish to use stronger words to condemn the authoritarian acts of the police. If the personal liberty of a Member of the Legislative Assembly is to be played with in this fashion, one can only wonder what may happen to lesser mortals! Police Officers who are the custodians of law and order should have the greatest respect for the personal liberty of citizens and should not flout the laws by stooping to such bizarre acts of lawlessness. Custodians of law and order should not become depredators of civil liberties. Their duty is to protect and not to abduct. However the two police officers, the one who arrested him and the one who obtained the orders of remand, are but minions, in the lower rungs of the ladder. We do not have the slightest doubt that the responsibility lies elsewhere and with the higher echelons of the Government of Jammu and Kashmir but it is not possible to say precisely where and with whom, on the material now before us. We have no doubt that the constitutional rights of Shri Bhim Singh were violated with impunity. Since he is now not in detention, there is no need to make any order to set him at liberty, but suitably and adequately compensated, he must be. That we have the right to award monetary compensation by way of exemplary costs 01 otherwise is now established by the decisions of this court in ***Rudul Sah v. State of Bihar and Anr. 1983 (3) SCR 508 and Sebestian M. Hongray v. Union of India 1984 AIR SC 1026.*** *When a person comes to us with the complaint that he has been arrested and imprisoned with mischievous or malicious intent and that his constitutional and legal rights were invaded, the mischief or malice and the invasion may not be washed away or wished away by his being set free. In appropriate cases we have the jurisdiction to compensate the victim by awarding suitable monetary compensation. We consider this an appropriate case.* ***We direct the first respondent, the State of Jammu and Kashmir to pay to Shri Bhim Singh a sum of Rs. 50,000 within two months from today****. The amount will be deposited with the Registrar of this court and paid to Shri Bhim Singh."*

Law of Torts Changed!

Bhim Singh's detention was declared illegal. The Supreme Court judgment introduced a revolutionary change in the 'Law of Torts' as it is applicable in the 'European and British' legal system of Criminal Law. Master's liability for the wrong done by the servant.

G.M. Shah met the same fate that met his predecessors, the Sheikh, Bakshi, Qasim and Farooq Abdullah. Mr. Rajiv Gandhi was trapped in NC net.

BLUNDERS 37

Rajiv-Farooq Accord, 1987

Mr. Rajiv Gandhi was not allowed by political upheavals to complete his full tenure as Prime Minister of India though he had won a huge majority in Lok Sabha after the horrifying assassination of India's great leader, Mrs. Indira Gandhi.

What Mrs. Gandhi had proposed was disposed by Mr. Rajiv Gandhi vis-à-vis Jammu and Kashmir. G.M. Shah was fired 20 months after his assuming Chief Minister's Office in 1986. Congress leadership of J&K was starving for power and sharing doles from Delhi. They convinced inexperienced but nobleman, Shri Rajiv Gandhi that Congress's future lies in sharing power and wealth with National Conference. Dr. Farooq Abdullah was installed in power in 1987. The leaders of the Panthers Party and Peoples Conference of Mr. A.G. Lone were detained in jails by Dr. Farooq Abdullah to please the Congress leaders. This was a turning point in the political philosophy of Mr. A.G. Lone that he lost faith in 'democracy'. The most tragic tale of two years ruthless rule of Farooq Abdullah with Congress coalition from 1987 to 1989. National Conference leaders found the right opportunity to browbeat National leadership claiming to be sole agents of India. Several hundred young boys who were demanding jobs were dispatched by the National Conference leaders to go to POK to seek armed training. Many of them are still active and have been working as double agents. This was exactly what Mrs. Gandhi had realized in 1984 about the hidden agenda of National Conference leaders.

The Rajiv-Farooq Accord made 'Farooq' arrogant and power-blind. He drove his opponents to jails. Rigged Assembly elections of

1987. Manipulated polls to keep out Panthers Party in Jammu and the MUF in Kashmir. He rigged Udhampur Parliamentary polls to ensure fraudulent victory of Congress candidate. It was the beginning of the start of militancy in Kashmir.

BLUNDERS 38

Rigging MUF Elections, 1987

"From 1953 to 1975, Prime Ministers and Chief Ministers of J&K had been nominees of power that be in Delhi. Their appointment to that post was legitimized by the holding of farcical and rigged elections in which the National Conference (1951-1965) and the Congress party (1965-1975) remained in power."

There have been widespread charges of election-rigging in Kashmir which have plagued all the elections from 1951 till date. It is noteworthy that Mr. B. K. Nehru, former Governor of J&K had acknowledged publicly that elections in Kashmir had indeed been rigged in the past. These were observations by one of the senior most diplomat and statesman, Mr. B. K. Nehru who acted as Governor of J&K from 1981 to 1984.

Mrs. Indira Gandhi, whose Congress Party governed the state from 1965-1975 accused the Chief Minister Farooq Abdullah, of large scale rigging in 1983 Assembly elections.

Dr. Farooq Abdullah with the help of Congress MLAs formed a government after dismissing G.M. Shah known to be an experienced administrator. The angry Kashmiri leadership which is identified with several factions of Hurriyat Conference formed a loose federal group and named it as Muslim United Front (MUF). The Muslim United Front which included Ali Shah Geelani, late Mirwaiz Moulvi Farooq (later assassinated by terrorists), Mr. Abdul Ghani Lone, a veteran political leader who remained Education Minister in the Congress Government till 1975 (who was assassinated by the terrorists), Dr. Qazi Nisar Mirwaiz of Anantnag (he also fell down to the guns of terrorists). The MUF emerged a strong force in body politics of Kashmir Valley.

Interestingly, Master Salahuddin, known as master mind of all the terrorism in the Valley also contested elections in 1987 to the State Assembly.

Naturally, everyone took oath of allegiance to the Constitution of India as well as the Constitution of J&K. Mr. Rajiv Gandhi was made to believe that the MUF shall take away the Kashmir Valley on a platter to Pakistan if elected. It was Dr. Farooq Abdullah who rigged the elections and the MUF leaders including M/s. Ali Shah Geelani, Abdul Ghani Lone, Mirwaiz Moulvi Farooq and everybody when lost all hopes in democracy in Jammu and Kashmir, changed their mind the gun-wielding youth who were trained in Pakistan, courtesy Dr. Farooq Abdullah.

This policy of treacherous politics and bungling, corruption, deceit that led to alienation of the common people from the mainstream. It was the greatest blunder committed by an innocent human being, Rajiv Gandhi in 1987 by imposing Farooq Abdullah in power with the support of Congress MLAs. A blunder that cannot be rectified which paved the roads of militancy, distrust, death and destruction in the peace-loving Valley.

Rigging Spree Continued

After his victory in fraudulent polls, Farooq Abdullah did not change his attitude towards to the style of his misrule. Congress MP, Pt. G.L. Dogra died. The Udhampur Lok Sabha seat fell vacant in 1988. This author supported by entire opposition fought Lok Sabha by-election in June, 1988 as Panthers Party candidate. He was supported by Shri H.N. Bahuguna, Shri Atal Bihari Vajpayee, Shri N.T. Ramarao, Shri O.P. Chautala, Mufti Mohd. Sayeed and Shri V.P. Singh, Shahi Imam of Delhi and several entire opposition of the country.

This author won by a margin of 32,000 votes yet he was declared defeated after polls and re-polls, counting and recounting for a month. It was Farooq Abdullah who convinced Rajiv Gandhi to this author's ouster.

This result of by-election shocked the conscience of the entire nation. National papers in their editorial condemned the rigging. Congress and NC demonstrated their old habit of rigging. This author won Lok Sabha by-election from Udhampur in 1988 by 32,000 votes, yet he was declared defeated by electoral manipulation and rigging.

BLUNDERS 39
Fraudulent Udhampur Poll, 1988

All Party's Memorandum to the President of India

Almost entire opposition of India met President of India at Rashtrapati Bhawan and urged him to name Prof. Bhim Singh as M. P. from Udhampur by dismissing the Congress M. P. who have been illegally and unconstitutionally installed by declaring Prof. Bhim Singh as defeated. The All Party delegation was led by Shri V. P. Singh, Leader of Jan Morcha (who a year later became Prime Minister of India) which included Shri Vidya Charan Shukla (Jan Morcha), M/s. P. Upendra, Madhav Reddy (Telugu Desam Patry), Ram Vilas Paswan, Harikesh Bahadur Singh (Janata Party), Sharad Yadav (Lok Dal), Vijay Kumar Malhotra (Bharatiya Janata Party). Ram Jethamalani, MP (Bharat Mukti Morcha), Dinesh Goswami (Asom Gana Parishad), K.P Unikrishnan (Congress-S), Saifuddin Choudhary (CPI-M).

The delegation submitted signed document to the President. The President showed helpless as he did not enjoy constitutional mandate to intervene.

"We consider it our duty to appraise you of certain matters pertaining to and arising out of the Lok Sabha held at Udhampur (J&K) and to appeal to Your Excellency to take appropriate action.

There are two broad aspects, which we, as representative of the opposition parties in the country, would like to bring into sharp focus for the urgent consideration of your Excellency.

That there have been serious malpractice and blatant subversion of the electoral process in Udhampur Parliamentary Constituency, which have exposed serious lacunae in the entire electoral system and which provide chilling evidence of gross missus of officially machinery, vulgar resort to money power, arrogant disregard for democratic principles, highly inflammable arousal of communal passions and shamelessly criminal recourse to electoral coercion and franchise fraud.

That the manner in which the ruling Congress (I) Party and the National Conference (F) resorted to basest forms of rigging was matched only by the biased manner in which the Election Commission of India, quasi–Judicial institution, conducted the Udhampur by election and partial re-poll, was calculated to ensure the defeat of the consensus opposition candidate, Mr. Bhim Singh, and did serious injury to the credibility of the Election Commission it self, shattered the faith of the public in the very concept of parliamentary democracy, underlined the need for an urgent re-appraisal of the composition and working methods of that august body and driven home the absolute necessity for significant electoral reforms.

We the representatives of the opposition parties of India, wish to convey and express our grave concern to you, as Head of state, about the persistent and pernicious attempts of the ruling party and its agents to intimidate voters through brute force, to resort to by-election bribery and blackmail, to incite communal passion, deploy government machinery in open support of the congress-I candidate and to do everything in its power to appoint pliant polling officers in order to get its in candidate elected by hook or by crook.

We are certain that Your Excellency is already aware of the salient points about the shocking sequence of events pertaining to the Udhampur by–election held on June 16, 1988. We take partial repoll in 14, polling booths held on July 12, 1988. We take the liberty of placing before you specific additional information.

That throughout the entire drama, the opposition parties kept the Chief Election Commissioner and his officers informed about misuse of official machinery and other malpractices, through telegrams, written communications and oral complaints.

That on June 13 itself, when the presiding officers in the districts of Udhampur and Doda were suddenly changed, the chief Election commissioner was duly informed about it about it and the apprehensions of the opposition parties was conveyed to him.

That on June 15, on the very eve of polling, Mr. Bhim Singh personally spoke to the CEC over telephone from Jammu and expressed his grave apprehensions over the possibility of foul play and rigging of the elections, particularly in Banihal and Gool-Gulabgarh Assembly segments of the Udhampur parliamentary constituency. This matter was also brought to the notice of the two Central Observers of the Election Commission.

That on June 16, one of Mr. Bhim Singh's representatives, Mr. Sanjoy Sachdeva, brought it to the notice of Central Observer, Mr. Vivekanand Patanayak that the ruling part was organizing massive and systematic rigging and several polling booths in the Banihal and Gool-Gulabgarh segments had been captured by agents of the Congress (I)-National Conference (F) ruling alliance. Mr. Patanayak could not visit many of the remote polling stations because of lack of motorable roads.

That on the same day, polling agents of the joint opposition candidate reported to the AROs about booth capturing at several stations, including Marwah-Dechhen, Gulabgarh and Banihal. Strangely enough, no notice was taken by the concerned officers of the specific complaints made on the spot.

That on June 17, the ballot boxes from all the segments of the Udhampur Constituency, with the conspicuous exception of the boxes from Banihal and Gool-Gulabgarh segments, were brought to the counting centre at Kathua. The counting agents of Mr. Bhim Singh pointed out to the Returning Officer about the undue delay in arrival of the boxes from the said two segments. In reply, the Returning Officer claimed that the delay was because of a breakdown of the vehicles, which were bringing the boxes to Kathua.

That on the morning of June 18, the counting process was initiated, despite the protest of Mr. Bhim Singh and his agents that counting should begin only after the boxes from Banihal and Gool-Gulabgarh arrived. The Returning Officer brushed aside the protest and directed that counting should begin.

That Mr. Bhim Singh wrote a letter to the Returning Officer there and then putting on record his apprehensions about the missing boxes. The Returning Officer replied to the letter only the next day, June 19, in which he sought to give a new explanation about the reason for delay in arrival of the ballot boxes in question. He said the boxes had been taken from Gulabgarh to Rajouri then on to is in itself highly suspicious. The Returning Officer informed that some of the boxes from Banihal were taken to Udhampur, instead of being brought to Kathua, on the directions of the Divisional Commissioner, Jammu.

That the Opposition parties protested to the Election Commission about the rigging in Banihal and Gulabgarh. A written complaint was lodged on June 18 with the Returning Officer, with copies served on the State and Central Observers of the Commission.

That the counting process came to a halt after ballot papers from 13-segments out of the total 15-segments of the Udhampur constituency had been counted. At that stage, Mr. Bhim Singh was leading by a margin of over 32,000 votes over the Congress-I candidate.

That no counting took place on June 19, mainly because it was an open secret that the uncounted votes from Banihal and Gool-Gulabgarh were fraudulent franchise.

That on the afternoon of June 18 itself, the matter was brought to the attention of the Chief Election Commissioner in New Delhi through two hand-delivered written complaints. After daylong deliberations on June 19, the CEC deputed the Commission's Secretary, Dr. R.P. Bhalla, to rush to Kathua to personally supervise the counting.

That on June 20, Dr. Bhalla arrived Kathua in a special BSF aircraft and gave an assurance that justice would be done. The counting process resumed and was completed by about midnight the same day.

That, as apprehended by the Opposition parties, the votes in the boxes from Banihal and Gool-Gulabgarh were obviously fake and attacked heavily in favour of the Congress (I) candidate, in sharp and stark contrast to the trend of voters preference in the 13 other segments of the same constituency.

That as a result of the flood of false votes, Mr. Bhim Singh's lead margin of over 32,000 was reduced to 2,229 at the completion of the counting process.

That when the result sheet was tabulated, Mr. Bhim Singh was found to have won the election by 2,229 votes. The Congress (I) candidate and his agents raised no objection at that time. To the utter shock of the Opposition candidate and his agents, however, or Bhalla went out of his way and beyond his brief by persuading the Congress (I) agents to raise a dispute. Dr. Bhalla personally assisted the Congress (I) candidate in drafting out a written complaint.

That about 2.00 a.m. on June 21, Dr. Bhalla called Mr. Bhim Singh to the Control Room and told him that the Congress (I) candidate had filed a complaint about the rejected votes and therefore he, Dr. Bhalla, would not allow the result to be declared. As a result, the matter was referred to the CEC in New Delhi.

That at New Delhi, Mr. Bhim Singh filed a detailed representation to the Chief Election Commissioner, giving sample statistics about the stark contrast between the voting pattern in the rigged segments of Banihal and Gool-Gulabgarh and the rest of the constituency. The representation furnished ample proof of rigging, malpractices and booth capturing in more than 31 polling stations in Banihal and 36 stations in Gool-Gulabgarh.

That the Chief Election Commissioner was not prepared to examine the evidence of malpractices furnished by Mr. Bhim Singh nor to take cognizance of the specific points brought to his notice by Opposition leaders who called on him.

That in the most unjust fashion and without applying his mind to crystal-clear evidence of large-scale malpractices, the CEC issued an arbitrary order on June 25, 1988, through which he ordered fresh polls in a more 14 polling stations, instead of in the entire segments of Banihal and Gool-Gulabgarh.

That the CEC chose to adopt double standards by ordering re-poll in as many as 161 polling stations in Faridabad Parliamentary Constituency, even though he had before him complaints regarding only 43 polling booths. Whereas in the case of Udhampur, he chose to ignore the timely and specific complaints of large-scale rigging throughout the two segments of Banihal and Gool-Gulabgarh, and ordered re-poll in only 14 stations, in a transparent attempt to favour the Congress (I).

That it is pertinent to invite Your Excellency's attention to the fact that the CEC, in his Order dated June 25, himself notes, in para 9, that in about 17 polling stations in Banihal and 5 polling stations of Gool-Gulabgarh, the polling percentage was between 81% and 89%. Such a high voter turnout in the far-flung mountainous terrain of the two segments was not only abnormal but truly incredible, particularly since most of the population of the areas concerned consists of nomadic herdsmen who migrate to the Kashmir Valley during the summer months.

That the CEC, in his above-mentioned order, goes out of the way to stress the need for urgent electoral reforms to check the evil of silent booth-capturing. Unless he was convinced in his heart that massive rigging had taken place, he would not conceivably have digressed in a formal order to dwell upon the need for electoral reform.

That going contrary to logic and the sacred norms of justice and fair play, the CEC imposed imaginary limitations upon himself and took the specious plea that the rules did not permit him to act at polling stations where the voter turnout was less than 90%. As Your Excellency is surely aware, the 90% yardstick for measuring abnormal voting was laid down in 1985 by the Election Commission to assist its officers to pinpoint abnormal voting whenever there is any ambiguity as to whether or not electoral malpractices have been committed. It was never intended to be a rigid rule to be applied with mathematical precision, to the exclusion of all other evidence of malpractices. It is the height of absurdity to say that polling is abnormal in one polling station where 90 voters out of 100 have cast their votes, whereas it is not abnormal in a neighbouring booth where 89 voters out of 100 have cast their votes. But this is precisely the absurd logic put forward by none other the Chief Election Commissioner of India. He has rigidly applied with scientific exactitude the 90% maxim to detect the fine art of rigging.

That on June 28, Mr. Bhim Singh filed review application against the above-mentioned order of the CEC and demanded that re-poll should conducted through out the Udhampur Constituency or at least in the entire segments of Banihal and Gool-Gulabgarh. The review application gave further detailed facts and figures to establish more than a prima facie case of large-scale electoral malpractices committed in the two segments in question.

That even before the review application on was submitted by a delegation of opposition leaders on June 28, Secretary Bhalla issued a press statement saying that the Commission would not entertain any review applications and that the commission would not budge even an inch from its order of June 25. This press statement was made by Dr. Bhalla on June 27 and appeared in the newspapers on the morning of June 28.

That after the review application was submitted by leaders of eleven Opposition parties personally to the CEC on June 28, the Commission showed no inclination of even considering the application.

That it was only after the Congress (I) filed a review application pertaining to Faridabad a full two days later, that the Election Commission sprung into action and fixed the dates for hearing of the review application relating to Faridabad and Udhampur. The biased attitude of the Commission's senior officers was manifest in their extreme reluctance to take cognizance of the Opposition petition and their contrasting alacrity to act swiftly the moment the ruling party moved its petition.

That it is pertinent that the dates fixed for the re-poll in Faridabad and Udhampur, July 3 and July 12 respectively, was in itself suspicious and malafide, since a full two weeks were made available to the ruling parties of J&K to bring back the migrant voters in time for the re-poll in 14 polling stations.

That the Commission, which had publicly resolved not to budge an inch from its June 25 Order, extended the date of polling for Faridabad re-poll from July 3 to July 12, to facilitate hearing of the review applications.

That it was clear at the very outset that the CEC had prejudged the issue and that the hearing of the review petition in the case of Udhampur would be no more than a futile ritual aimed at insincerely projecting an image of fairness and impartiality.

That on July 7, the CEC formally rejected Mr. Bhim Singh's review application without bothering to go deep into the serious and specific points raised therein. The Commission took the plea that it did not want to change the rules of the game while the game was in progress. This amounts to an implicit admission that the Commission was inwardly convinced that rampant rigging had taken place in the two segments of Udhampur Constituency.

That, immediately after the rejection of the review application, Mr. Bhim Singh requested the Commission to guard against booth capturing and to deploy CRPF personnel at all the 14 polling stations. In a press briefing, the Commission gave an assurance that CRPF personnels would be posted at each of the 14 polling stations where re-poll was to take place.

That despite this assurance, no CRPF men were seen anywhere in the Gulabgarh and other areas where re-poll took place on July 12. The Presiding Officer of Majrakund polling station has certified in writing that no CRPF personnel were at his polling station on polling day.

That on July 7, the Commission was informed telegraphically that workers of the Panthers Party had been assaulted in broad daylight at Banihal. The Commission was also informed that on July 9, the DC, Doda, visited Banihal and arbitrarily imposed Section 144 Cr. P. C. Neither the Returning Officer nor the CEC took any notice of these complaints.

That the CEC was also informed that highly placed State government officers were openly canvassing for the Congress (I) candidate in the re-poll areas. State government Ministers went to each of the polling areas and openly bribed the voters by ordering developmental work, including building of roads, laying of water pipelines, enhancement of ration quotas, up-gradation of primary schools, etc., in gross violation of election norms and blatant misuse and arrogance of power. Details of these pre-poll crimes were reported in the Indian Express editions dated July 9 and 10.

That on polling day, Mr.Bhim Singh was personally present at Gulabgarh and Khour polling stations. Only six unarmed police constables manned these booths and no CRPF men were on duty.

That violent booth capturing and rampant impersonation took place throughout the polling areas. Numerous complaints in writing and through telegrams and telephone calls were made before, during and after the July 12 polling, of specific instances of malpractices.

That the CEC did not care to give even cursory attention to the cast-iron proof of rioting and booth capturing in Gulabgarh, Khour, Majrakund, Khaned and other booths. Nor did he take any cognizance of charges of misuse of official machinery and massive impersonation.

That, to top it all, the CEC did not brother to find out the whereabouts of State Observer, Mr. G.D. Sharma, a distinguished District and Sessions Judge, who was stranded in rain-hit Gulabgarh for over a week. The Commission refused to wait for the report of Mr. G.D. Sharma, who, in his capacity as State Observer, was an eyewitness to the violence and rioting in Gulabgarh engineered by Congress (I) leaders.

That to seek justice, Mr. Bhim Singh went on indefinite fast outside the Election Commission headquarters in New Delhi. Instead of going through the complaints made by the opposition parties, the CEC ordered the counting process to be rushed through on July 18, even while Mr. Bhim Singh was on fast. The result was declared in favour of the Congress (I) candidate the same afternoon.

That it was only after the results had been declared that a helicopter was sent to Gulabgarh to rescue the stranded State Observer Mr. G.D. Sharma, who was brought to Kathua after 3.30 p.m.

Your Excellency has been given the above outline of what happened during the Udhampur parliamentary by-elections, in the hope and with the prayer that as Head of State, you will intervene in the matter in the interests of upholding the cherished values of democracy, justice and truth. We, the representatives of opposition parities in the country, would be glad to furnish further details and documentary material in support of our charge that wholesale rigging took place at the Udhampur Parliamentary by-poll and re-poll held on June 16 and July 12, 1988. We pray that Your Excellency should intervene suo-moto and institute a thorough inquiry by a sitting Judge of the Supreme Court. We pray that you should order cancellation of the fraudulent Udhampur by-elections and direct the concerned authorities to hold fresh polls in the entire constituency. We further pray that you should take a close look into the entire election machinery and take steps to plug the serious loopholes and lacunas in the electoral system, which enable the ruling party to rig elections through misuse of its power. In this context, we request you to keep a sharp eye on the Prime Minister declared moves to initiate electoral reforms in the forthcoming Session of Parliament. We apprehend that the Prime Minister may subvert the electoral system in the garb of reforms in order to enable his party to rig the General Elections due in December 1989.

We hope Your Excellency will take appropriate action in the interests of the 700 millions people of India and to safeguard the parliamentary democratic system in the country."

High Court Quashed Election of Congress MP

Soft spoken, highly cultured and determined judge of J&K High Court, Shri K.K. Gupta delivered a historic judgment, declaring election of the Congress candidate a 'void'. This is the only judgment in the political history of J&K that the High Court of J&K delivered on merit in the matter of an election dispute. The Congress succeeded in their delaying tactics even then judgment could not be installed. Alas, it came a little after the 'Lok Sabha' had been superceded. Roads of destiny must have been written differently had this author entered the sovereign seat of judgment, Lok Sabha in 1988, the political map of J&K would have been written in different colours and visions.

Judgment

"Parliamentary Constituency No.5 Udhampur fell vacant on the death of Sh. G.L. Dogra, M.P. and Election Commission of India in order to fill the said seat issued notification on May 16, 1988 for holding by-election. Petitioner filed his nomination as a candidate of J&K Panthers Party Respondent no.1, Shri Mohd. Ayub Khan filed his nomination papers as a candidate of Indian National Congress. Election was held and Respondent No.1 was declared elected. The Petitioner has by way of this election petitioner challenged the said election of Respondent no.1 on various grounds, including competency of Election Commission of India to order

for re-poll and corrupt practices. Respondent No.1 who only contested the petition refuted the allegations of the petitioner and this court on February 17, 1989 framed the following issues:

Whether the documents namely petition, schedules and the annexures annexed with the petition and the affidavit have been verified according to law? OPP.

Whether the order of Chief Election Commission of India dated 25.6.1988 amounts to noncompliance of election rules and representation of People Act and whether it has materially affected the result? OPP.

Whether the act on the part of the authorities concerned at the instance of respondent No.1 to shift the ballot boxes of 14 polling stations of Gulabgarh segment to Rajouri which is outside the jurisdiction of Udhampur Parliamentary Constituency and then shifting the said ballot boxes to Udhampur before bringing them to Kathua, the venue of counting, after three days from the date of poll amounted to corrupt practices? OPP.

Whether the petitioner can be declared elected on the basis of the total number of valid votes polled in favour of the petitioner at the end of counting of all 15-segments on the intervening night of 20th and 21st June, 1988? OPP.

Whether the secrecy of the poll after the entire result was declared and number of votes was also counted in 14 polling stations has completely been lost and re-poll amounted to corrupt practices? OPP.

Whether the votes on polling station No.11 and 12 were improperly received, if so what is its effect? OPP.

Whether the Presiding Officer of polling stations Thathar (Banihal) and polling station Khaned (Ramnagar) were also beaten up and locked up by the police and the revenue officials to rig the election in favour of respondent No.1 on the poll day i.e. 16th June, 1988 and it amounts to corrupt practices? OPP.

Whether the slogans used by Respondent No.1 and his supporters like 'Vote for Islam in Defense of Quran' amount to corrupt practices? OPP.

Whether the canvassing by Arun Govil who has acted as 'Ram' in Ramayan serial by addressing public meting at Udhampur and Katra amounted to corrupt practice? OPP.

Whether the use of Pawan Hans, a state helicopter, by Respondent no.1 and his supporters, Ministers in the Government and the Congress-I Party General Secretary Ghulam Nabi Azad, for the election campaign of Congress-I amounted to corrupt practice? OPP.

Whether the counting of 3 polling stations on 20th June was done by the secretary to the Chief Election Commission pertaining to Budan, Chasote and Chenani in Gulabgarh segment which was illegal, if so what is its effect? OPP.

Whether during re-polling at Gool-Gulabgarh polling agents of the petitioner were beaten up at the instance of Respondent No.1 and poling stand was ransacked and captured, if so what is its effect? OPP.

Whether the averments regarding alleged corrupt practices are vague, full particulars of which are not given, if so what is its effect? OPP.

Whether the allotment of symbol of hand to Respondent No.1 amounted to corrupt practice? OPP.

Under an order dated April 21, 1989 Issue No.3 was however, recast as under:

"Whether the authorities concerned shifted ballot boxes of 14 polling stations of Gool-Gulabgarh segment to Rajouri which is out side the jurisdiction of Udhampur parliamentary Constituency and afterwards shifted said boxes and Udhampur before bringing the same to Kathua, the venue of counting after three days from the date of poll of the instance of Respondent No.1 and whether result of the election has been materially effected by it? OPP

Issue Nos. 1, 2, 13 and 14 have been treated as preliminary issues and parties have led evidence in regard to the same.

I have heard the learned counsel for the parties and perused the record. Mr. J.P. Singh learned counsel appearing for the petitioner has taken only a legal plea that in accordance with Section 64-A of Representation of Peoples Act. Election Commission of India was not competent to order re-poll of certain stations when counting of votes had completed and in this manner because of the illegality committed by the Commission for ordering of re-poll of certain segments whole polling has become vitiated and the result declared on the basis of that polling became void. Mr. Bakshi learned counsel for Respondent no.1 has referred to Section 66 of the aforesaid act and according to him there was a direction of Election Commissioner for ordering of re-poll before announcement of the result and as such re-polling was ordered properly. His further plea in this regard is that both the parties had consented for re-polling and order of Election Commission in that regard cannot be said to be invalid in any manner.

Section 64-A of the above said Act reads as under:

"(i) If any time before counting of votes is completed any ballot paper used at a poling station or at a place fixed for the poll are unlawfully taken out of the custody of the Returning Officer or are accidentally or intentionally destroyed or lost or are damaged or tampered with to such an extent that the result of the poll at that polling station or place cannot be ascertained, the Returning Officer shall forthwith report the matter to the Election Commission.

(ii) ...."

The other relevant provisions requiring consideration is contained in Section 66, which is as under:

"When the counting of votes has been completed the Returning Officer shall, in the absence of any direction by the Election Commission to the contrary, forthwith declare result of the election in the manner provided by this Act of the rules made thereunder."

It is admitted case of both the parties that the Returning Officer had completed the process of counting of votes and after that a reference was made for re-polling in certain segments of the constituency. Chief Election Commissioner of India on such recommendations passed order for a fresh poll or certain polling stations vide his order dated 25.06.1988. The words in Section 64-A of Representation of Peoples Act, (Act hereafter), "of any time before counting of votes is completed" are very much pertinent. It is clear from these words that power of fresh poll of particular polling station can be exercised by Election Commissioner before counting of votes is completed. After the counting is complete, the Commission cannot order a re-poll, Mr. Bakshi wants this court to invoke the provisions contained in Section 66 of the Act as, according to him, there was a direction from Election Commission of India not rights not to declare the result even after counting of votes had taken place. I think Mr. Bakshi is not correct in his contention. There is nothing on record to show that there were instructions or directions to the Returning Officer by Election Commissioner not to declare the result. If such was the case there was hardly any reason for the Returning Officer to complete the process of counting. There is express provision in both the above-referred Section 64-A and 66 of the Act that the Returning Officer has to declare the result when counting of votes have been completed. There is thus a clear violation of the mandatory provision contained therein.

Mr. Singh wants me to hold that at the time of completion of counting of votes the petitioner had secured more votes than Respondent no. 1 and he was to be declared as elected member but I think it will not be proper to do so when the case is being disposed of on a legal point.

In view of the violation committed by the Election Commission of India of the express provisions contained in Section 64-A of the Act re-polling of certain segments of the constituency has become invalid and the election declared on that basis has also become void and it is held so. The parliament for which said election was held has since been dissolved and now parliament was subsequently constituted and as such no order can be passed either for re-poll or for only other purpose. This petitioner is, therefore, disposed of with the above said observations."

Sd/-
K.K.Gupta (Justice)
Jammu
15.10.1992

BLUNDERS 40

Five Militants Freed for Rubia's Release December 13, 1989

On December 8, 1989, Rubaiya daughter of Mufti Mohammad Sayeed, the then Home minister of India in the V. P. Singh government was kidnapped by JKLF. They were demanding release of five militants in exchange for Rubaiya's release. The negotiations opened through Zaffar Meraj a local journalist, while Shabnam Lone, daughter of A.B. Ghani Lone and Maulvi Abbas Ansari of the Muslim United Front were tapped as possible channels.

Later, a judge of the Allahabad High Court, Moti Lal Bhat, entered the picture. A friend of Mufti, he began negotiating directly with the militants on behalf of the Union Home minister December 13, 1989, two Union Cabinet Ministers, Inder Kumar Gujral and Arif Mohammad Khan, personally flew to Srinagar to persuade. The Chief Minister Farooq Abdullah who was opposed to the kidnappers' demand. He argued openly that surrender to the terrorists' demands would open the floodgates of such mischiefs.

The Dr. Farooq Abdullah's Govt. reluctantly followed the dictates of the Union Govt. headed by Mr. V. P. Singh to save his own neck and power. Accepted the demand of ghost kidnappers and released, unconditionally, ISI sponsored five militants from Srinagar jails namely Sheikh Abdul Hameed, a so called JKLF 'area commander', Ghulam Nabi Butt, younger brother of the late Maqbool Butt, Noor Muhammad Kalwal, Muhammed Altaf, and Javed Ahmed Zargar a Pakistani citizen.

December 13, 1989, Dr. Rubaiya Sayeed was set free, two hours after the government released the five jailed militants. Thousands of young men gathered at Rajouri, Kadal to take them out in a so-called victory procession. The procession was glorified in its national bulletin by 'DD' only channel available those days boosting the dying morale of the dying militancy. An unforgivable blunder!

BLUNDERS 41

Last Exodus of Kashmiri Pundits January 19, 1990

The power that be ignored the plight of the Kashmiri Pundits. A memorandum of Kashmiri Pundits dated January 16, 1990 addressed to the Governor General (retd.), Mr. K. V. Krishna Rao deserves a careful attention;

"The ineffectiveness of the State Government has not been able to check loot, arson and killing of innocent people. Instead of the Government, it is the militant who are the de facto rulers in the Valley today. The ruling political forces are solely concerned with their own survival avoiding the wrath of the secessionists. Happenings in Anantnag, Sopore, Baramulla, Tral, Nurran, Pulwama, Ishber, Vicharnag, Shopian and other places in the Valley are indicative of the fundamentalists' designs regarding their planned targets of attack on the minorities. On 15th December, 1989, in Shopian men, children and old women of the minority community were mercilessly attacked and women-folk molested. The murder of Mahant Keshav Nath, Tikka Lal Taploo, N. K. Ganjoo, Prem Nath Bhat, Ajay Kapoor and others, was to create scare and awe among the minority community to force them to leave the Valley. The pace of exodus has further accelerated now.

It is a sad commentary on the present administration that not even a single assailant of the minority leaders and others has either been identified or apprehended by the police till now."

Mr. Jagmohan took over as Governor on January 19, 1990, the day last exodus took place. Instead of strengthening administration, the Chief Minister, Dr. Farooq Abdullah resigned under the excuse of

Mr. Jagmohan's appointment. It was utter failure of the Union Government to provide security to the Kashmiri Pundits.

Tens of thousands of Kashmiri Pundits across the Valley were forced out of their thousands of years old ancestral homes and land to save their lives and religion from brutal tide of violence let loose by their centuries old ethnic neighbourers' fraternity. The horrifying bloodbath initiated by the ISI and its allies at the end of December, 1989 against the secular and nationalist Kashmiris slaughtered thousands of innocent people creating a communal divide. The Govt. in Delhi failed to judge the situation. Power hungry political hawks were helping the saboteurs of peace and harmony. Most of the leaders left the Valley to their safe havens in India and abroad. The minorities were left to their own destiny live or die. This was the utter failure of the Union leadership to provide social, physical or political protection to the Kashmiris, particularly the minorities. Hundreds of innocent pundits were killed and none felt secured. For life they decided to part with their motherland, Kashmir, the heavens on earth. It is pity that those who were ruling them till end of 1989, 'Quit Kashmir' of their own leaving the Kashmiris at the hands of the human killers aided, abetted and armed and financed by neighbouring country. The blunder committed by the Union Govt. headed by Mr. V. P. Singh cannot be ignored by the history of Kashmir. Instead of providing protection to the Kashmiri Pundits, the Central Govt. provided them safe exodus. Mr. Jagmohan, the Governor, appointed by the Central Govt. took over on January 1990, itself. In his own words he described the situation in Frozen Turbulence as, "Looking at the compact and enmeshed houses, and the by-lanes which acted like fine threads of a well-knit fabric, I wondered how these families, who had all their Gods and Goddesses here, and had deep roots in the soil, could leave and settle in distant and unfamiliar lands. Sometimes life is unaccountably cruel. And we human beings have, perhaps, no option but to suffer–suffer in silence, or wail." Where was the protective umbrella of the Central or State Authority?

Caravans of buses, trucks and taxies with puzzled and anguished men, women and children huddled in them looked like sheep being taken to the slaughter house. Searching questions seemed writ large all over the faces. What had they done to deserve such severe inhuman punishment? Why this banishment? The Kashmiri Muslim intelligentsia, the Muslim press dancing to the tune of the ISI commands, terrorists belonging to numerous outfits and the Kashmiri Muslim political leaders taking oaths of loyalty to the Indian Constitution but in the depth of the heart owing allegiance to anti-India subversive force spread the canard that the Kashmiri Pundits left Kashmir in search for safety for their children and women and coming generations. Their miseries and tears failed to find The Guru Teg Bahadur mat the end the 20th Century. There were no Sheikh Abdullah either to stand with a daring rod for their protection and safety. The echelons of power in Delhi failed to perform their duty that the Constitution had entrusted to them to provide security to the citizens of their country. The exodus, of Kashmiri Pundits, a rarest of the rare, I would say 'Race' in the universe with its thousands of years old cultural heritage and civilization full of fragrance, from their motherland shall always be recorded as naked assassination of a civilization in the 20th century when the man has reached the moon and mars.

This exodus of a great civilization has diluted the very essence of Kashmiriyat of which entire J&K felt proud of. The waters of entire Indian Ocean cannot wash their bloody hands soaked with the blood of history of exodus from their own land in their own secular country in the era of democracy. A horrorful blunder!

Blunders 42

Poll Boycott by NC, 1996

The militancy reached the skies by 1989. The government led by Dr. Farooq Abdullah literally collapsed. Prime Minister, V. P. Singh dispatched Shri Jagmohan to Kashmir as Governor. The City of Srinagar witnessed unprecedented violence, deaths and destruction. Dr. Farooq Abdullah resigned leaving lonely Governor to face the situation. Before his resignation, Dr. Farooq Abdullah had a meeting with Mr. Rajiv Gandhi who was still staying at 7, Race Course. This author was present in the room where the two leaders had a serious discussion on the new strategy of National Conference to deal with Mr. Jagmohan. Governor Rule was imposed in J&K to meet the challenge posed by National Conference and the militants. The Governor Rule continued till 1996. The Assembly was dissolved and the tenure of Legislative Council came to an end. There was complete constitutional breakdown. All the important leaders from the Valley left their homes for Delhi or elsewhere. It appeared as if they were waiting for a take over from a foreign country.

Elections to the Lok Sabha was declared in 1996. National Conference leader declared from London to boycott the elections. Mr. Narasimha Rao, considered one of the most genius statesmen failed to convince Dr. Farooq Abdullah to participate in the Lok Sabha polls. He declared from Burkin Paso, during his African tour, that he would grant autonomy to Kashmir with sky as the limit if National Conference participated in the Lok Sabha polls. Farooq Abdullah defied Mr. Narasimha Rao and did not participate in the elections. Interestingly, Election Commission of India refused to hold elections in J&K on the pretext that situation was not conducive to hold elections in J&K. This author sought intervention of the Supreme Court of India. The intervention of the Supreme Court of India (1996) 4 Supreme Court Cases 188 allowed the writ petition filed by this author and held that it was the prerogative of the Union of India to determine the situation and not that of the Election Commission of India. The blunders committed by NC leadership with malafide intention to weaken the State-Centre relations deserve to be placed on record for the information of those who are interested in the political history of J&K.

National Conference remained out and the Congress won all the seats from J&K by using their usual methods of rigging and manipulating elections. Later on the Prime Minister of India, Mr. H. D. Deve Gowda visited Kashmir and declared that dialogue shall be held with the elected representatives only. This author was the only political person from J&K who accompanied Mr. Deve Gowda in Army helicopter over the Valley to assess the situation. Dr. Farooq Abdullah had no choice but to join the election fray in 1996. The Central government failed to fulfill their commitment to hold free and fair polls. Candidates of National Conference were declared elected where polling did not exceed 2 to 4 persons in several constituencies. The National Conference became absolute ruler.

BLUNDERS 43

Dreaded Terrorists Exchanged for Hijacked Passengers December 31, 2000

On December 31, 2000, three detained dreaded terrorists, namely undergoing trial in different Courts in Delhi, Srinagar and Jammu were released unconditionally on the direction of the NDA Govt. headed by Shri Atal Bihari Vajpayee to secure the safe release of 154 Indians held hostages in the hijacked Indian Airlines aircraft by the ISI terrorists. NDA Ministers Mr. George Fernandes and some others rushed to Srinagar to persuade Dr. Farooq Abdullah to release two of the militants from Srinagar and Jammu jails, that too on Sunday, a holiday. The two militants namely, Mohd. Masood Azhar was released without any authority of law from Kotbhalwal Jail, Jammu and Mushtaq Ahmed Zargar was handed over to the Central agencies who was lodged in Srinagar Central Jail. Third one Ahmed Umar Sheikh was picked up from Tihar Jail Delhi.

The entire operation to transport the three militants to Kandhar was marked by secrecy. They were flown to Kandhar with the then External Affairs Minister, Mr. Jaswant Singh, after an agreement was reached with the hijackers for the safe return of the passengers. Hijackers were never identified.

Azhar came to Delhi in January, 1994 via Dhaka on a forged Portuguese passport, to supervise the merger of the two militant outfits; Harkat-Ul-Mujahideen and Harkat-e-Jihad-e-Islami (HUJI) under a new name of Harkat-ul-Ansar.

Ahmed Umar Sayeed Sheikh, a 28-year-old Harkat-ul-Ansar militant, was a British national of Pakistani origin. His brief was to abduct foreigners, to secure the release of Mohammad Azhar and other Harkat leaders lodged in the Indian jails. He was arrested on October 31, 1994 and lodged in Tihar jail.

This was a blunder of the NDA Govt. that a Union Minister carried three dreaded militants in his aircraft to Kandhar, capital of Afghanistan. The Govt. committed not only a blunder but infringed the constitutional mandate and rule of law by releasing the terrorists without following the procedure established by Law. That too worked as moral boost to the terrorists.

BLUNDERS 44

Manipulation of 2001 Census

The population of Kashmir Valley was less than the population of Jammu province. There was a difference of electorates as well. The difference in the number of electorates was nearly two lacs. The Valley was having less number. During the militancy period in the Valley from 1990 to 2000, half a million Kashmiri Pundits had left the Valley for survival whereas about 200,000 citizens mostly belonging to Muslim fraternity also left the Valley as they were feeling insecure and defenseless. The National Conference government headed by Dr. Farooq Abdullah first delayed the census process under the pretext of insecurity and militancy. Later on the Chief Minister managed to hold census on the table showing increase of over 10 lacs of population in the Valley as compared to Jammu province. The sad part of the story is that the leadership in Delhi failed to take cognizance of this grave offence rather than a blunder. Encourage by the NDA government in Delhi Dr. Farooq Abdullah managed to get the clearance of the census taken in Jammu and Kashmir from the Union Home Ministry headed by Shri L.K. Advani. This was an uncounted blunder of the NDA government for which every person in J&K has been penalized. Dr. Farooq Abdullah played another gamble by introducing ban on the Delimitation of the Assembly Constituencies as was done by the Parliament of India during the BJP headed government in the Centre. Strange that the same person has been harping for Greater Autonomy who himself was responsible to act as faithful and obedient soldier of the BJP leaders ruling in the Centre. It is also important to mention that Sheikh Mohd. Abdullah had extended the life of Assembly from 5 to 6 years during Emergency in 1976 to follow the act of the Parliament. When the Parliament changed the tenure from 6 to 5 during Janata rule in the Centre, the National Conference refused to follow the Central Law. These are the blunders which deserve attention of every citizen of India.

BLUNDERS 45

Bar on Delimitation

The 'Congress and BJP' combine supported 'National Conference' to adopt an obnoxious, discriminatory and highly undemocratic amendment in Section 47(3) of J&K Constitution barring Delimitation of the Assembly Constituencies till 2031, say 40 years. This was done to establish a ruthless, undemocratic and authoritarian political domination of Kashmir Valley over Jammu province and Ladakh region. NC leadership suffered a split after the dissolution of NC into the Congress in 1965 under the leadership of NC Prime Minister, G. M. Sadiq. Bakshi Ghulam Mohd. refused to reconcile to the idea of the Communist lobby.

Sheikh Mohd. Abdullah revived the NC when he was appointed Chief Minister by Mrs. Indira Gandhi in 1975. Both Congress and NC were the architects to ensure political domination of Jammu province. Kashmir had 42 Assembly seats, Jammu 32 and Ladakh 2. After an ad-hoc Delimitation in 1995, Jammu seat went upto 37 and Kashmir seats rose to 46. Ladakh got 4 political lever of power shall always remain with the Valley. Delimitation is barred to suit the Kashmir leadership alone.

BLUNDERS 46

India's Silence on Merger of Gilgit-Baltistan, 2009

The Gilgit-Baltistan Empowerment and Self-Governance Ordinance 2009 was promulgated by Pakistan granting so-called internal political autonomy to 'the Disputed Areas of Jammu and Kashmir'. The Ordinance violates UNCIP Resolutions because this area is not a part of Pakistan. The 1948 ceasefire line resulted in the division of J&K with Pakistan gaining control over some portion of the occupied territory. Pakistan occupied areas of J&K was subsequently divided in 1970 into two 'administrative zones'; 'Azad Jammu and Kashmir' (AJK) and 'Northern Areas'. 'AJK' is constitutionally not a part of Pakistan and is governed under an Interim Constitution of 1974. Northern Areas were brought under the direct control of Islamabad and now are governed by so-called elected Govt. as placed by the Empowerment Ordinance 2009. The Gilgit region has been struggling to free itself from the control of the Pakistani Government ever since 1947. The Government of Pakistan has extended and reinforced its control over the region through its illegal "Reform Package." Pakistan is not prepared to give the region an independent status or to enable its people to adopt a modern, transparent democratic system. Gilgit-Baltistan is now a de-facto province of Pakistan.

India committed a blunder by keeping silent on the grave violation of UNCIP Resolutions vis-à-vis POK in spite of repeated calls by Panthers Party and Balawaristan National Front and several others. Early Pakistan had leased out nearly 5000 sq. miles of Karakoram (J&K) territory to China in utter violation of the UNCIP Resolutions. India failed to intervene. China has since built National Highway connecting Beijing with Peshawar (Pakistan) thus creating road connectivity with Europe for the first time in history. The Highway has built 16 battle-helipads threatening the geo-security of India. India did not care to lodge a protest even in the United Nations on this grave violation of UNCIP Resolution of August 13, 1948. Allowing Pakistan to convert de-facto control of Gilgit-Baltistan (28000 sq. miles) in 2009 to de jure status has completed annexation process of this territory that the Maharaja had acceded to the Union of India in 1947.

The prison 'diary' of Brig. Ghansara Singh, the last J&K Governor in Gilgit already scripted in this book would suggest that the Indian leadership has learnt no lesson from their earlier blunders. They continue to repeat them in 2010 which was admittedly committed in 1947 vis-à-vis Gilgit-Baltistan.

BLUNDERS 47

With Last Abdullah, 2008

Imposing an inexperienced, unacceptable, inefficient and over ambitious young Abdullah as Chief Minister in J&K was the latest blunder that Delhi has committed.

Early Assembly polls were necessitated on the resignation of Chief Minister, Ghulam Nabi Azad when he lost majority on the floors of the Assembly. The credit for toppling Azad government goes to the Panthers Party who with their four MLAs showed exit to the Government.

The Assembly election of 2008 was fought with the help of the mobile voters and EVMs in Kashmir. EVMs and the faithful bureaucrats gave National Conference a larger margin than others. The Congress changed their equation and returned to their Union with National Conference. May be, this was the last blunder of the Congress leadership lying on heaps of volcanoes in the State.

Appointment of interlocutors by Government of India to provide oxygen to sinking power House in Kashmir, has demonstrated bankruptcy of the Union Ministry for Home.

WAY OUT

Accession and Merger

Jammu and Kashmir was a princely state which acquired an independent status after August 15, 1947 on the ground that the competent ruler did not accede before or by August 14, 1947 either with India or Pakistan. The Maharaja signed the Instrument of Accession to the Union of India on October 26, 1947. The Accession became final on its acceptance by the Governor General of India on October 27, 1947. The Instrument of Accession for all the States had similar format signed by the respective rulers of other States. The Constituent Assembly of J&K terminated monarchy on August 20, 1952 by adopting unanimous resolution under the leadership of National Conference leader, Sheikh Mohd. Abdullah. All the conditions, or any condition attached or stipulated by the Monarch came to an end rather stood terminated with the termination of the powers of the Monarch. In strict sense of the mandate of Section 3 of Constitution of J&K read with First Schedule, item-15 of Article-1 of the Constitution of India, Jammu and Kashmir formed **integral part** of India. According to India's Independence Act of British Parliament, after the Accession of a State got automatically merged in the Union. This happened in respect of all the Princely States which acceded to the Union of India or Pakistan in 1947. It was constitutional integration much more than the merger.

If there were no constitutional merger the Constituent Assembly of India could not have enacted a special provision for Jammu and Kashmir under Article 370.

Presidential Order of 1954 extended several provisions of the Indian Constitution for the reason that Article 370 had granted some temporary concessions to Jammu and Kashmir for political reasons. Article 324 of Constitution of India as applicable to J&K should not leave any doubt about the constitutional status of J&K as integral part of the Union of India. Word, 'integral' has been used only after J&K stood constitutional merged with the Union of India as its integral part.

Only 'Dispute'

The Parliament of India in 1994 under the leadership of the then Prime Minister, Shri P. V. Narasimha Rao adopted unanimous resolution to the effect that only dispute vis-à-vis Jammu and Kashmir with Pakistan was the liberation of the illegally occupied areas of Jammu and Kashmir from Pakistan. There is no other dispute with Pakistan on J&K.

That is the dispute, of course, bilateral. For the past 63 years Pakistan continued illegal occupation of nearly one-third of the Territory of J&K. Pakistan has been violating UNCIP Resolution right from day one. Pakistan defied UN Resolutions by refusing to vacate the occupied territories. Instead of withdrawing civilian settlers from POK and Gilgit-Baltistan, Pakistan settled thousands of retired army men in Askardu, Chitral, Hunza and others areas. It was on this defiance of UN Resolution that Owen Dixon was sent as UN representative to J&K who recommended so-called 'Dixon Plan' suggesting to create a 'Greater Kashmir' by dissecting Muslim majority areas of Jammu province and tagging them with Kashmir. It was Anglo-American strategy to appease Pakistan and create a safe ground for the Pentagon in the region to check the expansionist activities of China in the Himalayas.

Pakistan has been harping on the so-called 'dispute' vis-à-vis J&K. UNCIP Resolution of August 13, 1948 directing Pakistan to vacate all occupied territories of the State it forcibly occupied in 1947 is the only dispute on J&K.

The word, 'dispute' was brushed aside by Krishna Menon in his historic and eloquent rejoinders to Pakistan on the floors of the United Nations in 1957. 'Dispute' did not figure in Tashkent Agreement, 1966 or Simla Agreement, 1972. However, Anglo-American Bloc continued instigating and supporting ISI of Pakistan to keep situation boiling in Jammu and Kashmir with a purpose to implement the CIA-sponsored Dixon Plan, 1950, which intended to create an 'Islamic State' in the name of Greater Kashmir by tagging Muslim majority areas of Jammu Province with the proposed State. The Anglo-American Plot has been to establish their military base in Askardu (Baltistan) to keep watch on China's movement in the region. This was rejected by Pt. Jawahar Lal Nehru for obvious reasons. This was the only daring decision on Jammu and Kashmir.

Mrs. Indira Gandhi and Zulfiqar Ali Bhutto had, it is believed, nearly settled this issue by accepting the existence of LoC with minor adjustments along the river Kishanganga in the Valley. President Musharraf had almost (publicly) offered a similar formula to the Indian Prime Ministers, Shri Atal Bihari Vajpayee and later to Dr. Manmohan Singh. Neither Zulfiqar Ali Bhutto survived nor General Musharraf's stayed in the office of President to accomplish this unfinished agenda.

Mr. Krishna Menon's roaring speeches on the Floors of the General Assembly of the United Nations in 1957 left no doubt in the minds of international community about the real dispute. It was Mr. Narasimha Rao who showed roadmap for the settlement of the dispute, liberation from Pakistan of all illegally occupied territories of J&K, through war or peace.

Of course, there is an another dispute with Pakistan on the rehabilitation of the refugees, who are still called 'migrants', from POK numbering more than one million who were thrown out of the occupied areas during the Pak-occupation in 1947, 1965, 1971.

The dispute is about their comprehensive settlement by compensating them as was done in case of other refugees from Pakistan. Pakistan must compensate.

Thousands of them have been living in refugee camps in J&K. They have to be settled honourably in accordance with the command and mandate of international law for the rehabilitation and settlement of refugees. This problem does not exist in Kashmir province for the reasons that all these migrants have been residing in Jammu province ever since their displacement. There are about 85,000 refugees languishing in the border areas of Poonch, Rajouri, Jammu and Kathua who migrated from Pakistan in 1947 from across the international border to Jammu. They were rehabilitated by the orders of the Sheikh Mohd. Abdullah in 1947 when he was acting as administrator in J&K, appointed by Maharaja Hari Singh. These 'Pakistani' refugees and their descendents who were born and brought up in Jammu have remained deprived of all their basic, civil, political and fundamental rights. Those who were born in Jammu and Kashmir after 1947 have been suffering from the same discrimination, the Jammuites' suffered. This 'dispute' of human rights of 85,000 refugees and citizens of India is a burning problem that needs to be settled to honour the human rights as enshrined in the Charter of the United Nations. The Kashmir leadership is opposed to their rehabilitation and settlement for communal reasons. This problem also needs to be settled.

Two historic agreements were signed between India and Pakistan, in 1966, Tashkent and another after 1971 war in Simla. The word, 'dispute' which Indian Home Minister, Mr. Chidambaram has been using frequently and practiced by some other busybodies is neither relevant in law nor it is relevant for the resolution of the situation in Jammu and Kashmir. In Simla Agreement which was signed between Mrs. Indira Gandhi and Mr. Zulfiqar Ali Bhutto, word, 'settle of J&K situation' was used while proposing a frequent dialogue between the Heads of the two countries. The agreement had rejected any third country intervention or mediation. The word, 'Kashmir dispute' in relation to J&K did not find any space in the Tashkent Agreement also. The word, 'Kashmir dispute' was invented by those who have been trying to destabilize India in the name of J&K. Anyway, dispute on J&K is only on illegal occupation of one-third of J&K territories by Pakistan.

Settlement of LoC

India has two options to settle the status of LoC once for all. One is through war and another through peace. India and Pakistan fought three wars over Kashmir. The result was a status quo-ante each time, pressure of big powers. Pakistani aggression in the garb of infiltration started in 1990. It still continues. That is undeclared war though the people do not want war on either side. The people of both countries are against war, blood and bullets. This author has been interacting with the people of different walks of life in Pakistan as well as with the suffering people who have been living in a State of war for decades, none supported war. Can India or Pakistan afford nuclear war in 21st century when the world is looking for peace and progress? India has to unilaterally or bilaterally accept the international reality about the existence of 700 kms. long Line of Control. The option for the settlement of status of LoC without resorting to war is to accept its existence with minor adjustments as international border.

Dr. Manmohan Singh, the Prime Minister of India has made it clear that the borders shall not be readdressed. The mood in Pakistan is 'no' different from India's approach. The residents born and brought up in POK and taught a syllabi have grown differently as compared to those who are born and brought up in J&K (India). India or Pakistan cannot afford any 'transfer' of population in 21st century. The reality has to be accepted. Indian Parliament needs a unanimous approach to accept the reality on LoC.

The Kashmiri speaking majority in the Valley have no love lost for the Dogri-Punjabi-Pahari speaking population of J&K majority of whom reside in POK. If entire State of J&K as it existed before the Accession is allowed to reunite, the Kashmiri speaking Valley shall be reduced to minority. That is the psyche of the Kashmiri speaking leadership in general. There may be some exceptions but they don't matter. That was the reason that Sheikh Abdullah opposed the liberation of POK. That was the tragedy behind the division of the State. The people of POK and Gilgit shall be great sufferer after LoC is recognized as International Border without settling their (POK and

Gilgit) constitutional safeguards under POK Constitution. India must mobilize international opinion to seek the same special status for POK which is being enjoyed by J&K within the Union of India.

'Reorganization'

The State government claimed that they have terminated the feudal system and the Monarchy. Yet, the so-called Durbar (Civil Secretariat) has to move from Kashmir to Jammu and vice versa after every six months. The people of Kashmir continue to suffer because they remain cut off from the Civil Secretariat (Government) for six months and same is the plight of the people of Jammu who have to suffer for the remaining period of the year. This needs a change to satisfy the aspirations of the people of both the regions. There is need to continue functioning of the Civil Secretariat in both capital cities.

There has been a continuing political discrimination against Jammu region so far as the allotment of Assembly seats is concerned. Jammu province has 37 seats in the Assembly whereas Kashmir Valley has 46. The area of the Jammu province is double as compared to the area of the Valley. Delimitation has remained under the political dictates of the ruling parties which have been working under the dictate of Kashmir rulers since 1947. Kashmir Valley has three Members in the Lok Sabha whereas Jammu province has to be satisfied with two only. There are heaps of regional discriminations which need to be removed in the interest of survival of the State.

The local issues need to be settled amicably among the people of the three regions as early as possible. Reorganization is the only way out. Separation of power; legislative, political and financial is the only way out.

Separation of Powers Legislative, Political and Financial

So far as the political turmoil in J&K is concerned, it needs a respectable and honourable distribution of political, legislative and financial power to each region. Admittedly creation of J&K was an unnatural and heterogeneous combination in the history when it was formulated in 1846. There are three regions presently in J&K; Ladakh, Kashmir Valley and Jammu province. Each region enjoys distinguished cultural, social, linguistic and geographical identity. The identity of the each region has to be honoured in accordance with the mandate of the Constitution and aspiration of its people. Each region has its aspiration to grow in freedom, peace and democracy. Unnatural Union must end amicably and democratically. This can be achieved by reorganization of the entire State of J&K on the bases of cultural, linguistic, historic and geographical identity of each region. The demand of 'autonomy' or 'self-rule' shall be addressed with the aspirations or the wishes of the people of all regions through reorganization.

Re-organization of G&K

There is a constitutional mechanism that the State may be re-organized by amending Article 370 of the Constitution of India. Amendment in Article 370 can be affected by 'Presidential Order' without seeking a vote in the Parliament according to the mandate of Article 370. Through this amendment two separate Provincial Assemblies of 'Kashmir' and 'Jammu' may be established. Provincial Assembly should be vested with legislative, financial and political powers in respect of the subjects enumerated in the State List in the respective region. The items listed in the Concurrent List may be taken care by the State Assembly which shall comprise of the Legislators of the respective regions. So far as subjects in the Union List are concerned, it should be left for the Parliament to legislate in respect of such matters. There is practically no constitutional bar to have a separate Chief Minister for each region. One Governor and one Chief Justice may do good for the preservation of the unity of the State. Naturally, there shall be separate and independent Civil Secretariats in Srinagar and in Jammu. This is the only solution to end unnatural domination of a region over the other which has been a grave cause of conflict and tension between the regions. Both the districts of Kargil and Leh in Ladakh have already been granted Hill Council Status. The authority of the Hill Councils may be upgraded and institutionalized to encourage local participation and build confidence in the arrangement.

This will also harmonize the process of granting political representation to the Scheduled Tribe and granting Scheduled Tribe Status to the ethnic Pahari population spread in the bordering districts of Kupwara, Poonch and Rajouri. The Kashmiri Pundits may also be granted political reservation in the Assembly and reservation in government services to save this distinct cultural identity from total extinction. To save 'Jewish' distinct race, the UN granted them a State in Palestine. To save another distinct race, the Kashmiri Pundits, they should be granted, at least, legitimate representation inside the Legislative Assembly of Kashmir.

The Article 370 will survive with empowerment of Parliament to legislate on Central subjects whereas the State Legislature may take care of Concurrent matters. The Provincial Assemblies shall deal with the provincial subject under their jurisdiction. With separation of powers; legislative, political and financial, all the 'doubts' and 'suspicions' of regional discrimination may go. There shall be greater 'inter-regional' interaction and trust-deficit shall also disappear.

This author had a privilege to discuss this proposition with Prime Minister, Shri Narasimha Rao in depth. Shri Rao considered as one of the most genius political weights showed keen interest in this subject but he did not have sufficient number in the Parliament to take such a plunge. When the rumours were afloat about the dissolution of Lok Sabha in 2002, this author took this matter with Shri Atal Bihari Vajpayee the then Prime Minister. He asked for a detailed note in writing on my proposal which was submitted to him. Shri Vajpayee had two problems. Firstly he had problem with his own party which in its agenda and manifesto stood for complete abrogation of Article 370 from the Indian Constitution. The second problem as was understood by this author that he did not expect support from his own constituents in the NDA to amend Article 370. To realize such an amendment in the

Constitution of India it needed lot of courage and commitment to the cause of the nation and comprehensive understanding of the situation in J&K.

'Doubts' that have been created by vested interests in the minds of the innocent and suffering people of Kashmir shall evaporate when they shall find that 'Jammu' in no way dominates them or threatened their economic interest and vice-versa. Sans distrust and suspicions the State may prosper and harmony shall prevail.

Effects of Reorganization

The Reorganization shall introduce new era of development and tensionless atmosphere in the State. Regional conflicts and trust-deficit shall disappear. Discrimination shall have no scope in the new dispensation. There shall be separate allocations of Central finances.

(a) Each region shall have separate Public Service Commissions, Recruitment Boards, High Secondary Education Boards and Planning Commission.

(b) The Secretariat in each provincial capital shall function around the year so that the people in far-flung areas of Kashmir and Jammu province may have an easy access to the Secretariats for the redressal of their local problems.

(c) High Court and the Raj Bhawan shall continue their usual schedule and remain a subject matter of the State Assembly.

(d) Over a million refugees of 1947, 1965, 1971 and others from POK shall be settled comprehensively in accordance to international law and human dignity.

(e) Each province shall have independent 'Delimitation' of the Assembly Constituencies on the basis of equity, principles of natural justice, population and terrains.

(f) The regional history of the regional heroes of different fields shall be compulsory subject from the first standard to the University level. The national heroes of Ladakh, Kashmir and Dogra Desh shall be included in the respective syllabi.

(g) This is the only perfect constitutional mechanism that shall provide a 'genuine' representation to the SC and ST in each province in proportion to their population in each province.

(h) The minorities in each province shall also be compensated by adequate representation in recruitment and the legislature.

Wisdom Lies in Daring!

More than half a century has gone since the partition of India, thanks to the colonial empire that ruled the sub-continent for two centuries. The partition generated hatred more than anything else between two countries which resulted into bloody wars between the same civilization and people. The time has come when the leadership in India and Pakistan takes a determined stand to work jointly for peace and progress which is the need of the 21st century. The leadership in both the countries shall have to respond to the aspirations and wishes of their respective people who desire no more deaths, no more blood and no more bullets as the new generations are looking for peaceful co-existence and respective living. The message drawn from different treaties and agreements signed by the leadership of both countries, may it be Tashkent Agreement or Simla Accord. The emphasis has been on dialogue and honourable co-existence of two brotherly nations.

This is unfortunate that Pakistan could not enjoy a stable democratic and popular government for a reasonable period of time. However, even the military dictators had realized that India and Pakistan may have to live in peace and harmony in the interest of their respective nations. The initiatives taken by India recently deserve to be responded with an open heart by the leadership of Pakistan. The two leaderships have to bear in mind that Anglo-American Bloc has their national interests in the sub-continent and therefore peaceful co-existence between India and Pakistan does not suit them in the longer run. The leadership in India has shown their fundamental interest in generating a peaceful atmosphere so that India and Pakistan can live in peace by a healthy cooperation and coordination.

The dispute with Pakistan over LoC in Jammu and Kashmir shall be addressed once the leadership of both sides initiates a composite dialogue with a clear roadmap towards cooperation and peace.

The leadership of India deserves a favourable and trustworthy response from the leadership of Pakistan to bring an end to the outdated hatred and unhealthy distress. Wisdom lies in daring and both India and Pakistan have to prove their wisdom and courage to sign everlasting peace between the two. Their might may lead the entire world towards international peace and security. This will generate a new era of progress and democracy in Middle-East and African continent. The Indian Parliament should also show their wisdom and magnanimity by closing the narrow walls of their electoral ideologies and go for amendment of Article 370 to take people of all the three regions of Jammu and Kashmir into confidence. Let Pakistan also show its wisdom and commitment to the people living in the territory of Jammu and Kashmir under Pakistan's control. Their existence with their cultural and linguistic identity deserves a special attention too.

I close my entreats and echoes for peace and democracy of the world with a few lines that noble peace laureate wrote;

Where the mind is without fear
and the head is held high,
Where knowledge is free
Into that heaven of freedom,
my Father, let my country awake.

MAJOR EVENTS IN J&K FROM 1947-2010

12th August, 1947: Maharaja's Government offered Standstill Agreement to India and Pakistan.

14th August, 1947: India partitioned and a new theocratic State of Pakistan created.

15th August, 1947: At the stroke of the midnight hour India attained freedom. Pakistan accepted offer of standstill agreement.

16th August, 1947: Pak signed agreement with J&K.

9th September, 1947: Sheikh Mohammad Abdullah released from prison.

1st October, 1947: Sheikh Mohammad Abdullah declared at a public meeting at Hazuri Bagh, Srinagar: "Till the last drop of my blood I will not believe in the two nation theory" as propounded by Mohammad Ali Jinnah.

15th October, 1947: Justice Mehr Chand Mahajan took over as the Prime Minister of Jammu and Kashmir.

18th October, 1947: Maharaja's Government, through a telegram to Pakistan Prime Minister, protested against the violation of Standstill Agreement by Pakistan.

22nd October, 1947: Armed tribesmen, supported by Pakistani troops, invaded the State territory at several points.

23rd October, 1947: Muzaffrabad fell to the aggressors.

24th October, 1947: Invaders advanced towards Baramulla and Srinagar; State Forces, the only Power Station at Mohra destroyed by the raiders, plunging the Valley into darkness; Maharaja sent his Prime Minister to Delhi to seek military assistance.

25th October, 1947: V. P. Menon arrived in Srinagar from Delhi. Met the Maharaja and flew back the same day to Delhi.

26th October, 1947: Maharaja Hari Singh signed Instrument of Accession in Jammu.

27th October, 1947: Governor General Lord Mountbatten accepted the Instrument of Accession; the first batch of Indian troops, 1st Sikh Regiment, landed at Srinagar Airport at 8.15 in Dakota.

30th October, 1947: Maharaja Hari Singh appointed Sheikh Mohammad Abdullah as the Head of the Emergency Administration.

1st November, 1947: Brig. Ghansara Singh, Governor of Gilgit held prisoner by Muslim Scouts with the help of Pak-soldiers.

2nd November, 1947: K.H. Khurshid, Mr. Jinnah's Private Secretary arrested by Sheikh Abdullah in Kashmir.

3rd November, 1947: Pattan and Gulmarg freed from the raiders occupation.

7th November, 1947: Fierce battle around the Srinagar Aerodrome; raiders fled away after **12 hours battle** of Shalateng leaving behind 300 dead.

8th November, 1947: Baramulla liberated.

14th November, 1947: Invaders pushed beyond Uri.

1st December, 1947: Maharaja Hari Singh inaugurated Jammu Radio Station, which renamed as Radio Kashmir, Jammu.

16th December, 1947: Heavy fighting took place near Uri, 321 raiders killed.

1st January, 1948: India approached Security Council against Pakistan by declaring unilateral ceasefire.

17th January, 1948: Security Council passed resolution asking India and Pakistan to stop fight.

20th January, 1948: The Security Council set up a three member commission to investigate facts.

3rd February, 1948: Pakistani raiders pushed back from Samba and Kathua sectors.

5th March, 1948: Maharaja announced Interim Government with Sheikh Mohammad Abdullah as Prime Minister.

21st March, 1948: First jeep motored to Tragbal in Gurez.

23rd March, 1948: Indian troops liberated Teetwal.

1st July, 1948: Radio Kashmir, Srinagar inaugurated; Gurez liberated.

4th July, 1948: Brigadier Usman killed while fighting against Pakistani raiders and troops at Jhangar area of Rajouri district.

13th August, 1948: UNCIP through a resolution directed total withdrawal of Pakistani troops from all occupied areas.

1st November, 1948: Indian troops crossed 11578 feet high Zojila with tanks, recaptured Kargil.

8th November, 1948: Bimber Gali liberated.

9th November, 1948: Ramgarh Fort in Rajouri re-captured.

15th November, 1948: Drass liberated, links established with Kargil and Leh.

20th November, 1948: Link established with Poonch.

23rd November, 1948: Kargil and Mendhar liberated finally.

5th January, 1949: UNCIP passed resolution on holding of plebiscite with certain conditions that Pak shall vacate POK territories.

28th April, 1949: Maharaja Hari Singh left Jammu for Delhi? He never returned to J&K.

16th June, 1949: Sheikh Mohammad Abdullah, Maulana Masoodi, Mirza Afzal Beg and Moti Ram Baigra took seats in Indian Constituent Assembly at Delhi.

20th June, 1949: Maharaja Hari Singh signed Proclamation at Delhi making Yuvraj Karan Singh as the Regent.

27th June, 1949: Indo-Pak ceasefire agreement signed at Karachi.

13th July, 1950: Revolutionary Land Reforms adopted; Proprietary rights of 10,000 land-owners transferred to tillers without any compensation fixing sealing limit of 23 acres irrespective of irrigated or kandi agricultural land.

1st May, 1951: Proclamation directing formation of State Constituent Assembly issued.

15th October, 1951: National Conference won all the 75 Constituent Assembly seats unopposed.

31st October, 1951: Constituent Assembly Session began in Srinagar with Maulana Masoodi in chair.

19th August, 1952: Constituent Assembly approved unsigned Delhi Agreement which had no existence, which intended to delete fundamental rights from J&K Constitution.

20th August, 1952: Monarch terminated through a resolution of the Constituent Assembly. 106 year old hereditary rule abolished by a resolution moved by D. P. Dhar.

16th November, 1952: Yuvraj Karan Singh took over as Sadar-i-Riyasat on 16th November, 1952.

22nd June, 1953: Jan Sangh leader, Dr. Shyama Prasad Mukherjee died in Srinagar jail, the Jan Sangh called it as murder.

9th August, 1953: Sadar-i-Riyasat, Yuvraj Karan Singh dismissed Sheikh Mohammad Abdullah as Prime Minister and arrested him. Bakshi Ghulam Mohammad was sworn-in as Prime Minister.

6th February, 1954: Constituent Assembly ratified accession of the State to India.

14th May, 1954: Constitution (Application to J&K) Order issued by the President of India under article 370 extending some provisions of the Union Constitution to the State with some exceptions and modifications.

16th March, 1956: China's Chou En Lai said that the people of Kashmir have already expressed their will regarding accession to India.

17th November, 1956: State Constituent Assembly adopted Constitution, inter-alia, declaring State as integral part of India.

20th November, 1956: Former British Prime Minister Attlee says "Kashmir has definitely opted for Union with India."

22nd December, 1956: Vice President, Dr. Radha Krishanan declared open the Jawahar tunnel.

26th January, 1957: State Constitution of J&K promulgated. Section 3 of J&K Constitution declared that J&K is and shall be integral part of India.

8th January, 1958: Sheikh Mohammad Abdullah released from Kud Jail after five years of detention under Nehru's direction.

29th April, 1958: Sheikh Mohammad Abdullah re-arrested for violating his commitment.

1st May, 1958: Comptroller and Auditor General of India's jurisdiction extended to J&K.

19th June, 1958: Sheikh Mohammad Abdullah, Mirza Afzal Beg and twenty others charged with conspiracy against State.

26th January, 1959: J&K High Court brought at par with other High Courts in India.

1st April, 1959: Permit system for entry into the State abolished, thus ending closure at the State's border with the Punjab.

16th March, 1961: Prime Minister, Pt. Jawahar Lal Nehru and Ayub Khan, President of Pakistan held talks on J&K in London. The minutes not made in public.

26th April, 1961: Maharaja Hari Singh passed away in Bombay at the age of 64.

24th January, 1962: Sheikh Mohammad Abdullah and other co-accused in Kashmir conspiracy case committed to Sessions Court.

18th February, 1962: National Conference under the leadership of Bakshi Ghulam Mohd. won 38 Assembly seats uncontested.

27th April, 1962: Soviet delegates to Security Council said "Question of Kashmir as integral part of India has been decided by the people of Kashmir."

20th October, 1962: China launched attack in Ladakh and NEFA.

26the October, 1962: National emergency declared.

21st November, 1962: China declared unilateral ceasefire after occupying 14500 sq. miles in Ladakh.

2nd March, 1963: Pakistan illegally transferred 5000 sq. miles of State territory in Gilgit, under its illegal control, to China. This was a grave violation of UNCIP Resolution of 13th August, 1948 which had directed Pakistan to vacate all occupied areas of J&K.

4th October, 1963: Prime Minister, Bakshi Ghulam Mohammad resigned under Kamraj Plan.

12th October, 1963: Shamas-ud- Din sworn in as Prime Minister of J&K who did not lost three months.

8th April, 1964: Sheikh Mohammad Abdullah released.

26th May, 1964: Sheikh Mohammad Abdullah met President Ayub Khan of Pakistan in Rawalpindi.

27th May, 1964: Nehru died.

26th January, 1965: National Conference converted into J&K Pradesh Congress Committee with Syed Mir Qasim as its President.

30th March, 1965: State Constitution amended; Sadar-i-Riyasat and Prime Minister renamed as Governor and Chief Minister, respectively.

9th May, 1965: Sheikh Mohammad Abdullah arrested at Palam Airport while returning from Algiers where he had made provocative utterances.

5th August, 1965: Pakistan pushed armed guerrillas into J&K. They were dropped by the parachutes in Rajouri, Poonch and other areas.

3rd September, 1965: UN Secretary General Security Council confirmed that violations began with armed men invaded Ceasefire Line from Pakistan side.

4th September, 1965: Security Council urged immediate ceasefire and withdrawal of forces.

5th September, 1965: Indian troops crossed boundary in Lahore sector.

6th September, 1965: Indian troops entered Sialkote sector.

11th September, 1965: Ceasefire came into force.

10th January, 1966: Indian Prime Minister, Shri Lal Bahadur Shastri signed Peace Agreement with General Ayub Khan, President of Pakistan.

11th January, 1966: Prime Minister, Shri Lal Bahadur Shastri died at Tashkent under mysterious circumstances.

25th January, 1966: Old Ceasefire Line restored under Tashkent Agreement and Haji Peer, highly strategic territory handed over back to Pakistan, a greatest setback to India's security. India lost a great heroic Prime Minister, Shri Lal Bahadur Shastri who died immediately under mysterious circumstances after signing the Agreement.

15th May, 1967: 15 Mr. Baghwan Sahai took over as Governor of the State.

6th November, 1967: Gajendragadkar Commission was set up to inquire into the grievances of regional discrimination under the pressure of Dr. Karan Singh, the then Union Minister.

8th December, 1967: Sheikh Mohammad Abdullah released.

15th August, 1968: Judiciary separated from Executive in J&K.

3rd December, 1968: Gajendragadkar Commission Report presented to the Chief Minister, which remained kept in the dustbin till date.

19th December, 1968: Moulvi Mohammad Farooq became Mirwaiz of Kashmir.

8th January, 1971: Sheikh Mohammad Abdullah, Mirza Mohammad Afzal Beg and G. M. Shah externed from the State by the Congress Govt.

13th January, 1971: Militant outfit "Alfateh" unearthed and smashed.

30th January, 1971: Indian Airlines plane with 32 passengers on board hijacked to Lahore during its flight from Srinagar to Jammu.

1st April, 1971: Census Report showed State's populations 46,16,632, showing 29.65% increase in a decade.

17th May, 1971: Foundation stone of Rs. 5 crore HMT watch factory laid in Srinagar, which was destroyed by terrorists in 1992.

24th August, 1971: Article 226 of Indian Constitution extended to the State empowering High Court to issue respective writs.

3rd December, 1971: Pakistan attacked India; National emergency declared.

6th December, 1971: India recognized Bangladesh; Pak Air Force attacked Jammu.

12th December, 1971: Chief Minister G.M. Sadiq died; Mir Qasim sworn in as Chief Minister.

16th December, 1971: Unconditional surrender by Pakistani Forces in Bangladesh; India declared unilateral ceasefire on Western Front.

20th February, 1972: Pt. Prem Nath Dogra passed away of cancer in Jammu, leaving a vacuum of leadership.

15th July, 1972: Bakshi Ghulam Mohammad passed away of cardiac arrest in Srinagar ending an era of national renaissance.

2nd October, 1972: Jammu back on Railway map after 25 years. It had Jammu-Sialkote rail link till 1947.

11th December, 1972: India and Pakistan approved Line of Control in J&K.

3rd July, 1973: L.K. Jha took over as Governor.

10th November, 1973: Sheikh Mohammad Abdullah reiterated Kashmir's Accession to India as final.

10th June, 1974: Foreign Minister, Swarn Singh said that his talks with Sheikh Mohammad Abdullah convinced him about some basic common approaches on which constructive co-operation could be built.

2nd July, 1974: Sheikh Mohammad Abdullah said that some communal elements in J&K conspired to foil his efforts for amicable settlement with New Delhi.

24th September, 1974: Pakistan illegally merged Hunza Principality with it in Gilgit region.

13th November, 1974: Parthasarthy and Beg signed "Agreed Conclusions' as emissaries of Prime Minister Indira Gandhi and Sheikh Mohammad Abdullah thus paving the roadmap of Sheikh's return to J&K as Chief Minister.

24th February, 1975: Syed Mir Qasim tendered resignation to facilitate handing over power to Sheikh Mohammad Abdullah; State Congress Legislative Party expressed confidence in Sheikh Mohammad Abdullah who was invited to head government in J&K.

25th February, 1975: Sheikh Mohammad Abdullah took over as Chief Minister with 3 Cabinet Ministers, M. A. Beg, D.D. Thakur, Sonam Narboo.

13th March, 1975: Indira-Sheikh Accord was approved by Parliament and later by the State Legislature.

5th July, 1975: Plebiscite Front dissolved by Mirza Afzal Beg thus slogan of plebiscite was buried.

13th October, 1975: Four member Co-ordination Committee set up to ensure smooth implementation of Indira-Sheikh Accord.

13th April, 1976: Sheikh Mohammad Abdullah elected President of revived National Conference.

10th February, 1977: State Assembly extended its life from 5 to 6 years following the Act of Parliament to extend its life to six years.

25th March, 1977: Congress headed by Mufti Mohd. Sayeed withdrew support to Sheikh Government inside Assembly.

26th March, 1977: State Assembly dissolved; Governor's rule proclaimed by Governor B.K. Nehru.

26th April, 1977: Janata Party unit launched in J&K with Maulana Masoodi as its convenor.

25th June, 1977: Prime Minister Morarji Desai arrived in Srinagar for election campaign issued directive against any rigging.

30th June, 1977: Assembly polls held; massive victory for National Conference, this author was elected as opposition Member (INC) in 1977 from Chenani.

8th July, 1977: Governor invited Sheikh Mohammad Abdullah to form new Government.

6th September, 1978: Public Safety Ordinance promulgated, this author was first victim of PSA.

25th September, 1978: Sheikh Mohammad Abdullah sought resignation from Mirza Afzal Beg; Beg resigned and later was expelled.

14th January, 1979: Indian Airlines Service to Leh inaugurated.

20th June, 1979: Sikri Commission, instituted to look into alleged regional imbalances, just to dilute Gajendragadkar report.

23rd August, 1980: Government promulgated ordinance amending R. P. C. and Cr. P. C. to provide deterrent punishment for communal offences.

25th August, 1980: Sikri Commission on regional imbalances submitted its report to the Government. Remained unattended till day.

9th October, 1980: Legislative Assembly building at Srinagar gutted in a devastating fire after this author got an order of the Supreme Court to stay expulsion of Speaker Mohiuddin Malik. Mala and this author were attacked by government sponsored elements. Captain Tikku was the saviour.

22nd February, 1981: B.K. Nehru succeeded L.K. Jha as Governor.

1st March, 1981: Census puts State population at 59,87,389 with a decadal increase of 29.69 per cent. Dr. Farooq Abdullah elected President of National Conference.

8th September, 1982: Sheikh Mohammad Abdullah passed away; unprecedented scene of mourning witnessed in Kashmir; over a million joined the funeral; Dr. Farooq Abdullah sworn-in as Chief Minister. Mrs. Indira Gandhi joined the funeral procession. Mala and this author too joined the funeral.

5th June, 1983: Polling held for 76 Assembly constituencies. This author was elected as Panthers Party MLA from Chenani. BJP was completely washed out. Mrs. Indira Gandhi and Mr. Rajiv Gandhi were shocked on this author's victory.

26th April, 1984 : Jagmohan took over as Governor of J&K.

2nd July, 1984: Farooq Government dismissed; G M Shah sworn-in as Chief Minister with support of Congress-I.

31st July, 1984: This author and A.G. Lone were arrested by police. Not allowed to attend Assembly.

31st May, 1985: Historic Gulabgarh Palace complex in Old Secretariat, Jammu gutted in a fire.

6th March, 1986: Congress(I) withdrew support to G.M. Shah Government; Governor suspended Assembly. Governor rule imposed in the State.

7th September, 1986: President's rule under Article 356 imposed for the first time in the State after expiry of six months of Governor's rule.

7th November, 1986: President's rule revoked after Rajiv-Farooq Accord. National Conference (F)—Congress (I) alliance Government took over the reins of administration. A biggest blunder

23rd March, 1987: NC(F) and Congress-I alliance returned to power. NC (F) bagged 39 seats and Congress (I) 24 seats in mid term poll.

27th November, 1987: Former Finance Minister and M.P Mr. G.L. Dogra passed away.

13th February, 1988: Mr. P. Namgyal, the first Ladakhi, inducted into the Union Council of Ministers.

27th October, 1988: Bomb blasts and firing by militants in different parts of Srinagar; city engulfed with fear and terror.

7th October, 1989: Ladakh granted Scheduled Tribes status.

8th December, 1989: Union Home Minister, Mufti Mohammed Syed's daughter, Rubia Syed, allegedly abducted by militants in Srinagar.

13th December, 1989: Five militants freed in exchange of Rubia Syed's release by giving them undue publicity by glorifying terrorism.

16th January, 1990: Governor, K.V. Krishna Rao, resigned.

19th January, 1990: Jagmohan re-appointed as Governor; Dr Farooq Abdullah resigned in protest; Governor Rule imposed and State Assembly kept in suspended animation.

13th February, 1990: Director Doordarshan Srinagar, Lassa Koul, killed by militants.

19th February, 1990: State Assembly dissolved by Governor, Jagmohan.

6th April, 1990: Vice Chancellor, Kashmir University, Musheer-ul-Haq, his private secretary, Abdul Gani and General Manager, HMT, Srinagar H.L. Khera abducted by militants. They were later killed.

17th April, 1990: Jamat-i-Islami, Hizb-ul-Mujahideen, People's League, Islamic Jamat-i-Tulba, Islamic Students League banned.

21st May, 1990: Mirwaiz Moulvi Farooq gunned down by militants at his residence.

25th May, 1990: Governor Jagmohan resigned.

26th May, 1990: Girish Chander Saxena took over as new Governor.

18th July, 1990: Kashmir Valley declared disturbed area.

11th March, 1993: Governor G. C. Saxena resigned. Gen. (retd.) K. V. Krishna Rao, PVSM appointed new Governor.

19th March, 1994: Former Speaker, J&K Legislative Assembly, Wali Mohammed Itoo gunned in Jammu. Killers remained unidentified.

20th June, 1994: Islamic Scholar and Mirwaiz South Kashmir, Qazi Nissar gunned down by militants in Kashmir.

11th May, 1995: The historic 14th century Charar-i-Sharief Shrine torched by militants led by mercenary, Mast Gul, who managed to escape; Valley mourned the burning of the Shrine. This author was first to reach there.

20th July, 1995: Nineteen persons killed, 60 injured in Purani Mandi (Jammu) bomb blast.

10th November, 1995: The 3-member Election Commission decided not to hold Assembly Elections in J&K for the time being as the situation was not conducive for it. Only after the judgment of the Supreme Court on the petition of the JKNPP, election was held. NC boycotted the polls for Lok Sabha.

6th July, 1996: Prime Minister, Mr. H.D. Deve Gowda visited

Kashmir; announced Assembly election. This author accompanied the Prime Minister.

19th July, 1996: Election Commission announced four-phase Assembly elections in J&K to restore democratically elected Government.

26th November, 1996: J&K State Autonomy Committee, headed by Dr. Karan Singh, set up to examine the issue of greater autonomy within the Constitution.

6th January, 1997: Govt. announced setting up of the State Human Rights Commission.

29th June, 1997: A powerful bomb blast inside the MLA Hostel killing. NPP Provincial President Mohd. Ramzan with two other Panthers Party workers were killed. No one traced.

26th July, 1997: Prime Minister I.K.Gujral, laid foundation stone of Railway project at Qazigund; addressed public meeting.

7th August, 1997: Dr. Karan Singh resigned as the Chairman, State Autonomy Committee on personal reasons; State Works Minister, Ghulam Mohi-ud-Din Shah, replaced Dr Singh as the Chairman.

October, 2002: Election to the State Assembly was held. No one got majority. A coalition could only be formed with the support of Panthers Party four MLAs on the condition that the government shall implement Wazir Commission and constitute Delimitation Commission. The Congress led coalition betrayed the CMP. Panthers Party withdrew support with the result that the minority Government Chief Minister, Mr. Ghulam Nabi Azad had to resign in 2007.

October 2008: Congress revived its old friendship with the National Conference and imposed Omar Abdullah as the Chief Minister.

INDEX